D1372797

McDougal Littell

Grammar
for Writing

McDougal Littell
A HOUGHTON MIFFLIN COMPANY

McDougal Littell

Grammar for Writing

- **GRAMMAR**
- **USAGE**
- **MECHANICS**

McDougal Littell
A HOUGHTON MIFFLIN COMPANY

ISBN 13: 978-0-618-56616-7   ISBN 10: 0-618-56616-3

Printed in the United States of America.

Acknowledgments begin on page 323.

1 2 3 4 5 6 7 8 9—DCI—12 11 10 09 08 07

Contents Overview

Grammar, Usage, and Mechanics

We are learning to build Web sites and I'll be designing the home page.

4 Verbs 86

5 Adjectives and Adverbs 120

6 Prepositions, Conjunctions, Interjections   146

Wow! Awesome!

7 Subject-Verb Agreement 164

8 Capitalization 184

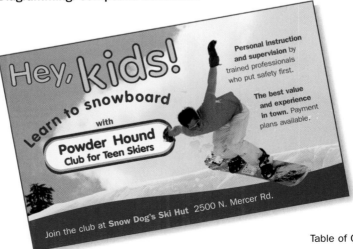

Quick-Fix Editing Machine

Special Features

Grammar Across the Curriculum

Grammar in Literature

Quick-Fix Editing Machine

Student Resources

Grammar, Usage, and Mechanics

Writing Machine

A machine doesn't run unless all of its parts work together. If even one part stops working, the machine can break down. Your writing won't make sense unless your words work together. Use the rules of grammar to avoid breakdowns in your writing.

3

The Sentence and Its Parts

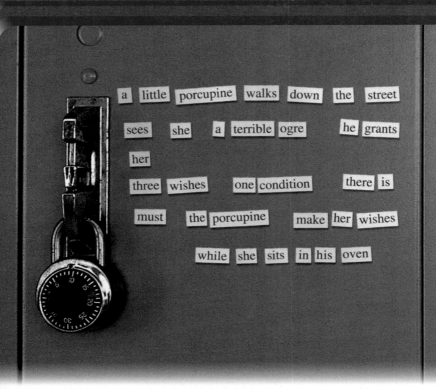

a little porcupine walks down the street

sees she a terrible ogre he grants

her

three wishes one condition there is

must the porcupine make her wishes

while she sits in his oven

Theme: Stories and Storytelling
Putting the Pieces Together

How would you arrange the words and phrases above to tell a story? Magnetic word blocks are fun because they let you group words together in any order. However, the words will only make sense if they are arranged in complete sentences. Sentences allow you to express complete thoughts. You can use different types of sentences to tell stories.

Write Away: Story Time
What do you think will happen to the porcupine? Write a brief story based on the words and phrases in the photograph. Place your completed story in your ▱ **Working Portfolio.**

For each underlined item, choose the letter of the term that correctly identifies it.

All <u>societies</u> have storytellers. In the Songhai Empire of West
(1)
Africa, griots <u>traveled from village to village</u>. These storytellers
(2)
<u>informed</u> people about historical and current events. Songhai kings
(3)
greatly valued their <u>work</u>. Some modern griots <u>have continued</u> this
(4)   (5)
tradition. Troubadours were European <u>storytellers</u> who performed
(6)
a similar role during the Middle Ages. <u>From their songs and stories</u>

<u>flowed all kinds of information.</u> <u>Sometimes they would tell funny</u>
(7)   (8)
<u>tales, other times they would explain herbal medicine.</u> They

<u>enlightened and entertained</u> audiences in market places and
(9)
palaces. <u>At one royal wedding, 426 troubadours performed</u>!
(10)

1. A. simple subject
   B. simple predicate
   C. complete subject
   D. complete predicate

2. A. simple subject
   B. simple predicate
   C. complete subject
   D. complete predicate

3. A. simple subject
   B. simple predicate
   C. complete subject
   D. complete predicate

4. A. predicate noun
   B. predicate adjective
   C. direct object
   D. indirect object

5. A. compound predicate
   B. verb phrase
   C. helping verb
   D. main verb

6. A. predicate noun
   B. predicate adjective
   C. direct object
   D. indirect object

7. A. fragment
   B. run-on sentence
   C. declarative sentence
   D. exclamatory sentence

8. A. fragment
   B. run-on sentence
   C. inverted sentence
   D. exclamatory sentence

9. A. complete subject
   B. complete predicate
   C. compound subject
   D. compound verb

10. A. exclamatory sentence
    B. interrogative sentence
    C. imperative sentence
    D. declarative sentence

❶ Here's the Idea

In order to share ideas and information successfully, you need to use complete sentences.

▶ **A sentence is a group of words that expresses a complete thought.**

Here is a group of words.

lost   her   slipper   Cinderella

These words cannot get a message across unless they have a structure. Here is a sentence made from the same words. Notice that the sentence communicates a complete idea.

Cinderella   lost   her   slipper

▶ **Every complete sentence has two basic parts: a subject and a predicate.**

1. The **complete subject** includes all the words that tell whom or what the sentence is about.

COMPLETE SUBJECT

The glass slipper fits only one person.

2. The **complete predicate** includes the verb and all the words that tell about the verb.

COMPLETE PREDICATE

The glass slipper fits only one person.

Here's How Finding Complete Subjects and Predicates

The prince searches for its owner.

1. **To find the complete subject, ask who or what does something (or is something).**
   Who searches for its owner? **The prince**

2. **To find the complete predicate, ask what the subject does (or is).**
   What does the prince do? searches for its owner

CHAPTER 1

② Why It Matters in Writing

You need to write complete sentences to share your ideas with others. When you revise your writing, make sure that each sentence has both a subject and a predicate.

STUDENT MODEL

There are over 500 European versions of "Cinderella."
Storytellers
∧Probably passed them around by word of mouth for
                                           appeared
centuries. The first written version∧in 1634.

③ Practice and Apply

CONCEPT CHECK: Complete Subjects and Predicates

Draw two columns on a sheet of paper. Label one "Complete Subjects" and the other "Complete Predicates." Write the complete subject and complete predicate for each sentence.

Cinderella in Asia
1. People around the world tell Cinderella stories.
2. The oldest version of all comes from China.
3. The main character's name is Yeh-Shen.
4. This lovely young woman lives with a cruel stepmother and a selfish stepsister.
5. Yeh-Shen receives help from a wise old man and a dead goldfish.
6. The bones of the dead goldfish grant the unlucky maiden's wish.
7. She goes to a party in a beautiful cloak and a beautiful pair of slippers.
8. One of the slippers falls off Yeh-Shen's foot.
9. A king seeks the slipper's owner.
10. You probably know the rest of the story.

➜ For a SELF-CHECK and more practice, see the EXERCISE BANK, p. 262.

Simple Subjects

LESSON 2

❶ Here's the Idea

You have learned that one basic part of a sentence is the complete subject. Now you will learn about the key part of the complete subject.

▶ **The simple subject is the main word or words in the complete subject.** Descriptive words are not part of the simple subject.

COMPLETE SUBJECT

Oral tales are important in Pueblo culture.
SIMPLE SUBJECT

This tradition has inspired Pueblo potters.
SIMPLE SUBJECT

 When a proper name is used as a subject, all parts of the name make up the simple subject.

SIMPLE SUBJECT
Mary Trujillo makes clay storyteller figures.

❷ Why It Matters in Writing

The simple subject gives important information. It tells the reader whom or what the sentence is about. When you revise your work, look out for unclear words used as simple subjects. Notice how a change in wording improves the sentence below.

Example: The clay object holds children on his lap.

Revision: The clay storyteller holds children on his lap.

CHAPTER 1

❸ Practice and Apply

A. CONCEPT CHECK: Simple Subjects

On a separate sheet of paper, write the simple subject of each sentence. Remember, descriptive words are not part of the simple subject.

Example: Desert tortoises are sneaky.
Simple subject: tortoises

> **A Traditional Pueblo Tale**
> **1.** A slow tortoise lived in the desert long ago.
> **2.** A nimble rabbit crossed his path one day.
> **3.** The rabbit challenged the tortoise to a race.
> **4.** Immediately, his tricky neighbor accepted the challenge.
> **5.** The mismatched animals agreed to hold the race four days later.
> **6.** The confident rabbit crossed the finish line.
> **7.** A big surprise awaited the rabbit.
> **8.** A smiling tortoise greeted him.
> **9.** The unsuspecting rabbit was the victim of a trick.
> **10.** His opponent's twin brother met him at the finish line!

➜ **For a SELF-CHECK and more practice, see the EXERCISE BANK, p. 262.**

B. WRITING: Creating Complete Sentences

Create four sentences by combining complete subjects with complete predicates from the table below. Underline the simple subject in each sentence.

Clay Storytellers	
Complete Subject	**Complete Predicate**
The storyteller figures	come from natural substances
Each Pueblo potter	pay thousands of dollars for some storyteller figures
The colors on the storyteller figures	are handmade and hand painted
Collectors	works in a different style

Simple Predicates, or Verbs

❶ Here's the Idea

You have learned about the simple subject of a sentence. You also need to know about the simple predicate.

▶ **The simple predicate, or verb, is the main word or words in the complete predicate.**

COMPLETE PREDICATE

Hercules **battles the nine-headed Hydra.**

SIMPLE PREDICATE

His nephew helps him in the struggle.

SIMPLE PREDICATE

▶ **A verb is a word used to express an action, a condition, or a state of being.** A **linking verb** tells what the subject *is.* An **action verb** tells what the subject *does,* even when the action cannot be seen.

Hercules arrived in a foreign city. (action you can see)

The ruler disliked Hercules. (action you cannot see)

Greek myths are timeless. (linking)

❷ Why It Matters in Writing

The verb is the most important word in a complete predicate because it tells what the subject does or is. When describing an event, choose powerful verbs that will help your readers imagine the action.

> **PROFESSIONAL MODEL**
>
> The Hydra **lunged** at Hercules with one of its deadly heads. Hercules **swung** his club. He **crushed** the skull. Two new heads quickly **sprouted** in its place.
>
> —Dee Stiffler

❸ Practice and Apply

A. CONCEPT CHECK: Simple Predicates, or Verbs

On a separate sheet of paper, write the simple predicate, or verb, for each sentence.

The Labors of Hercules
1. Hercules is the hero of many Greek myths.
2. He served King Eurystheus for 12 years.
3. The cowardly king hated Hercules.
4. He assigned the hero a series of dangerous tasks.
5. The Greeks called these tasks the labors of Hercules.
6. Hercules once captured a gigantic wild boar.
7. He also battled a flock of monstrous birds.
8. The birds showered Hercules with sharp bronze feathers.
9. Hercules held the sky on his shoulders during one of his labors.
10. The king was furious over Hercules' successes.

➡ **For a SELF-CHECK and more practice, see the EXERCISE BANK, p. 263.**

B. WRITING: Summarizing Information

The first column of this chart lists five gods and goddesses from Greek mythology. The second column lists a responsibility or role that each is known for. Use the information to write a sentence about each character. When you have finished, underline each simple predicate. Some possible verbs include the following: *protects, commands, represents, delivers.*

Mythic Figures	
God or Goddess	**Known As or For . . .**
Athena	goddess of wisdom and warfare
Demeter	protection of farmers and their crops
Hermes	delivery of important messages
Poseidon	command of the seas
Zeus	most powerful of the Greek gods

Athena

Verb Phrases

① Here's the Idea

The simple predicate, or verb, may consist of two or more words. These words are called a verb phrase.

▶ **A verb phrase is made up of a main verb and one or more helping verbs.**

VERB PHRASE

The princess had yawned loudly.

HELPING VERB ⬈   ⬉ MAIN VERB

Main Verbs and Helping Verbs

A **main verb** can stand by itself as the simple predicate of a sentence.

Her visitor talked for hours. (action)
        MAIN VERB

The tale was endless. (linking)
     MAIN VERB

Helping verbs help the main verb express action or show time.

VERB PHRASE

The tale might be endless.
HELPING VERB ⬈   ⬉ MAIN VERB

Her visitor had been talking for hours.

He will have been talking all day.

Notice that sometimes the main verb changes form when used with helping verbs. For more on these changes, see pages 96–106.

Common Helping Verbs	
Forms of *be*	is, am, was, are, were, be, been
Forms of *do*	do, does, did
Forms of *have*	has, have, had
Others	may, might, can, should, could, would, shall, will

❷ Why It Matters in Writing

You can use verb phrases to show when an action or event takes place. Notice how the verb phrases in this model move the action from the past to the present and the future.

PROFESSIONAL MODEL

Different versions of "The Endless Tale" have originated in various parts of the world. The hero of an English version can talk endlessly about locusts stealing corn. In Japanese folklore, you will find a similar hero who tells a never-ending story about rats.

PAST

PRESENT

FUTURE

—Etta Worthington

❸ Practice and Apply

CONCEPT CHECK: Verb Phrases

Write the verb phrase in each sentence below. Be sure to include all the helping verbs.

An Endless Tale
1. A beautiful princess was searching for a husband.
2. Her perfect suitor should be a good storyteller.
3. He must tell an endless tale to the royal family.
4. A poor young man did appear at the castle one day.
5. He would share a story about a well-built barn full of corn.
6. Just a single locust may fit through the barn's only hole.
7. The first locust could grab only a single grain of corn.
8. Soon a second locust has stolen another grain, and so on.
9. This man's boring story might have continued forever.
10. Fortunately, his marriage to the princess will interrupt it.

➜ **For a SELF-CHECK and more practice, see the EXERCISE BANK, p. 263.**

SENTENCE PARTS

❶ Here's the Idea

Sentences can have **compound subjects** and **compound verbs**.

▶ **A compound subject is made up of two or more subjects that share the same verb.** The subjects are joined by a conjunction, or connecting word, such as *and, or,* or *but.*

COMPOUND SUBJECT

Caroline **and Suzanne** are looking **for fables.**
SUBJECT   SUBJECT

The library or bookstore will have **a collection.**

▶ **A compound verb is made up of two or more verbs that share the same subject.** The verbs are joined by a conjunction such as *and, or,* or *but.*

COMPOUND VERB

Fables entertain **and teach.**
VERB   VERB

The animal characters speak **and** behave **like people.**

❷ Why It Matters in Writing

You can use compound subjects and verbs to get rid of unnecessary words. Notice how the writer of this paragraph combined sentences.

STUDENT MODEL

Aesop probably created ‚*or retold* some of the stories that made him famous. ~~He probably retold some others~~. However, he did not write any of them down. In his day, fables ‚*and myths* were part of the oral tradition. They were passed along by word of mouth. ~~Myths were also part of the oral tradition.~~

CHAPTER 1

❸ Practice and Apply

A. CONCEPT CHECK: Compound Sentence Parts

On a separate sheet of paper, write the compound subject or compound verb for each sentence.

The Ant and the Grasshopper

1. An ant and a grasshopper were in a field on a fine summer day.
2. The grasshopper hopped and sang.
3. The ant gathered and hauled seeds all day long.
4. The grasshopper relaxed or played in the meantime.
5. Cold winds and icy rains arrived in the winter.
6. The ant ate and enjoyed plenty of food.
7. The grasshopper starved and suffered.
8. His foolishness and laziness taught him a lesson.
9. Readers and listeners will probably guess what it is.
10. Discipline and hard work bring rewards in the future.

➜ For a SELF-CHECK and more practice, see the EXERCISE BANK, p. 264.

B. REVISING: Combining Sentences

This version of a fable by Aesop is a little wordy. Make it flow better by using compound subjects and verbs to combine sentences.

> The belly enjoyed food. So did the other body parts. Yet all meals went into the belly. Snacks also wound up there. One day the body parts decided to strike. The hands no longer obtained food. They didn't cook it either. The mouth refused to chew. The teeth stopped chewing as well. Soon the entire body grew uncomfortable. Now the body parts understood digestion. They appreciated digestion too. The strike was canceled. From then on, the body parts never blamed the belly. They also stopped complaining about it.

The Sentence and Its Parts **15**

Kinds of Sentences

❶ Here's the Idea

▶ **A sentence can be used to make a statement, to ask a question, to make a request or give a command, or to show strong feelings.**

Four Kinds of Sentences		
	What It Does	**Examples**
Declarative **.**	Makes a statement; always ends with a period.	Funny stories are popular everywhere. People from all cultures enjoy humor.
Interrogative **?**	Asks a question; always ends with a question mark.	Do you know any jokes? Which one is your favorite?
Imperative **. or !**	Tells or asks someone to do something; usually ends with a period but may end with an exclamation point.	Listen carefully. Stop interrupting me!
Exclamatory **!**	Shows strong feeling; always ends with an exclamation point.	You're really funny! That joke is a lot older than I am!

❷ Why It Matters in Writing

The four kinds of sentences enable you to express different feelings and attitudes in your writing. Notice the variety of sentence types used in this dialogue, or conversation, between a teacher and her student, who is a promising writer.

LITERARY MODEL

Miss Walker. What's wrong? I don't understand.

Lenore. I don't want to read my story. And I don't want to go to Thunder Bay!

INTERROGATIVE
DECLARATIVE
EXCLAMATORY

—Keith Leckie, *Words on a Page*

❸ Practice and Apply

A. CONCEPT CHECK: Kinds of Sentences

Identify each of the following sentences as declarative (D), interrogative (INT), exclamatory (E), or imperative (IMP).

Shoe Trouble

1. I found an amusing story in a book of folk humor.
2. Was it about a well-known judge who lived in China?
3. That's the one!
4. Remind me how the story goes.
5. One morning, the judge noticed that he was walking with a limp.
6. What could the cause be?
7. He was wearing two completely different shoes!
8. He asked his servant to run home and fetch a replacement.
9. The servant told him that there was no point in changing shoes.
10. The pair at home was exactly like this one!

➡ For a SELF-CHECK and more practice, see the EXERCISE BANK, p. 264.

B. WRITING: Creating Dialogue

When writers rewrite stories for the stage, they often use all four types of sentences. For example, imagine what the hedgehog might say when he discovers the creature in the stove. Different types of sentences help writers show the different feelings and attitudes of their characters. In your 🗀 **Working Portfolio,** find the story that you wrote for the **Write Away** on page 4. Write a brief skit based on this story. Use each type of sentence at least once in the dialogue.

Subjects in Unusual Order

CHAPTER 1

① Here's the Idea

In most declarative sentences, subjects come before verbs. In some kinds of sentences, however, subjects can come between verb parts, follow verbs, or not appear at all.

Questions

▶ **In most questions, the subject comes after the verb or between parts of the verb phrase.**

Is the story suspenseful?

VERB
⌢ PHRASE ⌢
Did you find it scary?
↖SUBJECT

To find the subject, turn the question into a statement. Then ask who or what is or does something.

Did the ending surprise you?

The ending did surprise you. (What did surprise you? *the ending*)

Commands

▶ **The subject of a command, or imperative sentence, is usually *you.*** Often, *you* doesn't appear in the sentence because it is understood.

(You) Turn down the lights.
↖ SUBJECT

(You) Sit perfectly still.

Inverted Sentences

In inverted sentences, the subject comes after the verb. Their usual order is reversed.

Inverted Subject and Verb	
Normal	A scratching **sound** came from the other side of the door.
Inverted	From the other side of the door came a scratching **sound.**
Normal	A large black **cat** rushed into the room.
Inverted	Into the room rushed a large black **cat.**

Sentences Beginning with *Here* or *There*

▶ **In some sentences beginning with *here* or *there*, the subject follows the verb.** To find the subject, look for the verb and ask *who?* or *what?*

WHAT COMES?

Here comes the scariest part.
　　VERB　　　　　　　　SUBJECT

WHAT GOES?

There goes our flashlight.
　　VERB　　　　SUBJECT

❷ Why It Matters in Writing

Most people would grow tired of eating the same meal every day. Variety is also important in writing. You should look for opportunities to vary the order of subjects and verbs in sentences. Notice how inverting a sentence in the model makes the paragraph more interesting to read.

STUDENT MODEL

DRAFT

　Miranda cautiously approached the abandoned barn. The hinges creaked and groaned as she opened the door. A pair of squeaking bats flew out. She ducked just in time.

REVISED

　Miranda cautiously approached the abandoned barn. The hinges creaked and groaned as she opened the door. **Out flew a pair of squeaking bats.** She ducked just in time.

❸ Practice and Apply

A. CONCEPT CHECK: Subjects in Unusual Order

In two columns on a separate sheet of paper, write the simple subject and verb (or verb phrase) of each sentence.

What a Nightmare!
1. Are your friends bored?
2. Tell a scary story.
3. Speak softly at first.
4. Then shock your listeners with a timely scream.
5. There are many scary stories.
6. Will you set yours in a cemetery?
7. In the shadows appear strange figures.
8. There is a mournful cry behind a tomb.
9. Are your friends afraid now?
10. At the end of the story is a terrible surprise.

➜ **For a SELF-CHECK and more exercises, see the EXERCISE BANK, p. 265.**

B. REVISING: Adding Variety

Follow the instructions to revise the model sentence.

Model: A headless man appears in the window.

1. Turn the sentence into a question.
2. Rewrite the sentence to begin with *There is.* (Hint: Remove the verb *appears.*)
3. Invert the sentence without using *there* so that the subject comes after the verb.

Now decide how your revisions affect the mood of the model sentence.

4. Which revisions could you use to give information?
5. Which revision asks for information?
6. Which revision seems the scariest?

Complements: Subject Complements

LESSON 8

① Here's the Idea

A **complement** is a word or a group of words that completes the meaning of a verb. Two kinds of complements are **subject complements** and **objects of verbs.**

▶ **A subject complement is a word or group of words that follows a linking verb and renames or describes the subject.** A linking verb links the subject with a noun or adjective that tells more about it.

LINKING VERB
Cowboy poetry is a Western tradition.
SUBJECT   COMPLEMENT

Common Linking Verbs	
Forms of *be*	am, is, are, was, were, being, been
Other linking verbs	appear, feel, look, sound, seem, taste

Predicate Nouns and Predicate Adjectives

Both nouns and adjectives can serve as subject complements.

▶ **A predicate noun follows a linking verb and defines or renames the subject.**

RENAMES
A popular cowboy poet is Rudy Gonzales.
SUBJECT   PREDICATE NOUN

▶ **A predicate adjective follows a linking verb and describes a quality of the subject.**

DESCRIBES
Most cowboy poetry is humorous.
SUBJECT   PREDICATE ADJECTIVE

Some of the poems are sad. (describes)

SENTENCE PARTS

❷ Why It Matters in Writing

Subject complements tell the reader much more about the subject.

LITERARY MODEL

One of Athene's pupils was a ▓man▓ called Daedalus. Even though he was ▓mortal,▓ he was almost as ▓remarkable▓ an inventor and craftsman as the god Hephaestus. He became ▓famous▓ throughout the world.

PREDICATE NOUN

PREDICATE ADJECTIVE

—Anne Rockwell, "The Boy Who Flew"

❸ Practice and Apply

A. CONCEPT CHECK: Subject Complements

Write the italicized word in each sentence and identify it as either a predicate noun (PN) or a predicate adjective (PA).

Poems on the Range
1. The cattle drives of the 1800s are *legendary*.
2. Life was *difficult* on the Western frontier.
3. It was also *colorful*.
4. Cowboy poets were the *storytellers* of the Old West.
5. Horses, hard work, and the cowboy life were their *themes*.
6. Their poems still seem so *vivid*.
7. The cowboy life remains an irresistible *subject*.
8. The stories of the Old West are *popular* once again.
9. Cowboy-poetry festivals are big *events* these days.
10. The future looks *bright* for this uniquely American art form.

➡ **For a SELF-CHECK and more practice, see the EXERCISE BANK, p. 265.**

B. REVISING: Using Subject Complements

Choose one of the following words to supply each missing subject complement below: *cowboys, veterinarian, authentic*.

It's no wonder that cowboy poets often sound so **(1)** (predicate adjective). Many of them are real **(2)** (predicate noun). The famous poet Baxter Black used to be a **(3)** (predicate noun) who treated livestock.

Complements: Objects of Verbs

LESSON 9

❶ Here's the Idea

In addition to subject complements, there are objects of verbs. Action verbs often need complements called direct objects and indirect objects to complete their meaning.

Direct Objects

▶ **A direct object is a word or group of words that names the receiver of the action.** A direct object answers the question *what* or *whom*.

CLIMBED WHAT?

Jack climbed the beanstalk.
DIRECT OBJECT

The giant's wife protected Jack. (protected whom? *Jack*)

Indirect Objects

▶ **An indirect object is a word or group of words that tells to whom or what (or for whom or what) an action is performed.** An indirect object usually comes between a verb and a direct object.

TO WHOM?

Jesse told his little cousins the story.
INDIRECT OBJECT   DIRECT OBJECT

Verbs that are often followed by indirect objects include *bring, give, hand, lend, make, offer, send, show, teach, tell, write,* and *ask*.

Here's How) **Finding Direct and Indirect Objects**

Jack showed his mother the magic beans.

1. Find the action verb in the sentence. *showed*
2. To find the direct object, ask, *Showed what? beans*
3. To find the indirect object, ask, *Showed to whom? mother*

SENTENCE PARTS

❷ Why It Matters in Writing

When you describe events, you can use direct objects and indirect objects to help readers understand relationships.

PROFESSIONAL MODEL

A strange-looking man offered Jack five beans for his cow. Jack immediately rejected this offer. Yet he changed his mind when he heard that the beans were magical. Jack's mother gave him a fierce scolding when he came home with the beans.

— Eric Scholl

DIRECT OBJECT

INDIRECT OBJECT

❸ Practice and Apply

CONCEPT CHECK: Objects of Verbs

For each sentence below, write each object and identify it as a direct object (DO) or an indirect object (IO).

Climbing the Beanstalk
1. Jack's mother tossed the beans away.
2. The boy saw a huge beanstalk outside his window the next morning.
3. He discovered a giant's castle at the top.
4. The giant's wife served Jack some breakfast.
5. She could have brought her hungry husband the boy.
6. Instead she offered Jack her oven for a hiding place.
7. The giant counted his gold coins.
8. This task gave him a great weariness.
9. Jack stole a bag of gold after the giant fell asleep.
10. He showed his delighted mother the gold at home.

➜ For a SELF-CHECK and more practice, see the EXERCISE BANK, p. 266.

Fragments and Run-Ons

LESSON 10

❶ Here's the Idea

Sentence fragments and run-on sentences are writing errors that can make your writing difficult to understand.

Sentence Fragments

▶ **A sentence fragment is a part of a sentence that is written as if it were a complete sentence.** A sentence fragment is missing a subject, a predicate, or both.

FRAGMENTS

The Bayeux Tapestry in an ancient French town.
(missing a predicate)

Tells the story of the Norman victory in England.
(missing a subject)

From the 11th century. (missing subject and predicate)

To make a complete sentence, add a subject, a predicate, or both.

REVISION

The Bayeux Tapestry hangs in an ancient French town. It tells the story of the Norman victory in England. The tapestry dates from the 11th century.

SENTENCE PARTS

Run-On Sentences

▶ **A run-on sentence is two or more sentences written as though they were a single sentence.**

RUN-ON

The English lost the historic battle, Duke William of Normandy became their new king.

REVISION

The English lost the historic battle. Duke William of Normandy became their new king.

REVISION

The English lost the historic battle, and Duke William of Normandy became their new king.

When combining two sentences with a conjunction, use a comma before the conjunction.

❷ Why It Matters in Writing

When you take notes or do prewriting, you often jot down ideas as fragments or run-on sentences. It is important to change your notes into complete sentences when you write your draft.

STUDENT MODEL

NOTES

Consists of 72 scenes and a fancy border. Over 1,500 people, animals, and other figures in it. Scholars value the tapestry as a great work of art, it is also an important historical document.

DRAFT

The Bayeux Tapestry consists of 72 scenes and a fancy border. Over 1,500 people, animals, and other figures appear in it. Scholars value the tapestry as a great work of art. It is also an important historical document.

❸ Practice and Apply

A. CONCEPT CHECK: Sentence Fragments and Run-Ons

On a separate sheet of paper, identify each of the following items as a fragment (F), run-on (RO), or complete sentence (CS).

A Storytelling Tapestry

1. William of Normandy led the Norman invasion of England in 1066.
2. In those days, Normandy was a small dukedom, today it is a region of France.
3. Bishop Odo of the town of Bayeux.
4. Was William's half-brother.
5. His teams of craftspeople made the enormous piece of needlework.
6. The tapestry is 231 feet long, it is only 20 inches wide.
7. This magnificent work tells the story of the invasion.
8. Is in many ways like a movie.
9. The thousands of details within the tapestry.
10. Have taught us a great deal about life in the Middle Ages.

➜ **For a SELF-CHECK and more practice, see the EXERCISE BANK, p. 266.**

CHALLENGE

Rewrite the exercise as a paragraph. Fix any fragments or run-on sentences.

B. REVISING: Fixing Fragments and Run-Ons

You and a classmate are working together on a presentation about the Bayeux Tapestry. You have taken the following notes. Correct any fragments or run-ons so that your partner will understand your notes.

SECTION 21 OF THE BAYEUX TAPESTRY

Shows soldiers from Duke William's army. They have just landed on the English coast, some are just getting out of their ships. One interesting detail the long oars within the ships. The Norman ships always fairly small in the tapestry. Historians tell us that they were actually around a hundred feet long.

Grammar in Literature

Using Different Types of Sentences

Whenever you ask a question, make a request, or express your excitement, you use different types of sentences. In writing, you need these types of sentences to show emotion and give information. Notice the types of sentences that Olivia E. Coolidge uses in retelling the Greek myth of Arachne.

ARACHNE
retold by Olivia E. Coolidge

Arachne was used to being wondered at, and she was immensely proud of the skill that had brought so many to look on her. Praise was all she lived for, and it displeased her greatly that people should think anyone, even a goddess, could teach her anything. Therefore, when she heard them murmur, she would stop her work and turn round indignantly to say, "With my own ten fingers I gained this skill, and by hard practice from early morning till night.... As for Athena's weaving, how could there be finer cloth or more beautiful embroidery than mine? If Athena herself were to come down and compete with me, she could do no better than I."

One day when Arachne turned round with such words, an old woman answered her. "... Take my advice and ask pardon of Athena for your words."

DECLARATIVE SENTENCE

INTERROGATIVE SENTENCE

IMPERATIVE SENTENCE

ACROSS the CURRICULUM LITERATURE

Practice and Apply

Using Different Types of Sentences

Retell your favorite fable, myth, fairy tale, or folktale, using at least three types of sentences. If you like, you can rewrite one of the following fables:

The Lion and the Mouse

One day a big lion caught a tiny mouse. The mouse pleaded with the lion to let her go and promised to return his kindness one day. The lion, of course, didn't believe the mouse could ever help him, but he let her go anyway. A few days later, he walked into a trap whose net closed tightly around him. The mouse heard the lion roar in frustration and hurried to him. She quickly began to gnaw through the net until the lion was able to escape. Moral: Even a small friend can be a great friend.

The Hare and the Tortoise

The hare was always making fun of the tortoise. He would laugh at the tortoise's short legs and call him slowpoke. One day, the tortoise claimed that even though he was slow, he could still beat the hare in a race. The hare thought the tortoise was joking, but he accepted the challenge to race. From the starting line, the hare far outdistanced the tortoise. But the tortoise kept going, slowly and steadily. The hare got so far ahead that he soon grew tired. Thinking he had lots of time, he ate some clover, sipped water from a stream, and sat down under a tree to rest. While the hare was fast asleep, the tortoise kept going, not stopping for food, water, or rest. Just before the tortoise reached the finish line, the hare woke up. He hurried down the road, but he was too late. The tortoise had won. Moral: Slow and steady wins the race.

The Sentence and Its Parts **29**

Mixed Review

A. Subjects, Predicates, and Compound Sentence Parts Read the passage; then write the answers to the questions below it.

A Cunning Spider

(1) Picture the following scene. (2) A king has discovered a crime in his household. (3) The guilty one climbs and escapes as a spider. (4) Who is this slippery trickster figure? (5) Folklore fans will recognize him as Anansi. (6) Stories about Anansi originated in West Africa. (7) Storytellers and listeners are quite fond of him. (8) This humorous character always tries to trick people. (9) He succeeds most of the time. (10) Sometimes he himself is the victim of a practical joke or a clever trick.

1. What kind of sentence is sentence 1?
2. What is the main verb of sentence 2?
3. What is the compound part of sentence 3?
4. What kind of sentence is sentence 4?
5. What is the helping verb of sentence 5?
6. What is the simple subject of sentence 6?
7. What is the compound part of sentence 7?
8. What is the complete subject of sentence 8?
9. What is the simple predicate of sentence 9?
10. What is the complete predicate of sentence 10?

B. Complements Identify each underlined word as a predicate noun, a predicate adjective, a direct object, or an indirect object.

An incident in "Anansi and the Crabs" is an **(1)** <u>example</u> of Anansi's trickery. At the end of the story, Anansi fears a harsh **(2)** <u>punishment</u> from Alligator. He tells **(3)** <u>Alligator</u> the lie that they are cousins. Alligator is **(4)** <u>suspicious</u>. He gives **(5)** <u>Anansi</u> this test. Supposedly, all alligators can drink boiling water. Therefore, Anansi must drink some boiling **(6)** <u>water</u>. Only then will Alligator believe him. Anansi seems **(7)** <u>cooperative</u>. He makes one **(8)** <u>suggestion</u>, however. According to Anansi, the water will become even **(9)** <u>hotter</u> after a long rest in the sun. Alligator agrees. Of course, the water becomes cooler instead. Anansi drinks the **(10)** <u>water</u> with ease!

For each underlined item, choose the letter of the term that correctly identifies it.

Have you considered storytelling as a hobby? Many students are
(1)   (2)
showing interest in this ancient art. Even a shy person could tell
(3)
stories before an audience. The following suggestions may be
helpful for beginners. You should consider the age of your
(4)   (5)
listeners. Myths and legends are good stories for younger
(6)
audiences. Practice telling the story over and over. Some
(7)
storytellers record their practice sessions on audiotape or
(8)
videotape. Speak clearly and directly, use appropriate gestures and
(9)
facial expressions. Look for a good location for your performance.
Schools, parks, libraries, and community centers often attract
enthusiastic crowds.
(10)

1. A. run-on sentence
   B. inverted sentence
   C. interrogative sentence
   D. declarative sentence

2. A. complete subject
   B. simple subject
   C. complete predicate
   D. simple predicate

3. A. complete subject
   B. simple subject
   C. complete predicate
   D. simple predicate

4. A. predicate adjective
   B. predicate noun
   C. direct object
   D. indirect object

5. A. complete predicate
   B. compound predicate
   C. helping verb
   D. verb phrase

6. A. compound subject
   B. compound verb
   C. direct object
   D. run-on sentence

7. A. declarative sentence
   B. interrogative sentence
   C. imperative sentence
   D. exclamatory sentence

8. A. complete subject
   B. simple subject
   C. complete predicate
   D. simple predicate

9. A. fragment
   B. run-on sentence
   C. inverted sentence
   D. declarative sentence

10. A. predicate noun
    B. predicate adjective
    C. indirect object
    D. direct object

SENTENCE PARTS

Student Help Desk

The Sentence at a Glance

A sentence has two parts: a complete subject and a complete predicate.

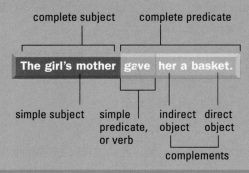

complete subject | complete predicate

The girl's mother gave her a basket.

simple subject | simple predicate, or verb | indirect object | direct object

complements

Subjects and Predicates — Story Line

Sentence Part	Example	How to Find It
Complete subject	**The sly wolf** slipped into the bed.	Ask who or what is or does something.
Simple subject	**wolf**	Find the main word(s) in the complete subject.
Complete predicate	Little Red Riding Hood knocked on the door.	Ask what the subject is or does.
Simple predicate	knocked	Find the verb(s) or verb phrase(s).

Complements Finishing Touches

	Type of Complement	Example	What It Does
Linking verbs	Predicate noun	The wolf is a **killer.**	Renames or defines the subject
Linking verbs	Predicate adjective	His teeth are **big.**	Describes the subject
Action verbs	Direct object	He ate the **grandmother.**	Completes the verb's action
Action verbs	Indirect object	She gave the **wolf** indigestion.	Tells to whom/what or for whom/what the action is done

Kinds of Sentences Different Voices

Declarative sentence	The story has a happy ending.
Interrogative sentence	How does it end**?**
Imperative sentence	**(You)** Tell me how it ends**.**
Exclamatory sentence	What a happy ending**!**

The Bottom Line

Checklist for Editing Sentences

Have I . . .

____ made sure that each sentence has a subject and a predicate?

____ corrected any fragments or run-on sentences?

____ combined any sentences with similar ideas by using compound subjects or verbs?

____ used different kinds of sentences and subject-verb order for variety?

____ used complements to make the meaning of sentences clear?

Nouns

Carmen's Diary
Thursday, July 23, 2001
On our trip Dad and I got lost
on the Greek island of Crete.
We wandered in the ruins looking
for the mosaic of the minotaur.
Because of the kindness of a
stranger, we finally found it.

Theme: Lost Cities and Civilizations

Finding Your Way

Poor Carmen! She and her father lost their way while exploring the ruins of a lost civilization on the island of Crete. Look at the different nouns in her diary. Which name people? Which name a place? Which name things? Which names an idea?

As you can see, nouns are an important part of language. You need nouns to name the people, places, things, or ideas you write about. Nouns are the signposts in your sentences. They keep you from getting "lost."

Write Away: Missing Out
Think about a time when you lost something important to you. You may have misplaced a treasured item, lost a contest or competition, or missed a big opportunity. Write a paragraph that describes this important event.

Save your writing in your  **Working Portfolio.**

For each numbered item, choose the letter of the term that correctly identifies it.

> Plato was a Greek philosopher. He wrote about an ancient
> (1)
> civilization called Atlantis. Long ago, he said, Atlantis had
> (2)
> disappeared beneath the waves. Plato's words have caused many
> (3)   (4)
> people to wonder about this lost place. Some people think Atlantis
> (5)
> was only a legend. Other people think it was indeed a real place.
> (6)   (7)
> There may be a very simple explanation for Atlantis. About 3,500
> years ago, a volcano erupted on Thera, an island near Greece.
> (8)
> The explosion completely destroyed the center of the island. So
> (9)
> Thera may be remembered as Atlantis, a civilization lost to a
> (10)
> natural disaster.

1. A. plural noun
   B. possessive noun
   C. common noun
   D. proper noun

2. A. singular noun
   B. proper noun
   C. possessive noun
   D. plural noun

3. A. noun as subject
   B. noun as direct object
   C. noun as object of preposition
   D. noun as predicate noun

4. A. common noun
   B. possessive noun
   C. predicate noun
   D. plural noun

5. A. plural noun
   B. possessive noun
   C. common noun
   D. proper noun

6. A. noun as subject
   B. noun as direct object
   C. noun as object of preposition
   D. noun as predicate noun

7. A. noun as direct object
   B. noun as subject
   C. noun as predicate noun
   D. noun as object of preposition

8. A. singular noun
   B. plural noun
   C. proper noun
   D. possessive noun

9. A. noun as subject
   B. noun as direct object
   C. noun as predicate noun
   D. noun as object of preposition

10. A. noun as predicate noun
    B. noun as direct object
    C. noun as object of preposition
    D. noun as subject

LESSON 1 What Is a Noun?

❶ Here's the Idea

▶ **A noun is a word that names a person, place, thing, or idea.**

PERSONS
archaeologist
Theresa

PLACES
site
Colorado

THINGS
pail
shovel

IDEAS
exploration
excitement

Common and Proper Nouns

A **common noun** is a general name for a person, place, thing, or idea. Common nouns are not capitalized.

A **proper noun** is the name of a particular person, place, thing, or idea. Proper nouns are always capitalized.

Common	people	home	state
Proper	Pueblo Indians	Cliff Palace	Colorado

Proper nouns make writing clear and precise.

COMMON NOUNS

People abandoned their home in the state.

PROPER NOUNS

Ancient Pueblo Indians abandoned the Cliff Palace in Colorado.

CHAPTER 2

❷ Why It Matters in Writing

Sentences without proper nouns are often too general. Notice how proper nouns make the following description more colorful and specific.

DRAFT	REVISION
I saw **the man** slowly hike up **the road** with **his students** to see the **houses** last **month**.	I saw **Mr. DeLalo** slowly hike up **Ruins Road** with **Rick and Theresa** to see the **Cliff Palace** last **August**.

❸ Practice and Apply

CONCEPT CHECK: What Is a Noun?

Write each noun, and label it as common or proper.

Quickly Lost, Slowly Found
1. Sometimes a place disappears quickly.
2. This happened to Pompeii, in Italy.
3. A volcano called Mount Vesuvius erupted almost 2,000 years ago.
4. Hot lava and ash shot out of the volcanic mountain.
5. The material rained down on the buildings of Pompeii.
6. Families were sitting down to eat bread and fish.
7. Some people ran to the sea and escaped in small boats.
8. Ash completely covered the town, and it was forgotten.
9. Pompeii was finally excavated in recent times.
10. Giuseppe Fiorelli found blackened rolls in a bakery.

Label each noun that you wrote above as a person, place, thing, or idea.

➡ For a SELF-CHECK and more practice, see the EXERCISE BANK, p. 267

Singular and Plural Nouns

❶ Here's the Idea

▶ **A singular noun names one person, place, thing, or idea. A plural noun names more than one person, place, thing, or idea.**

> A **tourist** walked down the cobbled **street.** (singular nouns)

> **Tourists** walked down the cobbled **streets.** (plural nouns)

To make sure you spell plural nouns correctly, follow the rules in the Quick-Fix Spelling Machine.

QUICK-FIX SPELLING MACHINE: PLURALS OF NOUNS

	SINGULAR	RULE	PLURAL
❶	ruin building	Add *-s* to most nouns.	ruins buildings
❷	trench dish	Add *-es* to a noun that ends in *s, sh, ch, x,* or *z.*	trenches dishes
❸	volcano	Add *-s* to most nouns that end in *o.*	volcanos
	echo	Add *-es* to a few nouns that end in *o.*	echoes
❹	city	For most nouns ending in *y,* change the *y* to an *i* and add *-es.*	cities
	stairway	When a vowel comes before the *y,* just add *-s.*	stairways
❺	shelf knife	For most nouns ending in *f* or *fe,* change the *f* to *v* and add *-es* or *-s.*	shelves knives
	chief	Just add *-s* to a few nouns that end in *f* or *fe.*	chiefs
❻	deer buffalo	For some nouns, keep the same spelling.	deer buffalo

▶ **The plurals of some nouns are formed in irregular ways.**

Singular	child	woman	man	foot
Plural	children	women	men	feet

❷ Why It Matters in Writing

Plural nouns are the cause of many spelling errors in writing. When you proofread, pay special attention to this challenge. Notice how plural nouns are spelled correctly in the model below.

LITERARY MODEL

Suddenly it seemed too late for Tito. The red hot **ashes** blistered his skin; the stinging **vapors** tore his throat. He could not go on. . . . In a moment Bimbo was beside him. . . . He licked Tito's **hands,** his **feet,** his face.

—Louis Untermeyer, "The Dog of Pompeii"

❸ Practice and Apply

A. CONCEPT CHECK: Singular and Plural Nouns

Rewrite the nouns in parentheses in their plural forms.

Have You Seen My Mummy?
1. The (priest) of Egypt put the (body) of dead kings in tombs.
2. (Egyptian) believed that a body had to be preserved in order to have life after death.
3. For this reason, they prepared their dead to be (mummy).
4. At first, only dead (king) and (queen) were wrapped in cloth.
5. After many (century), ordinary people were also mummified.
6. The mummies were buried with precious (object).
7. (Scientist) study mummies to learn about (disease).
8. They have found (rash) and (sore) caused by (parasite).
9. Egyptians with many (rich) often had short (life).
10. Perhaps the (story) about a mummy's curse got started because (archaeologist) were infected by ancient germs.

➡ For a SELF-CHECK and more practice, see the EXERCISE BANK, p. 267.

B. PROOFREADING: Spelling Plural Nouns

Ten plural nouns in the following passage are misspelled. Find them and write their correct spellings.

Garbage In, Knowledge Out!

Can you imagine archaeologists going through your trash? People who excavate, or dig up, lost citys do exactly that! They find artifacts that provide us with echos of the past. An artifact is any object mans, womans, and childs use in their daily lifes. Today's scientists examine pottery, tools, and other objects used by ancient communities. A future scientist may examine your mattresses, your toothbrushs, or your baby toys! A scientist today may look at bones to see which animals people ate, such as deers or buffalo. A future excavator may examine the leftover tomatos in your salad! Here's a hint. Keep your old dishs clean, in case they're ever seen!

C. WRITING: Describing Artifacts

On a social studies field trip, you saw the student archaeologist below. Write a description of the tools he used and the artifacts he found. Be sure to spell plural nouns correctly.

Social Studies Field Trip Notes

tools	artifacts
brush	bone
pick	pot

Possessive Nouns

❶ Here's the Idea

▶ **The possessive form of a noun shows ownership or relationship.**

The divers waited outside the [archaeologist's] tent.
    OWNERSHIP

The [archaeologist's family] had come to visit.
    RELATIONSHIP

You may use possessive nouns in place of longer phrases.

                                        ship's location.
The divers used a robot to find the ~~location of the ship.~~

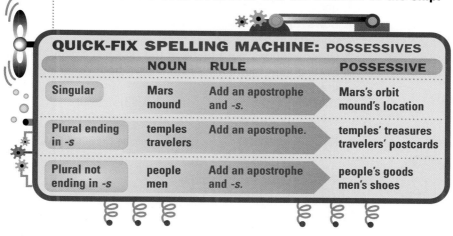

QUICK-FIX SPELLING MACHINE: POSSESSIVES

	NOUN	RULE	POSSESSIVE
Singular	Mars mound	Add an apostrophe and -s.	Mars's orbit mound's location
Plural ending in -s	temples travelers	Add an apostrophe.	temples' treasures travelers' postcards
Plural not ending in -s	people men	Add an apostrophe and -s.	people's goods men's shoes

❷ Why It Matters in Writing

When you write, be sure you have formed the possessive correctly. A misplaced apostrophe can confuse the reader. Notice how the revision in the model below clears up whether one or more people made the discovery.

> When the archaeologists opened the wooden chests, they found priceless relics. The explorer's discovery made headlines in newspapers across the country.

NOUNS

❸ Practice and Apply

A. CONCEPT CHECK: Possessive Nouns

Write the possessive form of each noun in parentheses. Then label each possessive noun singular or plural.

Risen from a Watery Grave

1. The *Mary Rose* was one of (England) finest warships.
2. She sank near the Portsmouth (Harbor) seabed during a battle with the French fleet in 1545.
3. Many (eyewitnesses) accounts told of her sad end.
4. The *Mary Rose* quickly became covered with the (seabed) mud and sand.
5. Alexander McKee located the (wreck) position in 1967.
6. In 1982 the ship was raised and stored in the (city) dry dock.
7. Bows, arrows, and other (archers) equipment were found on the gun deck.
8. Other weapons were found in the (sailors) cabins.
9. Netting kept the (*Mary Rose*) sailors from escaping when the ship sank.
10. The *Mary Rose* and its artifacts tell us about the (seamen) lives on board the ship.

➜ **For a SELF-CHECK and more practice, see the EXERCISE BANK, p. 268**

B. REVISING: Using Possessive Nouns

Use possessive nouns to make these phrases short enough to fit on labels for a social studies project.

Example: The Cliff Houses of Mesa Verde
Answer: Mesa Verde's Cliff Houses

1. The Capital City of the Aztecs
2. The Ruins of Pompeii
3. The Earth Mounds of Cahokia
4. The Royal Tomb of King Tut

Mesa Verde's Cliff Houses

Nouns and Their Jobs

❶ Here's the Idea

You use nouns every time you talk or write. Nouns name the people you meet, the places you visit, the sights and sounds you experience, and the ideas you have. Because nouns have many jobs, they are found in different places in sentences.

Nouns as Subjects

A **subject** tells whom or what the sentence is about. Notice the following sentences in which nouns act as subjects.

The Aztec Empire was located in the area now known as Mexico.

Tenochtitlán was the capital of the Aztec Empire.

Invaders entered Tenochtitlán in 1519.

Spanish soldiers destroyed Tenochtitlán during their conquest of Mexico.

Nouns as Complements

A **complement** is a word that completes the meaning of a verb. When a noun is a complement, it may be a predicate noun, a direct object, or an indirect object.

Nouns as Complements		
Predicate noun	renames or defines the subject after a linking verb	The Aztecs were fierce **warriors.**
Direct object	names the receiver of the action of the verb	Spanish soldiers defeated the **Aztec Empire** in 1521.
Indirect object	tells *to whom or what* or *for whom or what* an action is done	The Aztecs gave the **Spanish** gold and other precious goods.

Nouns as Objects of Prepositions

An **object of a preposition** is the noun or pronoun that follows the preposition. Nouns often appear in sentences as objects of prepositions.

The Aztec people settled in central Mexico.

PREPOSITION   OBJECT OF PREPOSITION

Aztec merchants traded with distant lands.

Among their valuable goods were gold and silver.

❷ Why It Matters in Writing

Using nouns in their various jobs can help you write a detailed explanation of any subject. Notice how the highlighted nouns in the model below add information to the sentences.

STUDENT MODEL

The Aztecs had many enemies. For this reason, they built their capital on an island. Long causeways led from the mainland to the island. Causeways are raised roads built across water. Aztec warriors guarded the ends of the causeways. In this way causeways provided the Aztec people protection.

SUBJECT
DIRECT OBJECT
INDIRECT OBJECT
PREDICATE NOUN
OBJECT OF PREPOSITION

❸ Practice and Apply

A. CONCEPT CHECK: Nouns and Their Jobs

Identify each underlined noun as a subject, a complement, or an object of a preposition.

Roadbuilders in the Sky
1. The Inca lived in the Andes Mountains in South America.
2. Cuzco was their capital.
3. The Inca were excellent record keepers.
4. They invented the quipu to keep track of their goods.

5. The <u>quipu</u> was a long <u>cord</u> with many <u>strings</u>.
6. Clerks tied <u>knots</u> in the strings in different patterns.
7. The Inca also built excellent <u>roads</u>.
8. Their <u>system</u> of roads carried <u>runners</u> across deep <u>gorges</u>.
9. <u>Officials</u> gave <u>runners</u> <u>messages</u> to carry hundreds of miles.
10. Some <u>roads</u> are still used today by Andean people.

➡ **For a SELF-CHECK and more practice, see the EXERCISE BANK, p. 268.**

Identify each complement in the exercise above as a predicate noun, a direct object, or an indirect object.

B. WRITING: Creating a Caption

Quetzalcoatl: Feathered-Serpent God
The photograph below shows Quetzalcoatl, a god worshiped by the Aztecs. Write a caption for a museum exhibit based on the information provided. Include nouns as subjects, complements, and objects of prepositions.

1. Quetzalcoatl = both snake and bird
2. Quetzal = brightly colored bird found in forests of Central and South America
3. long emerald feathers of quetzal highly valued
4. Quetzalcoatl = god of learning
5. Aztecs worshiped Quetzalcoatl

📁 **Working Portfolio: Revising** Find your **Write Away** paragraph from page 34. Revise your paragraph by adding specific complements that add to your explanation.

Grammar in Science

Using Nouns in Science

When you label diagrams, or identify specimens for science, chances are you use nouns. For example, nouns label the parts of the coniferous tree in the illustration. Some parts, or structures, are common to most plants. The illustrations show two types of plants; one coniferous plant (a pine tree) and one flowering plant (a rosebush). Notice the nouns used to label the pine tree.

needles

cone

trunk

roots

A flowering plant is similar to a coniferous plant.

(1) _____

(2) _____

(3) _____

(4) _____

Practice and Apply

A. USING NOUNS

Look at the diagrams of the pine tree and the rosebush. Copy the diagram of the rosebush on a separate sheet of paper. Then use the nouns below to write the words that label the rosebush. Use the labels on the pine tree diagram as a guide.

stem holds the plant upright, like the trunk of a pine tree

roots hold the plant in the soil and absorb water and nutrients from the soil to feed the plant

flower holds the seed of the plant, like the cone of the pine tree

leaves make plant food from sunlight and chlorophyll, like the needles on a pine tree

B. WRITING: Compare and Contrast in Science

A flowering plant carries its seeds in its flowers. A cone-bearing plant carries seeds in its cones. Write a paragraph in which you compare and contrast a pine tree and a rosebush. How are they alike? How are they different? Use the nouns you have learned in this lesson to refer to the parts that are alike and different.

NOUNS

Mixed Review

A. Kinds of Nouns Look at the cartoon, and answer the questions.

"Anyhow, according to the 'Science Times,' things would have turned out quite differently if that meteor had hit Earth."

© The New Yorker Collection 1999 Gahan Wilson

1. Which of the following is a proper noun?

   Earth,
   meteor,
   things

2. Which of the following is a common noun?

   Science Times,
   Earth,
   meteor

3. Which of the following is a plural noun?

   Science,
   things,
   meteor

4. Which of the following is the correct possessive?

   dinosaurs' pet,
   dinosaur's pet,
   dinosaurs's pet

5. Write a sentence telling what is going on in the cartoon. Underline the nouns, and identify how they are used.

B. Nouns and Their Jobs In each group of sentences, the same underlined noun is used in different ways. Label each noun as a subject, direct object, indirect object, predicate noun, or object of a preposition.

1. The <u>dinosaurs</u> had no cities or civilizations.
2. What happened to the <u>dinosaurs</u>?
3. The most popular animals in museums are <u>dinosaurs</u>.
4. We must give <u>dinosaurs</u> credit for surviving 160 million years.
5. Did an asteroid or other disaster kill the <u>dinosaurs</u>?
6. Other animals on Earth were <u>mammals</u>.
7. Ancient <u>mammals</u> were much smaller than the huge dinosaurs.
8. Finding food was easier for these <u>mammals</u>.
9. An earth without dinosaurs gave <u>mammals</u> much more space.
10. However, no blockbuster movie features small <u>mammals</u>!

For each numbered item, choose the letter of the term that correctly identifies it.

Roanoke Island lies off the coast of <u>North Carolina</u>. In 1587
(1)
English <u>colonists</u> started a colony on the island. John White was
(2)
the <u>leader</u> of the colony. <u>White's</u> ship *Hopewell* returned to
(3)   (4)
England in 1587 to get more supplies. In 1590 the ship was

bringing <u>supplies</u> to the new colony. However, White found no
(5)
colonists, only the <u>colonists'</u> possessions. A tree near the <u>fort</u> had
(6)   (7)
the name CROATOAN scratched in its bark. A storm prevented

the <u>ship</u> from reaching Croatoan Island. The disappearance of the
(8)
colony is a great <u>mystery</u>. Some <u>historians</u> believe the colonists
(9)   (10)
went to live with local Native American people in their villages.

---

1. A. proper noun
   B. common noun
   C. possessive noun
   D. plural noun

2. A. possessive noun
   B. plural noun
   C. singular noun
   D. proper noun

3. A. noun as direct object
   B. noun as predicate noun
   C. noun as object of preposition
   D. noun as indirect object

4. A. common noun
   B. plural noun
   C. possessive noun
   D. predicate noun

5. A. noun as subject
   B. noun as indirect object
   C. noun as direct object
   D. noun as object of preposition

6. A. singular noun
   B. proper noun
   C. possessive noun
   D. predicate noun

7. A. noun as object of preposition
   B. noun as predicate noun
   C. possessive noun
   D. noun as direct object

8. A. proper noun
   B. plural noun
   C. common noun
   D. possessive noun

9. A. noun as direct object
   B. noun as indirect object
   C. noun as object of preposition
   D. noun as predicate noun

10. A. noun as subject
    B. noun as direct object
    C. noun as indirect object
    D. noun as predicate noun

Student Help Desk

Nouns at a Glance

A noun names a person, place, thing, or idea.

Archaeologists in Egypt discovered a cemetery filled with mummies' tombs.

| Common Noun | Proper Noun | Singular Noun | Possessive Noun | Plural Noun |

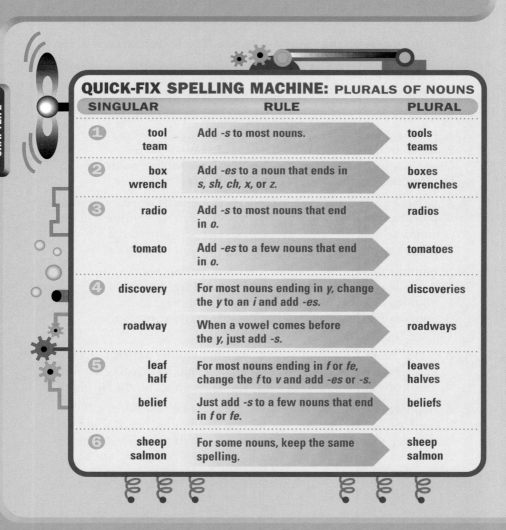

QUICK-FIX SPELLING MACHINE: PLURALS OF NOUNS

SINGULAR	RULE	PLURAL
① tool team	Add -*s* to most nouns.	tools teams
② box wrench	Add -*es* to a noun that ends in *s, sh, ch, x,* or *z.*	boxes wrenches
③ radio	Add -*s* to most nouns that end in *o.*	radios
tomato	Add -*es* to a few nouns that end in *o.*	tomatoes
④ discovery	For most nouns ending in *y,* change the *y* to an *i* and add -*es.*	discoveries
roadway	When a vowel comes before the *y,* just add -*s.*	roadways
⑤ leaf half	For most nouns ending in *f* or *fe,* change the *f* to *v* and add -*es* or -*s.*	leaves halves
belief	Just add -*s* to a few nouns that end in *f* or *fe.*	beliefs
⑥ sheep salmon	For some nouns, keep the same spelling.	sheep salmon

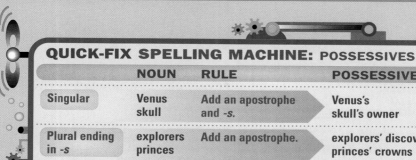

QUICK-FIX SPELLING MACHINE: POSSESSIVES

	NOUN	RULE	POSSESSIVE
Singular	Venus skull	Add an apostrophe and -s.	Venus's skull's owner
Plural ending in -s	explorers princes	Add an apostrophe.	explorers' discovery princes' crowns
Plural not ending in -s	children sheep	Add an apostrophe and -s.	children's games sheep's pasture

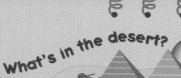

What's in the desert?

Nouns and Their Jobs

Nouns as . . .	Examples
Subject	The **cemetery** is more than 2,000 years old.
Predicate Noun	Dr. Salwah is an **archaeologist.**
Direct Object	He visited a **tomb.**
Indirect Object	He handed his **assistant** a flashlight.
Object of a Preposition	There were rows of **mummies.**

The Bottom Line

Checklist for Nouns

Have I . . .

____ chosen specific nouns?

____ spelled plural nouns
correctly?

____ used possessives to show
ownership or relationship?

____ used complements to
provide specific details in
explanations?

Pronouns

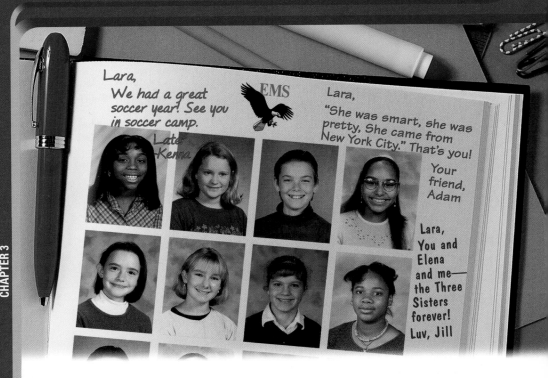

Lara,
We had a great soccer year! See you in soccer camp.
Later,
Kenna

EMS

Lara,
"She was smart, she was pretty. She came from New York City." That's you!

Your friend, Adam

Lara,
You and Elena and me—the Three Sisters forever!
Luv, Jill

Theme: Friendship

A Little Help from My Friends

A good friend has asked you to sign her yearbook. You have a writing space about the size of a large postage stamp. What if you couldn't use pronouns, like *I, we, you,* and *she,* but had to use everybody's name instead? Could you make your message fit?

Pronouns are little words that make a big difference. Be careful how you use them, though. Otherwise, your friends may misunderstand your messages.

Write Away: Thanks for the Memories!
Write a brief yearbook message for one or more of your friends. Use pronouns to make the most of your limited space. Place your work in your 📁 **Working Portfolio.**

Diagnostic Test: What Do You Know?

Choose the letter of the best revision for each underlined word or group of words.

Kevin and me did a report on peer pressure. Our teacher Mrs.
(1)
Lourdes asked him and me to do an oral presentation in class.
(2)
Peer means "equal in age or rank." Peer pressure is the influence

that people in you're own age group have on you. People want to
(3)
be accepted by their peer group. This here is why peer pressure is
(4)   (5)
so powerful. Peer pressure can be negative, but it's positive too.
(6)
One boy we interviewed said, "My buddy signed up for the

basketball team. Him and Daniel pressured me to sign up too.
(7)
Us buddies always do things together." Whom can resist the
(8)   (9)
pressure of two friends? "I'm glad I joined the team. The coach,

like the rest of us, is enjoying ourselves!"
(10)

1. A. Kevin and I
   B. Me and Kevin
   C. Us
   D. Correct as is

2. A. he and me
   B. him and I
   C. he and I
   D. Correct as is

3. A. yours
   B. youre
   C. your
   D. Correct as is

4. A. there
   B. theirs
   C. they're
   D. Correct as is

5. A. That there
   B. This
   C. These
   D. Correct as is

6. A. its
   B. its'
   C. it
   D. Correct as is

7. A. Daniel and him
   B. Daniel and them
   C. He and Daniel
   D. Correct as is

8. A. Them buddies
   B. We buddies
   C. Me and them buddies
   D. Correct as is

9. A. Who
   B. Which
   C. Whose
   D. Correct as is

10. A. himself
    B. theirselves
    C. myself
    D. Correct as is

What Is a Pronoun?

① Here's the Idea

> **A pronoun is a word that is used in place of a noun or another pronoun.** Like a noun, a pronoun can refer to a person, place, thing, or idea. The word that a personal pronoun refers to is called its **antecedent.**

REFERS TO

Alexis **is a great friend. She is so funny!**

REFERS TO

Alexis **read her jokes to the class.**

Personal Pronouns

> **Pronouns such as *we, I, he, them,* and *it* are called personal pronouns.**

Unlike nouns, personal pronouns change their forms to reflect **person, number,** and **case.**

Person and Number Personal pronouns have different forms for first person, second person, and third person. Pronouns can be singular or plural in number.

	Singular	Plural
First person:	**I went out.**	**We left early.**
Second person:	**You left too.**	**You are all leaving.**
Third person:	**He came by bus.**	**They came by car.**

Case Personal pronouns change their forms, or cases, depending on how they are used in a sentence. Each pronoun has three cases: subject, object, and possessive.

Subject:	**He just started middle school.**
Object:	**Scott met him on the first day.**
Possessive:	**Now Scott is his best friend.**

In the chart on the next page, notice how personal pronouns change according to their person, number, and case. You'll learn more about each case in the next three lessons.

CHAPTER 3

Personal Pronouns			
	Subject	**Object**	**Possessive**
Singular			
First person	I	me	my, mine
Second person	you	you	your, yours
Third person	he, she, it	him, her, it	his, her, hers, its
Plural			
First person	we	us	our, ours
Second person	you	you	your, yours
Third person	they	them	their, theirs

❷ Why It Matters in Writing

Without personal pronouns, the narrator of the passage below would need to repeat her friend's name and her own name several times! Instead, she uses forms of *I* and *you*.

LITERARY MODEL

Don't invite **me** to **your** birthday party because I'm not coming. And give back the Disneyland sweat shirt I said **you** could wear. If I'm not good enough to play on **your** team, I'm not good enough to be friends with.

—Judith Viorst, "The Southpaw"

❸ Practice and Apply

A. CONCEPT CHECK: What Is a Pronoun?

List the personal pronoun(s) in each sentence.

Definition of a Friend
1. Did you ever see the statue in front of Boys Town?
2. It shows one boy carrying a smaller boy.
3. Its caption says, "He ain't heavy, Father, . . . he's m' brother."
4. True friends are not burdens when they need help.

5. I interviewed my classmates about friendship.

6. "What is a friend?" I asked them.

7. They gave me different answers—all of them good.

8. "A friend stands by you no matter what," said Rachel.

9. "My friends want to be with me, and I want to be with them," Lenny said.

10. Sue said, "For me, friends are loyal, or they aren't friends."

➜ **For a SELF-CHECK and more practice, see the EXERCISE BANK, p. 269.**

B. REVISING: Substituting Pronouns for Nouns

Rewrite this student's draft of a social studies report. Change the underlined nouns to pronouns.

In ancient times, the idea of friendship was foreign to many people. **(1)** Many people didn't even have a word for "friend." In Old English, though, the word *friend* did exist. **(2)** The word *friend* first appeared in English in A.D. 1018.

Most ancient people lived in close communities. **(3)** Most ancient people had little contact with outsiders. These people did have a word for "stranger." **(4)** The word for "stranger" meant "enemy."

Today, we meet "strangers" all the time. Are these strangers enemies? Most of **(5)** these strangers are not. In fact, many strangers will become our friends.

C. WRITING: Dialogue

Write a dialogue between you and a friend of yours. In the dialogue, ask your friend for advice. When you're finished, underline all the personal pronouns you used.

Example:

You: Can <u>you</u> help <u>me</u>? <u>I</u> have a problem.

Friend: What is <u>it</u>? If <u>I</u> can help <u>you</u>, <u>I</u> will.

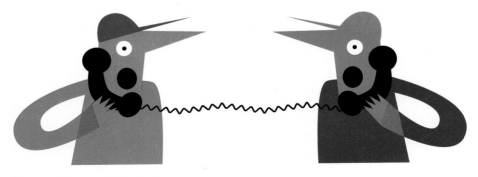

Subject Pronouns

❶ Here's the Idea

▶ **A subject pronoun is used as the subject of a sentence or as a predicate pronoun after a linking verb.**

Singular	Plural
I	we
you	you
he, she, it	they

Pronouns as Subjects

Use the subject case of a pronoun when the pronoun is the subject of a sentence. Remember, a pronoun can be part of a compound subject.

Friends often play on opposing teams. They compete hard against each other. (*They* replaces noun subject *Friends*.)

Charlene and I play on different teams.

We stay friends no matter what.

Predicate Pronouns

A predicate pronoun follows a linking verb and renames, or refers to, the subject. Use the subject case for predicate pronouns.

SUBJECT ⬎ ↘ RENAMES
Mrs. Sands is the coach. The coach is she.
PREDICATE PRONOUN ↗

RENAMES
The best players are Aaron and I.

RENAMES
The toughest opponents are Teresa and he.

Remember, the most common linking verbs are forms of the verb *be*; they include *is, am, are, was, were, been, has been, have been, can be, will be, could be,* and *should be*.

② Why It Matters in Writing

Sometimes subject pronouns may sound strange even though they are correct. As many writers have discovered, you can't rely on "sound" to choose the correct case.

STUDENT MODEL

Michael Jordan is a close friend of Charles Barkley. However, on court the fiercest competitors were ~~him~~ *he* and Charles. Off the court, Hermano and ~~me~~ *I* saw them laughing and playing golf together.

③ Practice and Apply

CONCEPT CHECK: Subject Pronouns

Write the correct form of the pronoun to complete each sentence.

Friends across the (Tennis) Net
1. I read about Martina Navratilova and Chris Evert. (Them, They) were the top two women tennis players in the early 1980s.
2. Martina and (her, she) played each other 80 times.
3. Rulers of the tennis courts were (they, them)!
4. My friend Elana and (me, I) are tennis rivals, too.
5. (We, Us) like to win but stay friends, just like Martina and Chris.
6. If Martina won, (she, her) would go over and comfort Chris.
7. Sometimes (they, them) would leave each other notes, like "Sorry," or "I'm sure you'll get me next time."
8. My brother is different. (He, Him) hates his rivals.
9. He's not like me and my friends. Best friends and tennis players are (us, we)!
10. Martina and (we, us) agree—be rivals on the court but stay close off the court.

➡ **For a SELF-CHECK and more practice, see the EXERCISE BANK, p. 269.**

Object Pronouns

LESSON 3

❶ Here's the Idea

▶ **Object pronouns are personal pronouns used as direct objects, as indirect objects, or as the objects of prepositions.**

Object Pronouns	
Singular	**Plural**
me	us
you	you
him, her, it	them

Direct Object: receives the action of a verb and answers the question *whom or what?*

> **True animal stories fascinate Jen.** (fascinate whom? *Jen*)
> DIRECT OBJECT

> **Do you like them too?** (like what? *them*)

Indirect Object: tells *to whom or what* or *for whom or what* an action is performed.

> TO WHOM?
> **Jen gave me a book about a dolphin who guided ships.**
> INDIRECT OBJECT

> **People gave him a hero's welcome.**

Object of a Preposition: follows a preposition (such as *to, from, for, against, by,* or *about*).

> **We'd like to hear more about him.**
> PREPOSITION   OBJECT

> **Can you tell the story to her and me?**
> PREPOSITION   OBJECT   OBJECT

Always use an object pronoun after the preposition *between.*

> **The books were divided between Mike and me.** (Not between Mike and I)

PRONOUNS

❷ Why It Matters in Writing

Using the pronouns *I* and *me* allows the writer to be up close and personal. In the passage below, Helen Keller uses these pronouns to describe when she first felt loved.

> **LITERARY MODEL**
>
> **I** stretched out my hand. . . . Someone took it, and **I** was caught up and held close in the arms of her who had come to reveal all things to **me,** and, more than all things else, to love **me.**
>
> —Helen Keller, *The Story of My Life*

❸ Practice and Apply

CONCEPT CHECK: Subject and Object Pronouns

Write the correct pronoun(s) for each sentence. Label each pronoun *subject* or *object.*

The Sailors' Friend

1. Jen told (we, us) a true story about a dolphin.
2. People gave (he, him) the name Pelorus Jack.
3. (He, Him) guided ships through the dangerous Cook Strait near New Zealand.
4. No one trained (he, him) to do this.
5. It was (he, him) who decided to guide ships.
6. Ships would come to the strait, and (he, him) would lead (they, them) out of danger.
7. Sailors watched (he, him) leaping through the waves.
8. Pelorus Jack swam swiftly in front of (they, them) and brought their ships through the strait.
9. (He, Him) was protected from harm by New Zealand law.
10. A movie was even made about (he, him)!

➜ **For a SELF-CHECK and more practice, see EXERCISE BANK, p. 270.**

CHALLENGE

Identify how each object pronoun you chose is used in the sentence: as a direct object, an indirect object, or an object of a preposition.

Possessive Pronouns

① Here's the Idea

▶ **Possessive pronouns are personal pronouns used to show ownership or relationship.**

Possessive Pronouns	
Singular	**Plural**
my, mine	our, ours
your, yours	your, yours
her, hers, his, its	their, theirs

The possessive pronouns *my, your, her, his, our,* and *their* come before nouns.

RELATIONSHIP

Some of my best friends live in other countries.

OWNERSHIP

All our correspondence is by e-mail.

OWNERSHIP

Even their old computers are on-line now.

The possessive pronouns *mine, ours, yours, his, hers,* and *theirs* can stand alone in a sentence.

The blue mouse pad is theirs. Ours is red.

Is that video game yours? Mine is broken.

Is his any good? Or should we play hers?

Possessive Pronouns and Contractions

Some possessive pronouns sound like contractions (*its/it's, your/you're, their/they're*). Because these pairs sound alike, writers often confuse possessive pronouns and contractions.

Remember, possessive pronouns *never* use an apostrophe. Contractions *always* use an apostrophe. Look at the examples in the Quick-Fix Spelling Machine on the following page.

QUICK-FIX SPELLING MACHINE

POSSESSIVE PRONOUNS		CONTRACTIONS	
its	Its modem is fast!	it's	It's fun to get new mail.
your	Your e-mails are funny.	you're	You're a good writer.
their	Their smiles are sideways! :-)	they're	They're full of funny faces.

❷ Why It Matters in Writing

Proofread your work carefully to be sure you haven't confused contractions and possessive pronouns. A computer spell checker will not catch these mistakes.

STUDENT MODEL

A circle of mountains lies deep under the Pacific Ocean between Japan and North America. It is known as the "ring of fire." If ~~your~~ *you're* wondering why, it's because the mountains are part of a circle of active volcanoes.

A volcanic eruption at sea can cause tsunami waves. ~~They're~~ *Their* danger is hard to see at first. A tsunami crossing the ocean is barely a ripple. But when it nears land, a tsunami can travel nearly 500 miles an hour and reach a height of over 100 feet. It destroys everything in ~~it's~~ *its* path.

In 1993 a tsunami struck Okushiri, Japan, and destroyed its wharf.

❸ Practice and Apply

A. CONCEPT CHECK: Possessive Pronouns

Write the correct pronoun or contraction for each sentence.

> **Cyber Friends**
> **1.** (Its, It's) now possible for schools throughout the world to be linked on the Internet.
> **2.** A school can partner with a "Sister School" overseas to learn about (its, it's) land and culture.
> **3.** If (your, you're) interested, contact the Society for International Sister Schools (SISS).
> **4.** (Your, You're) school can correspond with schools in Russia, Mexico, Korea, Ireland—almost anywhere!
> **5.** Your international Web pals write from (their, they're) computers, and you write from yours.
> **6.** Within minutes, (their, they're) sending you e-mails through cyberspace.
> **7.** Some schools post on-line surveys for (their, they're) Sister Schools to answer.
> **8.** *Hablo Español?* You can sharpen (your, you're) Spanish or other language writing skills.
> **9.** There are many native speakers in the program, and (their, they're) happy to help you!
> **10.** Maybe someday SISS will even have (its, it's) own virtual classroom!

➜ For a SELF-CHECK and more practice, see the EXERCISE BANK, p. 270.

B. PROOFREADING: Using Possessive Pronouns

For each sentence, write the correct form of the possessive pronoun or contractions. If a sentence contains no error, write *Correct*.

(1) Hey, Josie,
Your probably amazed finally to hear from me! I meant to answer your e-mail right away, but its been a crazy time. **(2)** Our class is doing a climate project for the Science Fair, and I am in charge of gathering data! **(3)** Our Sister School in Hirosaki, Japan, is helping us. **(4)** Its so great having a Sister School! **(5)** Their sending us information about their climate. **(6)** It's perfect because **(7)** their latitude is about the same as ours in Baltimore. **(8)** Your invited to see the exhibit when its done.

LESSON 5 Reflexive and Intensive Pronouns

1 Here's the Idea

Pronouns that end in *-self* or *-selves* are either **reflexive** or **intensive** pronouns.

Reflexive and Intensive Pronouns		
myself	yourself	herself, himself, itself
ourselves	yourselves	themselves

Reflexive Pronouns

▶ **A reflexive pronoun refers to the subject and directs the action of the verb back to the subject.** Reflexive pronouns are necessary to the meaning of a sentence.

REFLECTS

The **winners considered themselves** lucky.

REFLECTS

How do **you prepare yourself** for a game?

Notice that if you drop the reflexive pronoun, you change the meaning of the sentence. (*The winners considered lucky.*)

Intensive Pronouns

▶ **An intensive pronoun emphasizes the noun or pronoun in the same sentence.** Intensive pronouns are not necessary to the meaning of the sentence.

EMPHASIZES

I myself just keep saying, "We'll win!"

EMPHASIZES

The players themselves designed their uniforms.

Notice that when you drop the intensive pronoun, the sentence still makes sense. (*I just keep saying, "We'll win!"*)

Hisself and *theirselves* may look like real words, but they are not in the dictionary. Use *himself* and *themselves* instead.

CHAPTER 3

❷ Why It Matters in Writing

Notice how the student sportswriter uses reflexive and intensive pronouns to emphasize key words and ideas.

STUDENT MODEL

The U.S. women's soccer team won the 1999 World Cup in a final shootout. At the end, the players themselves were screaming for joy. Injured player Michelle Akers said: "I found myself hobbling out to the field to join my team. The 90,185 fans were going crazy. I was struggling to soak it all in and keep myself together."

INTENSIVE

REFLEXIVE

❸ Practice and Apply

CONCEPT CHECK: Reflexive and Intensive Pronouns

For each sentence, write the reflexive or intensive pronoun. Then label it *reflexive* or *intensive*.

All for One and One for All
1. My sister Emmy never pictured herself playing team sports.
2. Now Emmy herself admits that her best friends are her soccer teammates.
3. The players have to get themselves in step with the team.
4. One player can't win a match all by himself or herself!
5. Pro athletes themselves encourage young people to join teams.
6. Olympic soccer player Mia Hamm said: "Don't worry about how well you play; just enjoy yourself."
7. As a teen, pro basketball player Cynthia Cooper found herself imitating how the pros played.
8. She herself didn't try out for a team until she was 16.
9. I myself will never forget Sammy Sosa embracing Mark McGwire—his home-run rival!
10. Team players think of others besides themselves.

➡ For a SELF-CHECK and more practice, see the EXERCISE BANK, p. 271.

Interrogatives and Demonstratives

❶ Here's the Idea

Interrogative Pronouns

▶ **An interrogative pronoun is used to introduce a question.** Interrogative pronouns include *who, whom, what, which,* and *whose.*

> **Who has an animal for a friend?**
>
> **What do you like best about animals?**

Writers often confuse *who* and *whom.* The following guidelines can help you decide which form to use in your sentences.

Using *Who* and *Whom*

▶ ***Who* is always used as a subject or a predicate pronoun.**

> Subject: **Who gave you the parakeet?**
>
> Predicate pronoun: **It was who?**

 Don't confuse *who's* with *whose. Who's* is a contraction that means *who is* or *who has.* (*Who's missing?*) *Whose* is an interrogative or possessive pronoun. (*Whose is this?*)

▶ ***Whom* is always used as an object.**

> Direct object: **Whom do you ask about pet stores?**
>
> Indirect object: **You gave whom a turtle?**
>
> Object of preposition: **From whom did you buy it?**

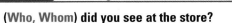

Here's How Choosing *Who* or *Whom* in a Question

(Who, Whom) did you see at the store?

1. If necessary, rewrite the question to put the subject first.
   You did see (who, whom) at the store?
2. Decide whether the pronoun is used as a subject or an object.
   You is already the subject. *Whom* is used as an object.
   You did see whom at the store? (direct object of *did see*)
3. Use the correct pronoun in the question.
   Whom did you see at the store?

Demonstrative Pronouns

▶ **A demonstrative pronoun points out a person, place, thing, or idea.**

Demonstrative pronouns—*this, that, these,* and *those*—are used alone in a sentence, as shown below.

Singular

This is my parakeet Newton.

That is his new cage.

Plural

These are his chewed-up toys.

Those are his favorite treats.

This and *these* mean that something is near, or here. *That* and *those* mean that something is far away, or there. Never use *here* or *there* with a demonstrative pronoun. The pronoun already points out which one; it doesn't need help.

This ~~here~~ is our cat.

That ~~there~~ is our crazy dog.

❷ Why It Matters in Writing

Knowing when to use *who* and *whom* can be tricky because many people use these pronouns incorrectly. Be careful to use the correct pronouns when you create questionnaires or surveys, like the one below.

STUDENT MODEL

Questionnaire for Friends

- Who is your oldest friend?   **SUBJECT**
- Who talks more—you or your best friend?
- With whom would you share your deepest   **OBJECT OF PREPOSITION**
  secret?
- Whom would you trust for advice?   **DIRECT OBJECT**

PRONOUNS

❸ Practice and Apply

A. CONCEPT CHECK: Interrogatives and Demonstratives

Write the correct pronoun to complete each sentence. Then identify it as an *interrogative* or *demonstrative* pronoun.

Four-Legged Versus Two-Legged Friends
1. **Aretha:** (Who, Whose) is your best friend?
2. **Cindy:** (That, That there) is easy: either Marsha Hanks or my dog Bandit.
3. **Aretha:** (Which, What) is it?
4. Besides, (who, whom) would prefer dogs as best friends?
5. **Cindy:** (Those, That) are the best kind.
6. (Who, Whom) loves you all the time? Only a dog.
7. (Who, Whom) can you play with anytime? A dog!
8. **Aretha:** (Those, Those there) are good arguments. I hadn't thought about it that way.
9. **Cindy:** By the way, your best friend is (who, whom)?
10. **Aretha:** (Who, Whom) would I choose? My parakeet Newton. I can talk to him about anything, and he talks back!

→ For a SELF-CHECK and more practice, see the EXERCISE BANK, p. 271.

B. WRITING: Science Questions and Answers

Write a five-question quiz based on the article below. Use each of these interrogative pronouns at least once: *who, whom, what,* and *which.* Underline the interrogative pronouns you use.

Example: <u>Who</u> learned sign language first—Koko or Michael?

In July 1972, Penny Patterson first met her good friend Koko. Penny was a graduate student at a major university. Koko was a one-year-old female lowland gorilla. Penny taught Koko sign language. Today, Koko knows more than 1,000 signs. She uses them to "talk" to humans and to her friend Michael, another lowland gorilla. Koko and Penny taught Michael to use sign language as well.

CHAPTER 3

Pronoun-Antecedent Agreement

LESSON 7

❶ Here's the Idea

▶ **The antecedent is the noun or pronoun that a pronoun replaces or refers to.** The antecedent can be in the same sentence or in a different sentence from the pronoun.

REFERS TO

Maria shared her favorite book, *The Friends*.
　ANTECEDENT　PRONOUN

REFERS TO

The story is set in Harlem. It tells about young girls growing up.

Pronouns must agree with their antecedents in number, person, and gender.

Agreement in Number

▶ **Use a singular pronoun to refer to a singular antecedent.**

REFERS TO

At first Phyllisia doesn't like her new classmate.

▶ **Use a plural pronoun to refer to a plural antecedent.**

REFERS TO

Later the girls share their dreams together.

Agreement in Person

▶ **The person of a pronoun must be the same as the person of the antecedent.**

3RD PERSON

The author is Rosa Guy. She was born in Trinidad.

2ND PERSON

Do you write stories about your life?

Avoid switching from one person to another in the same sentence or paragraph.

Incorrect:
> **Students like strong plots. We want to know what happens.** (*Students* is third person; *we* is first person.)

Correct:
> **Students like strong plots. They want to know what happens.** (*Students* and *they* are both third person.)

Agreement in Gender

▶ **The gender of a pronoun must be the same as the gender of its antecedent.**

Personal pronouns have three gender forms: masculine (*he, his, him*), feminine (*she, her, hers*), and neuter (*it, its*).

> **Anne is mad because she lost her book.**

> **Jim gave his extra copy to Anne.**

Don't use only masculine or only feminine pronouns when you mean to refer to both genders.

DRAFT:
> **Every student has his own opinion.**
> (Student could be male or female.)

There are two ways to correct this sentence.

1. Use the phrase *his or her*.
   Every student has his or her own opinion.

2. Rewrite the sentence using a plural antecedent and a plural pronoun. Be careful! Other words in the sentence may also need to be made plural.
   Students have their own opinions.

❷ Why It Matters in Writing

It's easy to make mistakes with person or number. Proofread your writing carefully. Avoid the common errors that the student writer made in the model on the following page.

Best **friends** come in all shapes and sizes.
~~You~~ *They* may be opposites of each other. For

instance, you might not like **someone** at first.
Then later on ~~they~~ *he or she* become, your best friend.

> *Friends* is third person plural.

> *Someone* is singular and could be male or female.

❸ Practice and Apply

CONCEPT CHECK: Pronoun-Antecedent Agreement

For each sentence, write the personal pronoun and its antecedent.

Number the Stars
1. This story is by Lois Lowry. It is set in Denmark during World War II.
2. Annemarie Johansen and her best friend Ellen Rosen live happily—until the Nazis come.
3. Then the girls are scared as their lives turn upside down.
4. Ellen is in special danger because her family is Jewish.
5. The Nazis have targeted all Jews as their enemies.
6. Annemarie's parents hide Ellen in their home.
7. The Johansens know that they must also try to protect Ellen's family.
8. Uncle Henrik uses his boat to carry some Jews to safety.
9. When Annemarie is asked to go on this dangerous ride, she agrees.
10. She must find the strength to save her best friend's life.

➡ For a SELF-CHECK and more practice, see the EXERCISE BANK, p. 272.

Write the number and person of each pronoun.

NUMBER THE STARS
Lois Lowry
LAUREL-LEAF ⬥ NEWBERY

PRONOUNS

Indefinite Pronoun Agreement

❶ Here's the Idea

▶ **An indefinite pronoun does not refer to a specific person, place, thing, or idea.**

Indefinite pronouns often do not have antecedents.

Everyone should know about the men of the *Endurance*.

Anybody would be amazed by the story of this shipwreck.

▶ **Indefinite pronouns can be singular, plural, or either singular or plural.**

Indefinite Pronouns			
Singular		**Plural**	**Singular or Plural**
another	neither	both	all
anybody	nobody	few	any
anyone	no one	many	most
anything	nothing	several	none
each	one		some
either	somebody		
everybody	someone		
everyone	something		
everything			

Pronouns containing *-one, -thing,* or *-body* are always singular.

Singular Indefinite Pronouns

▶ **Use a singular personal pronoun to refer to a singular indefinite pronoun.**

REFERS TO

Anyone in trouble depends on his or her friends.
(*Anyone* could be masculine or feminine.)

REFERS TO

On the *Endurance*, everybody had to keep up his spirits while waiting for rescue. (There were only men on the ship.)

Plural Indefinite Pronouns

▶ **Use a plural personal pronoun to refer to a plural indefinite pronoun.**

REFERS TO

Many shared their food and clothing.

REFERS TO

None realized they would not return home for 20 months.

Singular or Plural Indefinite Pronouns

▶ **Some indefinite pronouns can be singular or plural.**
Often the phrase that follows the indefinite pronoun will tell you whether the pronoun is singular or plural.

Most of the mast had lost its sail.
  ⬆ SINGULAR INDEFINITE PRONOUN   ⬆ SINGULAR PERSONAL PRONOUN

Most of the masts had lost their sails.
  ⬆ PLURAL INDEFINITE PRONOUN   ⬆ PLURAL PERSONAL PRONOUN

❷ Why It Matters in Writing

Agreement can help keep your facts and ideas clear. Make sure that all pronouns agree with their indefinite antecedents in number.

STUDENT MODEL

Many wonder how well ~~he~~ *they* would do in a crisis. The men aboard the ship *Endurance* had a chance to find out. Everyone did ~~their~~ *his* best to keep up hope. The leaders and crew battled wind, ice, and darkness. No one wanted to let ~~their~~ *his* friends down.

❸ Practice and Apply

A. CONCEPT CHECK: Indefinite-Pronoun Agreement

Choose the pronoun that agrees with the indefinite pronoun antecedent.

The Ordeal of the *Endurance*

1. In 1915, all of the men became trapped with (his, their) ship in the Antarctic ice.
2. No one could send (his, their) family a message.
3. Few of them were able to avoid sleeping on the ice in (his, their) wet clothes.
4. When spring came, all the men had to board three lifeboats. (He, They) sailed toward a splinter of land.
5. Each was relieved when (he, they) reached the land safely.
6. Shackleton chose a few of the men and asked (him, them) to row 800 icy miles to get help.
7. Each was chosen for (his, their) special courage.
8. One used (his, their) carpentry skills to make new boat parts from packing crates!
9. Some of the waves were 50 feet high. The men had to face (it, them) in only a lifeboat!
10. Incredibly, nobody in Shackleton's crew lost (his, their) life during the voyage.

→ For a SELF-CHECK and more practice, see the EXERCISE BANK, p. 272.

B. PROOFREADING: Agreement Errors

This paragraph contains four pronoun-antecedent errors. Rewrite the sentences to correct the errors.

Rescue in the Antarctic!

Ernest Shackleton chose five men to sail with him on a fearsome journey to find help. Many left on the island had his troubles too. Everyone had to eat penguins and seals for their daily diet. Several men had frostbite. One needed medical attention for his infected wound. Everyone in the remaining crew anxiously awaited their rescue. Nearly five months after Shackleton left, all of the men had his dream come true. Shackleton and the others came back for them!

LESSON 9 Pronoun Problems

① Here's the Idea

We and Us with Nouns

The pronouns *we* and *us* are sometimes followed by a noun that identifies the pronoun (*we students*, *us students*).

▶ **Use *we* when the noun is a subject or a predicate noun. Use *us* when the noun is an object.**

We volunteers like to help out.
　　　↖SUBJECT

Do you have work for us volunteers?
　　　　　　　↖OBJECT OF PREPOSITION

> **Here's How** Choosing *We* or *Us*
>
> **You can join (we, us) students tomorrow.**
>
> **1.** Drop the identifying noun from the sentence.
>
> **You can join (we, us) tomorrow.**
>
> **2.** Decide whether the pronoun is used as a subject or an object. In this sentence, the pronoun is the object of the verb *join*.
>
> **You can join us tomorrow.**
>
> **3.** Use the correct pronoun with the noun.
>
> **You can join us students tomorrow.**

Unclear Reference

▶ **Be sure that each personal pronoun refers clearly to only one person, place, or thing.** If there is any chance your reader will be confused by whom or what you are talking about, use a noun instead of a pronoun.

Confusing:

Noah and Rodrigo came to the work site, but he didn't stay. (Who didn't stay? Noah or Rodrigo?)

Clear:

Noah and Rodrigo came to the work site, but Noah didn't stay.

PRONOUNS

❷ Why It Matters in Writing

When you write instructions or directions, make sure you use the right case and keep your pronoun references clear. You don't want to confuse your readers, as this writer did.

STUDENT MODEL

Heads up! Hands out!

~~Us~~ *We* youth volunteers need help. Can

you join us? Call Nicki at 555-2222 or

Ann at 555-0000. ~~She~~ *Nicki* has an answering

machine, so leave a message!

> Use *we* as the subject.

> *She* could mean either Nicki or Ann. Name the person to avoid confusion.

❸ Practice and Apply

A. CONCEPT CHECK: Pronoun Problems

Write the correct pronoun or noun.

Helping Hands
1. (We, Us) students help out in lots of ways.
2. That garden was planted by (we, us) volunteers.
3. Carlos worked with Joe to clean the river, even though (he, Carlos) had never done that kind of work before.
4. Some of (we, us) athletes offered to coach youngsters.
5. Stacey always beats Terese to work, but (she, Terese) still gets there on time.

➜ For a SELF-CHECK and more practice, see the EXERCISE BANK, p. 273.

B. REVISING: Correcting Pronoun Errors

Correct the four pronoun errors in the following paragraph.

Cleaning up on the River!
Us swimmers are determined to clean up the riverbanks. The garbage there has disgusted we kids for a long time. For months, the mayor and the parks commissioner talked about doing something, but he didn't take any action. Danielle worked with Margo to pick up junk along the shore. She filled three trash bags in one hour!

More Pronoun Problems

LESSON 10

❶ Here's the Idea

Using Pronouns in Compounds

People often make mistakes when they use pronouns as parts of compound subjects and compound objects.

▶ Use the subject pronouns *I, she, he, we,* and *they* in a compound subject or a compound predicate pronoun.

Shawn and he are on the same study team.

The leaders of the team are he and I.

▶ Use the object pronouns *me, her, him, us,* and *them* in a compound object.

Our friends saw Darlene and me at the library.

The librarian gave Shawn and her some books.

To choose the correct case of a pronoun in a compound subject or object, mentally screen out the other noun or pronoun. Then choose the correct case.

Shawn gave an article to ~~Darlene and~~ (I, me). (*Me* is the object of the preposition *to*—therefore, *to Darlene and me* is correct.)

Phrases that Interfere

Sometimes words and phrases come between a subject and a pronoun that refers to it. Don't be confused by the words in between.

REFERS TO

Darlene, ~~like the others,~~ is working on her report.
(*Her* agrees with *Danielle* and not with *others*.)

REFERS TO

Harriet Tubman, ~~unlike many people,~~ risked her life to free slaves. (*Her* agrees with *Harriet Tubman* and not with *people*.)

PRONOUNS

❷ Why It Matters in Writing

Some people think *I* sounds more correct than *me* in a compound object. "I" is only correct when used as a subject or predicate pronoun. Watch out for this common mistake when you write.

> **STUDENT MODEL**
>
> You and I make great study partners. It's easy to divide
> the work between you and ~~I.~~ *me* I ask the questions. You find
> the answers!

❸ Practice and Apply

A. CONCEPT CHECK: More Pronoun Problems

Choose the correct pronoun to complete each sentence.

A Friend to Her People

1. Our social studies teacher asked Danielle and (I, me) to do a report on Harriet Tubman.
2. The librarian helped (her, she) and me with the research.
3. Both (she, her) and I knew that Tubman led slaves to freedom on the Underground Railroad.
4. Many facts about Tubman were new to (she, her) and me.
5. More than 300 slaves, including Harriet's own sister, owed (their, her) freedom to Tubman.
6. (She, Her) and the runaways had to move secretly from one house to another along the Underground Railroad.
7. Tubman, like other conductors, wouldn't let any of (her, their) runaways turn back.
8. Slave owners placed a $40,000 reward on her head. That fact surprised Danielle and (me, I).
9. John Brown, another of the freedom fighters, praised Tubman in (his, their) letters and speeches.
10. The librarian gave copies of some letters to Danielle and (I, me).

➜ **For a SELF-CHECK and more practice, see the EXERCISE BANK, p. 274.**

B. PROOFREADING: Correct Use of Pronouns

On a separate sheet of paper, correct the underlined pronoun errors.

<u>Darren and me</u> read about the Underground Railroad. <u>Him and I</u> soon realized that it was not "underground" and it was not a "railroad." Instead, it was a secret network of escape routes for slaves. This network of escape routes had <u>their</u> beginning in the South. The paths of the Underground Railroad crisscrossed <u>its</u> way through the North. Eventually, many routes ended in Canada. Canada, unlike the United States, had outlawed slavery within <u>their</u> borders.

The Underground Railroad was a hard journey for runaway slaves. Abolitionists and <u>them</u> were tracked by slave hunters. Anyone caught could be tried and sentenced to death!

C. WRITING: SOCIAL STUDIES: Drafting from a Time Line

Read the following biographical time line. Then write a paragraph about Harriet Tubman, based on the information. Underline any pronouns you use.

Example: Harriet Tubman was born around 1820 in Dorchester County, Maryland. <u>She</u> ran away for the first time when <u>she</u> was about six or seven years old.

1820?
Born in Dorchester County, Maryland.

1849
Harriet flees to Pennsylvania and freedom. Many people help Harriet along the Underground Railroad.

| 1820 | 1830 | 1840 | 1850 | 1860 |

1827?
Runs away for the first time, but goes back. Is punished by the farm owners Harriet worked for.

1844
Marries John Tubman. Wants John to run away with her. John refuses and stays in Maryland.

1850–1860s
Serves as a conductor on the Underground Railroad. Brings more than 300 people out of slavery. People admire Harriet. People call Harriet "Moses."

Grammar in Literature

Using Pronouns in Dialogue

You can use **dialogue,** or conversation, in stories and plays to show what your characters think and feel. Pronouns can make your dialogue sound more natural and make your characters seem more realistic. As you read this excerpt from *Damon and Pythias: A Drama,* notice how the use of pronouns makes the conversation between the two friends seem real.

DAMON
AND
PYTHIAS

RETOLD BY FAN KISSEN

Damon. Oh, Pythias! How terrible to find you here! I wish I could do something to save you!

Pythias. Nothing can save me, Damon, my dear friend. I am prepared to die. But there is one thought that troubles me greatly.

Damon. What is it? I will do anything to help you.

Pythias. I'm worried about what will happen to my mother and my sister when I'm gone.

Damon. I'll take care of them, Pythias, as if they were my own mother and sister.

Pythias. Thank you, Damon. I have money to leave them. But there are other things I must arrange. If only I could go to see them before I die! But they live two days' journey from here, you know.

Damon. I'll go to the king and beg him to give you your freedom for a few days. You'll give your word to return at the end of that time. Everyone in Sicily knows you for a man who has never broken his word.

Top left: Detail of statue of Diadoumenos (440 B.C.), unknown artist. Roman copy of Greek original, pentelic marble, The Metropolitan Museum of Art, Fletcher Fund, 1925 (25.78.56). Copyright © The Metropolitan Museum of Art. Top right: Detail of Chiron the centaur teaching Achilles to play the lyre (first to third century A.D.), Roman fresco from Pompeii, Museo Archeologico Nazionale, Naples, Italy. Photo copyright © Erich Lessing/Art Resource, New York.

Practice and Apply

WRITING: Using Pronouns in Dialogue

When actor Clifton Davis was a boy in the 1950s, he was
the only African American in his middle school class. For
graduation, the class was going to Glenn Echo Amusement
Park in Maryland. Then Clifton learned that he would not be
allowed into the park because he was black. He went back to
his room, crying.

When he told his friend Frank what was wrong, Frank said
he wouldn't go to the park either. Clifton knew how badly
Frank wanted to go, but his friend was firm. Frank also told
the other boys, and they all refused to go to the park. Clifton
felt proud that he had such loyal friends.

Write a dialogue between Clifton and Frank that dramatizes this
story. When you are finished, underline the pronouns you used.
How did they help make the dialogue sound more realistic?

Frank: Hey Clifton, why do you seem down?

Clifton: I just found out that I can't go with
the rest of you to the amusement park.

Mixed Review

A. Pronouns Choose the correct pronoun for each sentence.

1. Everyone in our class had to write (his or her, their) report on a myth.
2. Shirell and I worked together. (We, Us) chose a myth about Damon and Pythias.
3. Between you and (I, me), this myth turned out to be really good.
4. Damon and Pythias, each from a noble family, had vowed (his, their) undying loyalty to each other.
5. Pythias, sentenced to death by Dionysius, asked permission to leave the city to put (his, their) affairs in order.
6. Damon promised to die in place of Pythias if (he, Pythias) did not return on time.
7. Pythias, unexpectedly delayed, almost failed to keep (his, their) word.
8. Damon was nearly killed in (his, their) place.
9. Pythias saved (him, he) by arriving just in time.
10. Dionysius marveled at their friendship. He pardoned Pythias and asked the two to become (his, their) friends.

B. Revising: Using Pronouns Correctly This passage contains six errors in pronoun usage. Rewrite the paragraph to correct the errors.

STUDENT MODEL

Between you and I, the idea of reading "ancient stories" sounded boring to me. Then us students read a few Greek myths in class. It was the first time a teacher explained the stories to Kirsten and I. The action kept us interested. Her and I really liked the heroic characters Hercules and Jason. The two of they were always doing something exciting, like fighting monsters. Some of my friends like to act out his or her favorite characters. These myths would make great TV movies!

Mastery Test: What Did You Learn?

Choose the correct replacement for each underlined word in the passage, or indicate if it is correct as is.

Whom knows the story of Sacajawea? Ellen, Terri, and me saw
(1)   (2)
a movie about she. Sacajawea befriended Lewis and Clark in 1804
(3)
and helped guide they to the Pacific Ocean. In the early 1800s,
(4)
most of the land west of the Mississippi River was unexplored. The

idea to map the territory was who's? President Jefferson was the
(5)
one who ordered the expedition.

Us students couldn't believe how lucky Lewis and Clark were.
(6)
Them and their men crossed icy rivers and traveled through
(7)
hostile lands. Only one of the travelers lost his life. Sacajawea and
(8)
her husband even took they're baby on the trail! Ellen, along with
(9)
the rest of us, couldn't believe our ears when Sacajawea asked
(10)
Clark to raise her son as his own in St. Louis.

1. A. What
   B. Who
   C. Whose
   D. Correct as is

2. A. us
   B. I
   C. Me, Ellen, and Terri
   D. Correct as is

3. A. her
   B. we
   C. hers
   D. Correct as is

4. A. him
   B. he
   C. them
   D. Correct as is

5. A. whose
   B. who
   C. whom
   D. Correct as is

6. A. Us
   B. Them students
   C. We students
   D. Correct as is

7. A. Him
   B. They
   C. He
   D. Correct as is

8. A. their
   B. her
   C. his or her
   D. Correct as is

9. A. they
   B. their
   C. them
   D. Correct as is

10. A. her
    B. my
    C. their
    D. Correct as is

Student Help Desk

Pronouns at a Glance

Subject Case		Object Case		Possessive Case	
I	we	me	us	my, mine	our, ours
you	you	you	you	your, yours	your, yours
he	they	him	them	his	their, theirs
she		her		her, hers	
it		it		its	

Use this case when
- the pronoun is a **subject**
- the pronoun is a **predicate pronoun**

Use this case when
- the pronoun is a **direct object**
- the pronoun is an **indirect object**
- the pronoun is the **object of a preposition**

Use this case for
- pronouns that show **ownership or relationship**

Me and my Shadow

Pronoun-Antecedent Agreement

A pronoun should agree with its antecedent in number, person, and gender.

A singular antecedent takes a singular pronoun.

Tanya says **her** best friend is a yo-yo champ. (singular)

A plural antecedent takes a plural pronoun.

The **friends** stick together through **their** ups and downs. (plural)

At times the reference will include both genders.

Each has **his or her** special talent.

They have **their** special talents.

Types of Pronouns

"I'm Nobody. Are You Nobody too?"

Intensive & Reflexive	Interrogative	Demonstrative	Indefinite
myself	who	this	someone
herself	whom	that	anyone
himself	what	these	each
itself	which	those	several
yourself	whose		many
ourselves			all
yourselves			most
themselves			none

For a list of indefinite pronouns, see p. 72.

Pronoun Problems

Friends by the Case

We:	Subject/predicate pronoun	**We** guys stick together.
Us:	Object	Nothing comes between **us** guys.
Who:	Subject/predicate pronoun	**Who** is your oldest friend?
Whom:	Object	For **whom** would you do anything?

PRONOUNS

The Bottom Line

Checklist for Pronouns

Have I . . .

____ used the subject case for pronouns that are subjects and predicate pronouns?

____ used the object case for pronouns that are objects?

____ used the possessive case to show ownership or relationship?

____ made sure that pronouns agree with their antecedents in number, person, and gender?

____ used who and whom correctly?

____ used the correct cases in compound subjects and objects?

Verbs

WE MOVE YOU

Theme: On the Move

Moving Words

Verbs make sentences move. Just as a truck can't go anywhere without an engine, a sentence can't go anywhere without a verb. In this chapter, you will learn how to use verbs to move your sentences.

Write Away: Getting There

In a paragraph, describe your favorite way to get around. You can describe any form of transportation—your own two feet, a bike, rollerblades, a train, a car, or even a spaceship. Put the paragraph in your **Working Portfolio.**

Choose the best way to rewrite each underlined word or group of words.

> For more than a hundred years, science fiction writers <u>will predict</u> new ways of transportation. In 1865 Jules Verne <u>wrote</u> a
> (1)
> novel called *From the Earth to the Moon*. Verne <u>is getting</u> many
> (2)
> scientific details right. Science fiction writers today <u>had described</u>
> (3)
> journeys to other galaxies. Someday we <u>are traveling</u> to those
> (4)
> (5)
> distant places, just as we really <u>did travel</u> to the moon more than 30
> (6)
> years ago. Science fiction <u>will contribute</u> to transportation on Earth
> (7)
> as well. In 1903 H. G. Wells <u>maked</u> up military tanks in his short
> (8)
> story "The Land Ironclads." A decade later, during World War I,
> Winston Churchill remembered that story and <u>began</u> the research
> (9)
> that led to tanks. Surely other fictional means of transportation
> <u>are becoming</u> realities in the future.
> (10)

1. A. have predicted
   B. predict
   C. are predicting
   D. Correct as is

2. A. writed
   B. have written
   C. will write
   D. Correct as is

3. A. will get
   B. got
   C. getted
   D. Correct as is

4. A. were describing
   B. will describe
   C. have described
   D. Correct as is

5. A. will travel
   B. have traveled
   C. travel
   D. Correct as is

6. A. should travel
   B. will travel
   C. do travel
   D. Correct as is

7. A. should contribute
   B. is contributing
   C. has contributed
   D. Correct as is

8. A. made
   B. will make
   C. is making
   D. Correct as is

9. A. will begin
   B. has begun
   C. beginned
   D. Correct as is

10. A. became
    B. will become
    C. have become
    D. Correct as is

What Is a Verb?

LESSON 1

① Here's the Idea

▶ **A verb is a word used to express an action, a condition, or a state of being.** The two main types of verbs are **action verbs** and **linking verbs.** Both kinds can be accompanied by helping verbs.

Action Verbs

An **action verb** tells what its subject does. The action it expresses can be either **physical** or **mental.**

Early humans moved constantly. (physical action)

They carried their few possessions with them. (physical action)

These people worried about survival. (mental action)

They feared large animals. (mental action)

Linking Verbs

A **linking verb** links its subject to a word in the predicate. The most common linking verbs are forms of the verb *be.*

Linking Verbs	
Forms of *be*	be, am, is, are, was, were, been, being
Verbs that express condition	appear, become, feel, grow, look, remain, seem, smell, sound, taste

LINKS

Early humans were food gatherers.
LINKING VERB

They often felt hungry.

CHAPTER 4

Some verbs can serve as either action or linking verbs.

Animals appeared at their campsites.
ACTION VERB
LINKS

Some animals appeared friendly.
LINKING VERB

Helping Verbs and Verb Phrases

Helping verbs help main verbs express action or precise shades of meaning. The combination of one or more helping verbs with a main verb is called a **verb phrase.**

VERB PHRASE
Animals could carry the humans' heavy loads farther.
HELPING   MAIN

Then people would travel farther.

Some verbs can serve both as **main verbs** and as **helping verbs.** For example, *had* stands alone in the first sentence below but is a helping verb in the second sentence.

People had tools now.
MAIN VERB

They had mastered many skills.
HELPING VERB

Common Helping Verbs	
Forms of *be*	be, am, is, are, was, were, been, being
Forms of *do*	do, does, did
Forms of *have*	have, has, had
Other	could, should, would, may, might, must, can, shall, will

VERBS

❷ Why It Matters in Writing

When writing, use verbs that are strong and lively. Notice this author's use of *soared, rushed,* and *swirled,* which are more specific than some other verbs, like *dived, went,* and *flowed.*

> **LITERARY MODEL**
>
> We **soared**. The water **rushed** past my face and **swirled** around my body, and I felt the streaking lines of speed.
>
> —Don C. Reed, "My First Dive with the Dolphins"

❸ Practice and Apply

A. CONCEPT CHECK: What Is a Verb?

Write the verb or verb phrase in each of the following sentences.

They Got Around
1. Transportation developed along with civilization.
2. Half a million years ago, humans traveled frequently.
3. They searched for food like nuts and berries.
4. They hunted animals on foot.
5. Later they used beasts of burden.
6. They must have invented sledges about 5000 B.C.
7. These sledlike vehicles could move tons of weight.
8. Around 3500 B.C., someone created the wheel.
9. With wheels on vehicles, people could travel long distances.
10. The wheel was one of the most important inventions ever.

Label each verb above as *Action* or *Linking.*

CHALLENGE

➔ For a SELF-CHECK and more practice, see the EXERCISE BANK, p. 274.

B. REVISING: Using More Specific Verbs

Write a more specific verb to replace each underlined verb in the paragraph below.

Animal Travel
   Most animals travel. Dolphins <u>swim</u> through the water. Eagles <u>fly</u> in the sky. Horses can <u>move</u> for great distances. Snakes <u>go</u> through the grass. Butterflies <u>fly</u> from flower to flower.

Action Verbs and Objects

❶ Here's the Idea

Action verbs are often accompanied by words that complete their meaning. These **complements** are called direct objects or indirect objects.

Direct Objects

▶ **A direct object is a noun or pronoun that names the receiver of a verb's action.** The direct object answers the question *what* or *whom*.

LOVE WHAT?

Americans love the automobile.

ACTION VERB   DIRECT OBJECT

Cars changed our society.

Indirect Objects

▶ **An indirect object tells *to what* or *whom* or *for what* or *whom* an action is done.** Verbs that often take indirect objects include *bring, give, hand, lend, make, send, show, teach, tell,* and *write.*

Sue gave a ride. (gave to whom?)

TO WHOM?

Sue gave her sisters a ride.

INDIRECT   DIRECT
OBJECT   OBJECT

TO WHOM?

Sue gave them a ride.

 WATCH OUT

If the preposition *to* or *for* appears in a sentence, the word that follows it is *not* an indirect object. It is the object of the preposition.

Martin's mother taught the rules of the road to him.

OBJECT OF PREPOSITION

Martin's mother taught him the rules of the road.

INDIRECT OBJECT

VERBS

Verbs **91**

Transitive and Intransitive Verbs

An action verb that has a direct object is called a **transitive verb.** A verb that does not have a direct object is called an **intransitive verb.**

Good drivers avoid accidents.
TRANSITIVE VERB ⬈   ⬉ DIRECT OBJECT

They stay alert.
          ⬉ INTRANSITIVE VERB (No object)

Sometimes an intransitive verb is followed by a word that looks like a direct object but is really an adverb. An adverb tells where, when, how, or to what extent; a direct object answers the question whom or what.

DRIVE WHAT?
Some people drive trucks.
TRANSITIVE VERB ⬈   ⬉ DIRECT OBJECT

DRIVE HOW?
Some people drive carelessly.
INTRANSITIVE VERB ⬈   ⬉ ADVERB

❷ Why It Matters in Writing

The correct use of direct objects will help you make it clear to your readers exactly who did what. Notice how the model below uses a direct object to show what the automobile provides.

> **PROFESSIONAL MODEL**
>
> Today the automobile provides convenient,   **VERB**
> relatively inexpensive, and enjoyable
> transportation for people from all walks of life.   **DIRECT OBJECT**
>
> —*Understanding Science & Nature: Transportation*

❸ Practice and Apply

A. CONCEPT CHECK: Action Verbs and Objects

Identify the action verbs in these sentences. Then write
15 complements and label them as direct or indirect objects.
Identify each as a direct object or an indirect object.

The First Accidents
1. Experience tells us the risks of different vehicles.
2. In 1769 Nicolas-Joseph Cugnot showed the world the first automobile.
3. His vehicle had three wheels.
4. Steam power gave the vehicle a speed of about three miles an hour.
5. The auto had difficulties, however.
6. This fact gave Cugnot another place in history.
7. His car hit a wall in the world's first car accident.
8. In 1865 Pierre Lallemont made a test of his bicycle in Connecticut.
9. He hadn't given it brakes.
10. He hit a surprised team of horses in the first bike accident ever.

➡ **For a SELF-CHECK and more practice, see the EXERCISE BANK, p. 275.**

B. REVISING: Finding Direct Objects

Read the paragraph below. From the list of words at the top, select a direct object to fill each blank.

passengers, rumble seats, luggage, seat, name

Rumble Seats
In the 1930s many cars had no back ___(1)___. A
rider unfolded the ___(2)___ at the rear of the car.
A rumble seat held only one
or two ___(3)___. Sometimes
people carried ___(4)___ in
a rumble seat. The bumpy
ride in these little seats
explains the ___(5)___.

CORBIS/Schenectady Museum; Hall
of Electrical History Foundation

Linking Verbs and Predicate Words

❶ Here's the Idea

The complement that a linking verb connects its subject to is called a **subject complement.** The subject complement identifies or describes the subject. Some common linking verbs are *is, feel, seem,* and *look.*

IDENTIFIES

Barnstormers were **stunt pilots** in the 1910s and 1920s.
SUBJECT   VERB   SUBJECT COMPLEMENT

DESCRIBES

Their job looked **dangerous.**
SUBJECT   VERB   SUBJECT COMPLEMENT

Predicate Nouns and Predicate Adjectives

A subject complement can be a **predicate noun** or a **predicate adjective.**

▶ **A predicate noun is a noun that follows a linking verb and identifies, renames, or defines the subject.**

IDENTIFIES

Harriet Quimby was **a drama critic.**
SUBJECT   VERB   PREDICATE NOUN

She became **a stunt pilot** in 1911.

▶ **A predicate adjective is an adjective that follows a linking verb and modifies the subject.**

MODIFIES

Quimby was **natural** at the controls.
SUBJECT   VERB   PREDICATE ADJECTIVE

She felt **happy** in the air.

CHAPTER 4

❷ Why It Matters in Writing

You can use a predicate noun to tell more about your subject. Notice how the predicate nouns add information about the subjects.

Bessie Coleman was an African-American pilot who broke barriers of racial prejudice. She once said, "The air is the only place free from prejudices."

❸ Practice and Apply

CONCEPT CHECK: Linking Verbs and Predicate Words

Identify each linking verb, predicate noun, and predicate adjective in the sentences below.

A Flying First
1. The first African-American woman pilot was a Texan.
2. Her name was Bessie Coleman.
3. She became a pilot in 1921.
4. Coleman seemed an unlikely candidate.
5. She was a poor girl from Texas.
6. World War I pilots became her heroes.
7. American flying schools were too biased to let her in.
8. She seemed more welcome in France.
9. Coleman became an expert at stunt flying and parachuting.
10. Her goal became equality in the air.

➡ For a SELF-CHECK and more practice, see the EXERCISE BANK, p. 275.

VERBS

Principal Parts of Verbs

LESSON 4

❶ Here's the Idea

▶ **Every verb has four basic forms called its principal parts: the present, the present participle, the past, and the past participle.** These principal parts are used to make all of the forms and tenses of the verb. Here are some examples.

We live in a mobile society.
PRESENT

People are traveling more all the time.
PRESENT PARTICIPLE

Automobiles lent travelers more freedom.
PAST

Drivers have enjoyed this freedom for years.
PAST PARTICIPLE

The Four Principal Parts of a Verb			
Present	**Present Participle**	**Past**	**Past Participle**
move	(is) moving	moved	(has) moved
travel	(is) traveling	traveled	(has) traveled

Notice that helping verbs are used with the present participle and the past participle.

Regular Verbs

There are two kinds of verbs: regular and irregular.

▶ **A regular verb is a verb whose past and past participle are formed by adding -ed or -d to the present.** The present participle is formed by adding -ing to the present.

Present	Present Participle	Past	Past Participle
walk	(is) walk + ing	walk + ed	(has) walk + ed

You will learn about irregular verbs in the next lesson.

CHAPTER 4

② Why It Matters in Writing

The principal parts allow you to form verbs that show changes in time. In the news report below, notice how the writer uses the past and the present to show a shift in time.

Yesterday's Auto Expo showcased all the new cars plus some futuristic models. The sports models remain the most popular exhibit at the car show.

PAST

PRESENT

③ Practice and Apply

VERBS

CONCEPT CHECK: Principal Parts of Verbs

For each underlined verb in the paragraph below, name the principal part.

Gas, Food, Lodging
Henry Ford Museum in Dearborn, Michigan, **(1)** has showcased transportation since its early stages. For years, its exhibit "Automobile in American Life" **(2)** has appealed to visitors. The exhibit **(3)** started with more than 100 historic cars. The 15-millionth Model T **(4)** stands there. The exhibit **(5)** features a 1946 diner. Jukeboxes in the diner **(6)** are playing old songs. The exhibit also **(7)** shows a 1960s motel room. The details of a camper's cabin **(8)** make it special. Plastic ants **(9)** are crawling across the bureau. An open suitcase **(10)** is sitting on a rumpled bed.

➜ For a SELF-CHECK and more practice, see the EXERCISE BANK, p. 276.

Irregular Verbs

❶ Here's the Idea

> Irregular verbs are verbs whose past and past participle forms are not made by adding *-ed* or *-d* to the present.

The following chart shows you how to form the past and past participle forms of many irregular verbs.

Common Irregular Verbs			
	Present	**Past**	**Past Participle**
Group 1 The forms of the present, past, and past participle are all the same.	burst	burst	(has) burst
	cut	cut	(has) cut
	hit	hit	(has) hit
	hurt	hurt	(has) hurt
	let	let	(has) let
	put	put	(has) put
	set	set	(has) set
	split	split	(has) split
	spread	spread	(has) spread
Group 2 The forms of the past and the past participle are the same.	bring	brought	(has) brought
	buy	bought	(has) bought
	catch	caught	(has) caught
	dig	dug	(has) dug
	feel	felt	(has) felt
	flee	fled	(has) fled
	have	had	(has) had
	keep	kept	(has) kept
	lay	laid	(has) laid
	lead	led	(has) led
	leave	left	(has) left
	lose	lost	(has) lost
	make	made	(has) made
	say	said	(has) said
	sell	sold	(has) sold
	sit	sat	(has) sat
	sleep	slept	(has) slept
	teach	taught	(has) taught
	think	thought	(has) thought
	win	won	(has) won
	wind	wound	(has) wound

CHAPTER 4

Common Irregular Verbs *(continued)*

	Present	Past	Past Participle
Group 3 The past participle is formed by adding *-n* or *-en* to the past.	**bite** break choose lie speak steal tear wear	bit broke chose lay spoke stole tore wore	(has) **bitten or bit** (has) broken (has) chosen (has) lain (has) spoken (has) stolen (has) torn (has) worn
Group 4 The past participle is formed from the present, often by adding *-n* or *-en*.	**blow** do drive eat fall give go know ride rise see take throw write	**blew** did drove ate fell gave went knew rode rose saw took threw wrote	(has) **blown** (has) done (has) driven (has) eaten (has) fallen (has) given (has) gone (has) known (has) ridden (has) risen (has) seen (has) taken (has) thrown (has) written
Group 5 The last vowel changes from *i* in the present to *a* in the past and to *u* in the past participle.	**begin** drink ring shrink sing sink swim	**began** drank rang shrank sang sank swam	(has) **begun** (has) drunk (has) rung (has) shrunk (has) sung (has) sunk (has) swum

The Irregular Verb *Be*

	Present	Past	Past Participle
The past and past participle do not follow any pattern.	**am, are, is**	**was, were**	(has) **been**

VERBS

② Why It Matters in Writing

Writers must use the correct irregular verb forms to make their writing sound right. The best way to avoid mistakes is to memorize the principal parts of the most common irregular verbs. Notice the irregular forms used in this pilot's account of her first transatlantic flight.

LITERARY MODEL

I **brought** Harmony down to 7,000 feet, and then 5,000 feet, but the air **was** thick with clouds. I **came** down to 3,000 feet, then 2,000 feet, then 1,000 feet. Still there **were** clouds—and a real danger of crashing.

—Vicki Van Meter with Dan Gutman, adapted from
Taking Flight, My Story

③ Practice and Apply

CONCEPT CHECK: Irregular Verbs

In the sentences below, choose the correct forms of the verbs in parentheses.

Moving Through History
1. Transportation (beginned, began) before civilization.
2. For centuries, people walked and (runned, ran) everywhere.
3. They first (rode, rided) in dugout canoes and reed boats nearly 10,000 years ago.
4. They (letted, let) animals carry their loads by 3000 B.C.
5. They (drived, drove) chariots with solid wheels by 2500 B.C.
6. They (dug, digged) canals for ship traffic soon thereafter.
7. Spoked wheels (maked, made) their appearance around 2000 B.C.
8. The Greeks (built, builded) light, fast ships around 400 B.C.
9. The Roman Empire (saw, seen) advances in road building.
10. In A.D. 80, Roman gladiators in the Colosseum (rose, raised) to the arena on elevator-like lifting platforms.

➡ **For a SELF-CHECK and more practice, see the EXERCISE BANK, p. 276.**

Simple Tenses

❶ Here's the Idea

▶ **A tense is a verb form that shows the time of an action or condition.** Verbs have three **simple tenses:** the present, the past, and the future.

Understanding Simple Tenses

One biker **pedals** faster than anyone else.

She **sped** past the pack 50 feet ago.

Soon she **will cross** the finish line alone.

Simple Tenses

The present tense shows an action or condition that occurs now.

The past tense shows an action or condition that was completed in the past.

The future tense shows an action or condition that will occur in the future.

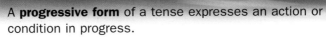

A **progressive form** of a tense expresses an action or condition in progress.

The crowd **is cheering.**

The winner's parents **were holding** their breath.

They **will be celebrating** later.

Progressive Forms

Present Progressive

Past Progressive

Future Progressive

VERBS

Forming Simple Tenses

The present tense of a verb is the present principal part. The past tense is the past principal part. To form the future tense, add *will* to the present principal part.

Forming Simple Tenses		
	Singular	**Plural**
Present (present principal part)	I skate you skate he, she, it skates	we skate you skate they skate
Past (present part + *ed/d*)	I skated you skated he, she, it skated	we skated you skated they skated
Future (*will* + present part)	I will skate you will skate he, she, it will skate	we will skate you will skate they will skate

To make the progressive form of one of these tenses, add the present, past, or future form of *be* to the present participle.

Present Progressive: **I am skating.**

Past Progressive: **I was skating.**

Future Progressive: **I will be skating.**

❷ Why It Matters in Writing

When you are stating a sequence of events, change tenses to show clearly when things happen in relation to each other. Notice how this student has revised the model to change from past to present to future tense.

> STUDENT MODEL
>
> Yesterday I ~~ride~~ *rode* my bike to my friend Lynn's house. I often walk to her house on weekends. She lives two miles away. Next Saturday, we *will* bike together along the lakefront.

❸ Practice and Apply

A. CONCEPT CHECK: Simple Tenses

Identify the tense of each underlined verb below by labeling it *Present, Past,* or *Future.*

> **Move Over, Superman**
> 1. Long ago, people <u>walked</u> everywhere.
> 2. They <u>covered</u> three or four miles an hour on foot.
> 3. Later, people <u>rode</u> horses.
> 4. They <u>traveled</u> up to 30 miles in an hour.
> 5. Now most adults <u>drive</u> everywhere.
> 6. Many other adults as well as most kids <u>bike</u> around town.
> 7. In the future, <u>will</u> people <u>travel</u> on high-speed monorails?
> 8. An early monorail <u>carried</u> people in Lyons, France, in 1872.
> 9. Maybe we <u>will fly</u> through the airways in vehicles like cars in the future.
> 10. In any case, we <u>will find</u> other ways for faster, more efficient travel.

➡ **For a SELF-CHECK and more practice, see the EXERCISE BANK, p. 276.**

B. REVISING: Correcting Simple Tenses

Revise the following paragraph by correcting the verb tenses.

> **Rocket Belts**
> In A.D. 1280, the Syrian writer al-Hasan al-Rammah **(1)** <u>will give</u> instructions for making rockets. In the 1960s the U.S. Army **(2)** <u>tests</u> rocket belts. They **(3)** <u>will carry</u> a soldier 360 feet forward in each hop. Some experts say that someday we **(4)** <u>saw</u> rocket belts in wide use. In the future, some people **(5)** <u>travel</u> only in virtual reality through their computers.

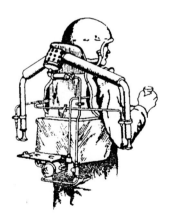

🗐 **Working Portfolio:** Find your **Write Away** from page 86 or a sample of your most recent work. Identify any errors in using simple tenses and correct them.

Perfect Tenses

LESSON 7

❶ Here's the Idea

Understanding Perfect Tenses

The **present perfect tense** places an action or condition in a stretch of time leading up to the present.

Hot-air balloons have existed for 300 years.	Balloons existed in the past; they still exist.

The **past perfect tense** places a past action or condition before another past action or condition.

After scientists had used weather balloons for years, people discovered them for sport.	*Had used* is farther back in the past than *discovered*.

The **future perfect tense** places a future action or condition before another future action or condition.

However, many more people will have tried the sport before it becomes ordinary.	*Will have tried* will occur before it *becomes ordinary*.

This balloon has finished first.

This balloon will have finished before dark.

Forming Perfect Tenses

To form the present perfect, past perfect, and future perfect tenses, add *has, had, have,* or *will have* to a past participle of the verb.

Forming Perfect Tenses	Singular	Plural
Present perfect (*has* or *have* + past participle)	I have floated you have floated he, she, it has floated	we have floated you have floated they have floated
Past perfect (*had* + past participle)	I had floated you had floated he, she, it had floated	we had floated you had floated they had floated
Future perfect (*will* + *have* + past participle)	I will have floated you will have floated he, she, it will have floated	we will have floated you will have floated they will have floated

In a perfect form, the tense of the helping verb *have* shows the verb's tense.

We often have seen balloons in the Arizona skies.

❷ Why It Matters in Writing

When writing about an event, you can use perfect tenses to help your readers understand when the event occurred in relation to other events. In the model, notice the effective use of the past perfect tense in relation to the past tense.

> **LITERARY MODEL**
>
> By a miracle the two companions had escaped   **PAST PERFECT**
> the dangerous side streets and were in a more
> open space. It was the forum. They rested here   **PAST**
> awhile—how long he did not know.
>
>   —Louis Untermeyer, "The Dog of Pompeii"

❸ Practice and Apply

A. CONCEPT CHECK: Perfect Tenses

Write the tense of each underlined verb: present perfect, past perfect, or future perfect.

Up, Up, and Away

1. People <u>had wanted</u> flight for hundreds of years, even though they were flightless.
2. The Montgolfier brothers <u>had launched</u> small balloons in 1782 before they sent up a balloon carrying a sheep, a duck, and a rooster in 1783.
3. Now pilots <u>have circled</u> the world nonstop in a balloon.
4. In March 2009 it <u>will have been</u> ten years since Brian Jones and Bertrand Piccard's historic flight.
5. Piccard's grandfather <u>had piloted</u> a balloon to a height of nearly 52,000 feet in 1931, almost 70 years before his grandson's feat.
6. Weather scientists <u>have learned</u> much about the earth's atmosphere from balloon flights.
7. They <u>have taken</u> air samples around the globe.
8. Plant scientists <u>have used</u> balloon rafts for exploration of the trees in the rain forest.
9. Their discoveries <u>have inspired</u> new medicines.
10. About 75,000 weather balloons <u>will have gone</u> up by the end of this year.

➜ For a SELF-CHECK and more practice, see the EXERCISE BANK, p. 277.

B. WRITING: Using Perfect Tenses

Rewrite each underlined verb in the tense named in parentheses.

Airships

By the time of the first airplane, airships <u>fly</u> (past perfect) for years. The first engine-powered balloon <u>take</u> (past perfect) to the air on September 24, 1852, over 50 years before the first successful engine-powered airplane flight. Engineers <u>build</u> (present perfect) different types of airships. Rigid airships <u>see</u> (present perfect) better days. Nonrigid airships, or blimps, <u>soar</u> (future perfect) over many sports events before their era ends.

Using Verb Tenses

❶ Here's the Idea

A good writer uses different verb tenses to show that events occur at different times. If you do not need to show a change of time, do not switch from one tense to another.

Writing About the Present

▶ **The present tenses show actions and conditions that occur in the present.** You can write about the present using the present tense, the present perfect tense, and the present progressive form.

Bullet trains are common in Japan.	The **present tense** places the action in the present.
They reach speeds of more than 130 miles per hour.	

Subways have carried commuters to work for decades.	The **present perfect tense** places the actions in a period of time leading up to the present.
They have given workers a fast trip to work.	

Traffic engineers are improving mass transportation.	The **present progressive forms** show the actions or conditions in progress now.
They are making subways more pleasant.	

VERBS

Writing About the Past

▶ **The past tenses show actions and conditions that came to an end in the past.** When you write about the past, you can use past verb forms to indicate the order in which events occurred.

In the 1850s batteries propelled some tram railways. The first cable cars appeared in San Francisco in 1873.	The **past tense** shows action that began and was completed in the past.

Until subways made commutes easy, workers had lived near their jobs. People had crowded Boston's streets before its subway opened.	The **past perfect tense** places the actions before other past actions.

Officials were encouraging mass transit for years before highways got too crowded. They were preparing cities for worse traffic as the population grew.	The **past progressive forms** show that the actions in the past were in progress.

CHAPTER 4

Writing About the Future

▶ **The future tenses show actions and conditions that are yet to come.** By using the future verb forms, you can show how future events are related in time.

People always will need to get from home to work. **But many of them will commute fewer than five days a week.**	The **future tense** shows that the actions are yet to come.
Home offices will have become popular before subways are overloaded. **By the time subways are full, workers will have learned to "commute" by computer.**	The **future perfect tense** places the actions or conditions before other future actions or conditions.
More people will be working at home several days a week. **Telecommuters will be sending their work to the office by computer.**	The **future progressive forms** show that the action or condition in the future will be continuing.

VERBS

❷ Why It Matters in Writing

When you are writing for social studies, use tenses correctly to show that you know the sequence of important events.

1880	1900	Today	2025
Steam provided power for trains.	Electricity provided power for subways.	Electromagnetic energy provides power for high-speed trains.	What kind of energy will move vehicles in the future?

A. CONCEPT CHECK: Using Verb Tenses

In each sentence, choose the correct verb form in parentheses.

> **It's Off to Work They Go**
> **1.** Commuters (have used, will use) mass transit since the 1800s.
> **2.** The first electric subway (opens, opened) in London, England, in 1890.
> **3.** In 1897 Boston (will become, became) the first U.S. city with a subway.
> **4.** After subways (had run, ran) for a few decades, they improved.
> **5.** They (ran, will run) faster and were better ventilated.
> **6.** Now many cities (had enjoyed, enjoy) computer-controlled trains.
> **7.** These automatic commuter trains (carry, had carried) millions of people every day.
> **8.** Bullet trains like those in Japan now (have traveled, travel) around 160 miles per hour over long distances.
> **9.** The next generation of subway trains (had moved, will move) without engines or rails.
> **10.** These "maglev" trains (will float, were floating) on a magnetic cushion at 300 miles per hour.

Name the tense of each verb you chose in part A.

➜ **For a SELF-CHECK and more practice, see the EXERCISE BANK, p. 278.**

B. EDITING: Arranging Verb Tenses

The following sentences tell about a commuter train ride. List the sentence numbers in a logical order so that the tenses of the verbs make sense. (Hint: Read all the sentences before you begin.)

> **1.** The train started before Mrs. Bakiloff had sat down.
> **2.** "Are you hurt?" said Mrs. Bakiloff.
> **3.** "Ouch! That's hot!" he exclaimed.
> **4.** After the train had stopped, 12 passengers rushed up the train steps to get the best seats.
> **5.** She fell toward Mr. Indigo, spilling her coffee.

LESSON 9

Troublesome Verb Pairs

① Here's the Idea

Some pairs of verbs seem similar, but are actually different words with different meanings. Troublesome verb pairs include *lie* and *lay, rise* and *raise, sit* and *set,* and *learn* and *teach.*

Lie and *Lay*

Lie means "to recline." It does not take an object.
Lay means "to put or place." It does take an object.

Pat lies on the floor with her model cars.

She lays a van on top of a carrier truck.

Lie and *Lay*		
Present	**Past**	**Past Participle**
lie Pat lies down.	lay Pat lay down.	lain Pat has lain down.
lay Pat lays the car down.	laid Pat laid the car down.	laid Pat has laid the car down.

 WATCH OUT

Lie and *lay* are confusing because the present principal part of *lay* is the same as the past principal part of *lie.*

Rise and *Raise*

Rise means "to move upward" or "to go up." It does not take an object. *Raise* means "to lift up." It usually takes an object.

Helicopters rise above the trees.

The pilot raises the flaps on the airplane's wings.

Rise and *Raise*		
Present	**Past**	**Past Participle**
rise The plane rises.	rose The plane rose.	risen The plane has risen.
raise Jo raises the car's hood.	raised Jo raised the hood.	raised Jo has raised the hood.

VERBS

Sit and Set

Sit means "to be seated." It does not take an object.

Set means "to put or place." It does take an object.

Jeff sits next to the flat tire.

He sets the lug wrench on the ground.

Sit and *Set*		
Present	**Past**	**Past Participle**
sit Let's **sit** up front.	sat We **sat** up front.	sat We have **sat** up front.
set Bob **sets** down the keys.	set Bob **set** down the keys.	set Bob has **set** down the keys.

Learn and Teach

Learn means "to gain knowledge or skill."

Teach means "to instruct" or "to help someone learn."

Sam learned to skateboard.

Leisha taught Sam to skateboard.

Learn and *Teach*		
Present	**Past**	**Past Participle**
learn Maria **learns** to ski.	learned Maria **learned** to ski.	learned Maria has **learned** to ski.
teach Mr. Lu **teaches** math.	taught Mr. Lu **taught** math.	taught Mr. Lu has **taught** math.

❷ Practice and Apply

A. CONCEPT CHECK: Troublesome Verb Pairs

Choose the correct word in parentheses in each of the following sentences.

Going Up?

1. The origin of modern elevators (lies, lays) in the invention of skyscrapers.
2. Only elevators could (raise, rise) to the upper floors.
3. Engineers (learned, taught) how to build hydraulic elevators.
4. These elevators (raised, rose) only freight, not people.
5. Workers (sat, set) the goods on the elevator floor and sent them up or down.
6. People were afraid to (sit, set) in boxes held up only by ropes.
7. Then Elisha Graves Otis (lay, laid) their fears to rest.
8. Otis (learned, taught) builders how to make elevators safe.
9. In 1857 he installed the world's first passenger elevator, which (rose, raised) five stories at 40 feet per minute.
10. For many years, elevators had cushioned places where riders (sat, set).

➡ For a SELF-CHECK and more practice, see the EXERCISE BANK, p. 278.

B. PROOFREADING: What Do They Mean?

List the five verbs that are used incorrectly in the following paragraph. Then change them to the correct verb forms.

Escalator Up

In St. Petersburg, Russia, the subway lays far underground. Passengers set in subway trains. When they get out, an escalator rises the passengers 195 feet up. As they raise, they may be distracted sometimes. But they teach quickly to pay attention when they step off the escalator at the top.

VERBS

Grammar in Physical Education

Using Action Verbs to Describe Motion

Whether you watch the playoffs on TV, read the sports page, or learn how to play a sport in gym class, you need verbs to express what is happening. Verbs explain physical movement, tell what something is, or link ideas. What verbs might you use to describe the following cheerleading jumps?

J-U-M-P!

Split

Herky

Full "C"

Pike

Bambi

Banana

CHAPTER 4

Practice and Apply

A. USING VERBS IN INSTRUCTIONS

Hooray! You got through tryouts and made the cheerleading squad. There's only one hitch—the coach's handout of basic jumps does not have any written directions. Study the illustration on page 114. Then write five steps explaining how to do one of these jumps. Use verbs from the list below that precisely describe the motion of your arms, legs, body, and head.

Action Verbs

raise	shake	straddle	thrust	leap
lower	land	clench	kick	squat
bend	hop	twist	split	crouch
straighten	cross	lift	drop	bounce
extend	lunge	push	point	vault
turn	twirl	roll	spin	swing
clasp	wrap	step	scoop	touch
pivot	move	jump	switch	lock
grab	place	stretch	stand	pull

B. USING VERBS IN A PLAY-BY-PLAY

With a partner, role-play two radio sports announcers. Do a play-by-play broadcast, or a running account of the action of a sports event as it unfolds, for the class. Narrate the action of one of the following sports highlights or another of your choice.

• a winning goal in a soccer match
• a home run in a tie softball game
• a record-breaking finish in a race

Use precise, vivid verbs that describe the action that takes place. Remember that you want your classmates to be able to picture in their minds what is happening.

VERBS

A. Revising Incorrect Verb Parts Find and correct the 10 incorrect verbs and verb forms in the following sentences. Watch out for irregular verbs and troublesome verb pairs.

Space: The Final Frontier

1. Fifty years ago, scientists will wonder whether humans could survive in outer space.

2. So they sended a dog named Laika up in a rocket in 1957.

3. Yuri Gagarin becomes the first person in space in 1961.

4. Just eight years later, astronauts are landing on the moon.

5. Today they had traveled in the space shuttle.

6. Unlike the older spacecraft, the shuttle was being reused again and again, like an airplane.

7. Some experts predict that we had a base on the moon in the 21st century.

8. Rockets will sit down tourists and businesspeople every day.

9. Some say we flew beyond our solar system someday.

10. Who knows where the human race has gone after that?

B. Using Tenses Using the ideas in the phrases listed below, write five sentences about the picture. Tell what happened before the scene shown in the picture, what is happening in it, and what might happen next.

puts on spacesuit

steps out into space

locks feet into foot holder on robot arm

rides robot arm to repair location

returns to the shuttle after fixing the problem

Choose the best way to rewrite each underlined word or group of words.

We now <u>are living</u> in the age of the automobile, but some people
(1)

<u>had worried</u> about that fact for a while. Cars give us freedom and
(2)

mobility, but they also <u>gave</u> us pollution, accidents, and road rage.
(3)

Before the automobile age, there <u>will be</u> almost no pavement in
(4)

the United States. Now we have 2.4 million miles of paved roads,

which <u>costed</u> $200 million per day to keep up and add to. Some
(5)

futurists believe that as roads get more crowded, more people <u>have</u>
(6)

<u>turned</u> to mass transit. Even now, subways, trains, and buses

<u>pollute</u> less per person than automobiles do. Other people predict
(7)

that communities <u>had become</u> more self-sufficient. After people
(8)

finally work near their homes, they <u>abandoned</u> their cars. The air
(9)

will be cleaner, and people <u>will have been</u> healthier.
(10)

VERBS

1. A. will live
   B. have lived
   C. will be living
   D. Correct as is

2. A. worry
   B. will worry
   C. have worried
   D. Correct as is

3. A. had given
   B. will give
   C. give
   D. Correct as is

4. A. had been
   B. are
   C. have been
   D. Correct as is

5. A. will cost
   B. cost
   C. will have costed
   D. Correct as is

6. A. turn
   B. had turned
   C. will turn
   D. Correct as is

7. A. had polluted
   B. will pollute
   C. polluted
   D. Correct as is

8. A. have become
   B. will become
   C. are becoming
   D. Correct as is

9. A. will abandon
   B. have abandoned
   C. are abandoning
   D. Correct as is

10. A. were
    B. have been
    C. will be
    D. Correct as is

Student Help Desk

Verbs at a Glance

A verb expresses action, condition, or state of being.

The two main kinds of verbs are **action verbs** and **linking verbs**.

Many people **drive** cars.
  ACTION VERB

Cars **are** very handy.
  LINKING VERB

Principal Parts of Regular Verbs

Present	Present Participle	Past	Past Participle
present	helping verb + present + *-ing*	present + *-ed* or *-d*	helping verb + present + *-ed* or *-d*
bike	(is) biking	biked	(has) biked
blast	(is) blasting	blasted	(has) blasted
dive	(is) diving	dived	(has) dived
float	(is) floating	floated	(has) floated
gallop	(is) galloping	galloped	(has) galloped
lift	(is) lifting	lifted	(has) lifted
move	(is) moving	moved	(has) moved
roll	(is) rolling	rolled	(has) rolled
travel	(is) traveling	traveled	(has) traveled
walk	(is) walking	walked	(has) walked

Keeping Tenses Straight   Travel Time

Tense	Definition	Example
Present	Action or condition occurring in the present	We **travel** everywhere.
Past	Action or condition occurring in the past	We **traveled** to Maine.
Future	Action or condition occurring in the future	We **will travel** to California next year.
Present perfect	Action or condition occurring in the period leading up to the present	We **have traveled** often.
Past perfect	Past action or condition coming before another past action or condition	We **had traveled** to Washington, D.C., before I turned 12.
Future perfect	Future action or condition coming before another future action or condition	We **will have traveled** to every state before I'm 21.

The Bottom Line

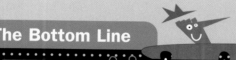

Checklist for Verb Usage

Have I . . .

____ used action verbs to express an action?

____ used linking verbs with predicate nouns and predicate adjectives?

____ used direct objects and indirect objects to answer the questions *whom, what, to whom,* and *to what?*

____ used the correct principal parts of irregular verbs?

____ used tenses correctly to express the time of actions and conditions?

____ used *sit* and *set, lie* and *lay, rise* and *raise,* and *learn* and *teach* correctly?

Adjectives and Adverbs

Dear Alice,

We hiked and camped. We saw flowers and climbed trails.

—Gomez

GRAND TETON NATIONAL PARK, WYOMING

CHAPTER 5

Theme: The Great Outdoors

Tell Me More

What would you think if you received the postcard message above? It's kind of boring, isn't it? To give a better sense of what it was like to be there, the writer could add words describing what he saw and did.

We hiked *endlessly* and camped *late*. We saw *mountain* flowers and *carefully* climbed *steep* trails.

The words writers use to describe people, places, and things are adjectives. The words they use to describe actions are adverbs. What adjectives and adverbs would you use to describe the picture on the postcard above?

Write Away: Wish You Were Here!

Create a postcard of one of your favorite outdoor places. On one side, describe the place and what you did there. Illustrate the other side with a picture of what you have described. Save your postcard in your 🗂 **Working Portfolio.**

For each underlined item, choose the letter of the term that correctly identifies it.

Yellowstone National Park is the oldest <u>national</u> park in the
(1)
United States. Opened on March 1, 1872, <u>this</u> park attracts
(2)
millions of people each year. Visitors are <u>wild</u> about the hot
(3)
springs, mud pots, and geysers. Old Faithful is popular because it
erupts <u>more regularly</u> than other geysers in the park. One of the
(4)
<u>neatest</u> sights is the colorful rainbow in Grand Prismatic Spring
(5)
that is made by algae. Tourists also enjoy <u>the</u> animals, including
(6)
bison, elk, <u>large</u> bears, and bighorn sheep. Although fires <u>badly</u>
(7)   (8)
burned many acres of the park in 1988, this <u>American</u> treasure is
(9)
now <u>healthier</u> than ever. Yellowstone will continue to delight
(10)
generations of visitors.

ADJ. & ADV.

1. A. adverb modifying *oldest*
   B. adverb modifying *is*
   C. adjective modifying *Idaho*
   D. adjective modifying *park*

2. A. pronoun used as adjective
   B. adverb
   C. proper adjective
   D. article

3. A. proper adjective
   B. demonstrative pronoun
   C. predicate adjective
   D. comparative adjective

4. A. comparative adverb
   B. superlative adverb
   C. comparative adjective
   D. superlative adjective

5. A. adjective modifying *one*
   B. adjective modifying *rainbow*
   C. adjective modifying *sights*
   D. adverb modifying *is*

6. A. proper adjective
   B. article
   C. demonstrative pronoun
   D. adverb

7. A. adjective modifying *bears*
   B. adverb modifying *including*
   C. adverb modifying *enjoy*
   D. adjective modifying *animals*

8. A. adverb telling how
   B. adverb telling when
   C. adverb telling where
   D. adjective telling how much

9. A. possessive adjective
   B. superlative adjective
   C. proper adjective
   D. noun used as adjective

10. A. comparative adjective
    B. comparative adverb
    C. superlative adverb
    D. superlative adjective

What Is an Adjective?

❶ Here's the Idea

▶ **An adjective is a word that modifies, or describes, a noun or a pronoun.**

MODIFIES

A **heavy** **rainstorm** soaked the campsite.
ADJECTIVE ⬏   ⬑ NOUN

Adjectives help you see, feel, taste, hear, and smell all the experiences you read about. Notice how adjectives make the second sentence in this pair more descriptive.

Coyotes startled the campers.

Noisy coyotes startled the sleepy campers.

Adjectives answer the questions *what kind, which one, how many,* and *how much.*

Adjectives			
What kind?	**green** backpack	**sturdy** tent	**spicy** stew
Which one or ones?	**last** hamburger	**third** hike	**every** lantern
How many or how much?	**two** flashlights	**many** insects	**little** moonlight

What kind?
waterproof floor
round roof

Which one or ones?
only door
each window

How many?
several stakes
two people

Articles

The most commonly used adjectives are the **articles** *a, an,* and *the. A* and *an* are used with singular nouns. Use *a* before a word beginning with a consonant sound.

a tent　　　**a candle**　　　**a lamp**

Use *an* before a word beginning with a vowel sound.

an axe　　　**an elephant**　　　**an unusual night**

The is an article that points to a particular person, place, thing, or idea. You can use *the* with singular or plural nouns.

The hiker tripped on the trail and dropped the cameras.

Use *the* when you want to refer to a specific person, place, thing, or idea. Use *a* and *an* when you want to be less specific.

Did the team leader bring a first-aid kit?
　　↑ ONE SPECIFIC LEADER　　↑ ANY FIRST-AID KIT

Proper Adjectives

Many adjectives are formed from common nouns.

Nouns and Adjectives	
Noun	**Adjective**
rain	rainy
scene	scenic
beauty	beautiful

A proper adjective is formed from a proper noun. Proper adjectives are always capitalized.

Proper Nouns and Proper Adjectives	
Proper Noun	**Proper Adjective**
China	Chinese
Ireland	Irish
Mars	Martian

ADJ. & ADV.

❷ Why It Matters in Writing

Adjectives provide important details about the nouns they describe. Imagine this description without adjectives.

Max came last. He was lugging a **new** knapsack that contained a **cast-iron** frying pan, a packet of hot dogs, and a box of **saltine** crackers—plus **two** bottles. **One** bottle was mustard, the other, **celery** soda. He also had a bag of Tootsie Rolls and a **shiny** hatchet. "To build a lean-to," he explained.

—Avi, "Scout's Honor"

❸ Practice and Apply

CONCEPT CHECK: What Is an Adjective?

Write each adjective and the noun or pronoun it modifies. Do not include articles when you write the adjectives.

Urban Wilderness
1. Central Park is now an American landmark.
2. It was once a dirty swamp that was filled with ugly shacks and much garbage.
3. In 1858 there was a national competition for a plan to turn the spot into an attractive park.
4. People tried to imagine a place where New Yorkers could enjoy the great outdoors.
5. The park took the builders sixteen years to complete.
6. The landscape includes green meadows, lakes, ponds, woods, and beautiful gardens.
7. There is also an Egyptian statue.
8. Other attractions include a colorful carousel and a zoo.
9. The zoo features an African exhibit with birds and monkeys.
10. Many monuments are scattered throughout the park.

➡ For a SELF-CHECK and more practice, see the EXERCISE BANK, p. 279.

Write the proper adjectives that appear in sentences 1, 7, and 9.

CHALLENGE

Predicate Adjectives

LESSON 2

❶ Here's the Idea

▶ **A predicate adjective is an adjective that follows a linking verb and describes the verb's subject.** The linking verb connects the predicate adjective with the subject.

DESCRIBES

A volcanic eruption is violent.
       SUBJECT   LINKING VERB

DESCRIBES

It is explosive.

Predicate adjectives can follow linking verbs other than forms of *be*. Forms of *taste, smell, feel, look, become,* and *seem* are often used as linking verbs.

DESCRIBES

The lava looks thick.
LINKING VERB   PREDICATE ADJECTIVE

DESCRIBES

Lava becomes hard when it cools.

For more about linking verbs, see page 94.

❷ Why It Matters in Writing

Writers often use predicate adjectives to tell more about a person's character, as in this author's description of her parents.

LITERARY MODEL

    Both my parents had grown up poor, and they also knew what it was to be **lonely.** They cared deeply about other people and were always **ready** to lend a helping hand to anyone. Mama couldn't bear to think of her children ever being less than **kind** and **caring.**
    "Don't ever be **indifferent**," she would say to Keiko and me. "That is the worst fault of all."

               —Yoshiko Uchida, "Oh Broom, Get to Work"

ADJ. & ADV.

❸ Practice and Apply

A. CONCEPT CHECK: Predicate Adjectives

Write each predicate adjective in these sentences, along with the noun or pronoun it modifies.

> **Look Out!**
> **1.** For more than 120 years, Mount St. Helens, a volcano in Washington, was inactive.
> **2.** Then the volcano became dangerous.
> **3.** In 1980 eruptions were responsible for widespread damage.
> **4.** The blasts were thunderous.
> **5.** After hot ash started fires, the air smelled smoky.
> **6.** The sky became very dark as ash fell like snow.
> **7.** Long after the eruption, pumice, a kind of volcanic rock, still felt hot.
> **8.** Following the blast, tall forests looked very flat.
> **9.** Thick, fast mudslides seemed deadly.
> **10.** The volcanic eruptions of Mount St. Helens were very destructive.

➡ **For a SELF-CHECK and more practice, see the EXERCISE BANK, p. 280.**

B. WRITING: Creating Riddles

On a piece of paper, write three sentences about yourself, using linking verbs and predicate adjectives. Underline each predicate adjective. Then fold the paper and put your sentences into a hat along with those of your classmates. Take turns drawing a piece of paper out of the hat. Try to guess the name of the author.

Example: I am <u>female</u> and very <u>tall</u>, and my hair is <u>red</u>. It is also extremely <u>long</u> and <u>curly</u>. To many people, I seem <u>quiet</u>, but often I feel <u>adventurous</u>.

In your 🗀 **Working Portfolio,** find the postcard you wrote for the **Write Away** on page 120. Add or change predicate adjectives to make your description clearer.

Other Words Used as Adjectives

LESSON 3

❶ Here's the Idea

Many pronouns and nouns can be used as adjectives. They can modify nouns to make their meanings more specific.

Pronouns as Adjectives

Demonstrative Pronouns *This, that, these,* and *those* are demonstrative pronouns. They can be used as adjectives.

MODIFIES

This canoe is made of wood and leather.

MODIFIES

These canoes are made of aluminum.

Possessive Pronouns *My, our, your, her, his, its,* and *their* are possessive pronouns. They are used as adjectives.

MODIFIES   MODIFIES

My skateboard is newer than your bicycle.

Indefinite Pronouns Indefinite pronouns such as *all, each, both, few, most,* and *some* can be used as adjectives.

MODIFIES

Most people in my family enjoy exploring caves.

MODIFIES

All members of my family enjoy picnicking.

ADJ. & ADV.

Nouns as Adjectives

Like pronouns, nouns can be used as adjectives. In the expression "mountain climber," for example, the word *mountain* (normally a noun) modifies *climber*. Notice the nouns used as adjectives in the sentences below.

MODIFIES

Rock climbers practice indoors on winter nights.

MODIFIES   MODIFIES

They use a rock wall made from construction materials.

MODIFIES

Climbing an indoor rock wall

❷ Why It Matters in Writing

By using nouns as adjectives, a writer can pack a lot of important information into just a word or two. Notice what information the nouns that are used as adjectives add to the passage below.

LITERARY MODEL

In the same week, my brother made the **baseball** team of his junior high school, Father started taking driving lessons, and Mother discovered **rummage** sales. We soon got all the furniture we needed, plus a **dart** board and a 1,000-piece **jigsaw** puzzle (fourteen hours later, we discovered that it was a 999-piece **jigsaw** puzzle).
—Lensey Namioka, "The All-American Slurp"

❸ Practice and Apply

A. CONCEPT CHECK: Other Words Used as Adjectives

Write each noun or pronoun that is used as an adjective in these sentences. Then write the word it modifies.

Climb Every Mountain
1. Most climbers climb mountain formations.
2. "Urban climbers" scale city buildings.
3. Many climbers participate in skill training.
4. Gyms allow these people to train on rock walls.
5. My friends prefer to test their skills on mountains.
6. Some climbs occur on glacier ice.
7. Those climbers want to enjoy a mountaintop view.
8. Their equipment includes this harness and that helmet.
9. Our goal is to learn correct body positions.
10. Each skill involves muscle strength and concentration.

→ For a SELF-CHECK and more practice, see the EXERCISE BANK, p. 280.

B. REVISING: Adding Nouns as Adjectives

Make this message more detailed by adding nouns from the list below to modify each of the nouns in boldface type.

mud   steel   neighborhood   park   safety

> Dear Tammi,
>
> You won't believe what happened today! I was roller-blading on a **sidewalk**, and a **kid** on a **skateboard** lost his balance and fell. The skateboard flew into my **helmet,** and I fell into a **puddle.**

C. WRITING: Creating a Safety Poster

Using the information below, create a safety poster about bicycle helmets. Include adjectives to show how helmets can protect bike riders from injury.

Liner absorbs shock of fall

Outer shell protects skull from impact

Chin strap holds helmet firmly in place

What Is an Adverb?

❶ Here's the Idea

▶ **An adverb is a word that modifies a verb, an adjective, or another adverb.**

MODIFIES

Explorers eagerly chase adventure.
　　　　　ADVERB　　VERB

MODIFIES

Some explorers visit amazingly beautiful places.
　　　　　　　　　ADVERB　　ADJECTIVE

MODIFIES

Others quite bravely explore the unknown—space.
　　　　ADVERB　ADVERB

Adverbs answer the questions *how, when, where,* or *to what extent.*

Adverbs	
How?	suddenly, carefully, sadly
When?	now, later, soon
Where?	there, up, ahead
To what extent?	completely, totally, fully

Adverbs can appear in different positions in sentences.

The tourists boarded the bus eagerly. (after verb)

The tourists eagerly boarded the bus. (before verb)

Eagerly, the tourists boarded the bus. (at beginning)

Adverbs that modify adjectives or other adverbs usually come directly before the words they modify. They usually answer the question *to what extent.*

MODIFIES

Marco Polo told really wonderful tales of China.

MODIFIES

People were very eager to hear his stories.

MODIFIES

They nearly always hung on every word.

Forming Adverbs

Many adverbs are formed by adding the suffix *-ly* to adjectives. Sometimes a base word's spelling changes when *-ly* is added.

QUICK-FIX SPELLING MACHINE: ADVERBS

ADJECTIVE	RULE	ADVERB
near	Add *-ly*.	nearly
gentle	Drop the *e* and add *-ly*.	gently
easy	Change *y* to *i* and add *-ly*.	easily

❷ Why It Matters in Writing

Use adverbs to record what you observe in science. Notice how one scientist used adverbs to record details about the behavior of spiders.

PROFESSIONAL MODEL

The spider can remain **perfectly** still for hours, waiting for its prey. When an insect does **accidentally** stumble into the web, the spider can move **swiftly**, injecting poison **rapidly** into its prey and wrapping it **tightly** in spider silk.

❸ Practice and Apply

A. CONCEPT CHECK: What Is an Adverb?

Write each adverb and the word it modifies. Identify the modified word as a verb, an adjective, or an adverb. There may be more than one adverb in a sentence.

The Wild West

1. Thomas Jefferson became very curious about the West after he took office as president.

2. He studied maps and explorers' journals quite often.

3. He soon asked Meriwether Lewis to explore the new territory of the 1803 Louisiana Purchase.

4. In preparation for the trip, Lewis quickly learned many skills.

5. On May 14, 1804, Lewis, William Clark, and a team of explorers headed west.

6. Team members gathered truly valuable information.

7. Their remarkably complete journals told what they saw.

8. Sometimes, the explorers sent specimens, such as live prairie dogs, to President Jefferson.

9. Finally, in 1806, the difficult 8,000-mile expedition ended.

10. Because the journey was so completely successful, Lewis and Clark became famous.

➡ **For a SELF-CHECK and more practice, see the EXERCISE BANK, p. 281.**

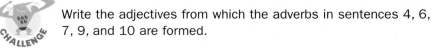

Write the adjectives from which the adverbs in sentences 4, 6, 7, 9, and 10 are formed.

B. WRITING: Adding Adverbs

Choose one adverb from the list to fill in each of the blanks.

carefully   soon   rather   often   upward

Starstruck

As a young child, Maria Mitchell gazed **(1)** (<u>answers where</u>) at the sky. **(2)** (<u>answers when</u>), she visited her father's observatory in Nantucket, Massachusetts. At the age of 12, she **(3)** (<u>answers how</u>) recorded information about an eclipse. On October 1, 1847, the grown-up Mitchell, an astronomer, made a **(4)** (<u>answers to what extent</u>) rare discovery—a new comet. She was **(5)** (<u>answers when</u>) elected to the American Academy of Arts and Sciences, the first woman to be so honored.

Making Comparisons

❶ Here's the Idea

Adjectives and adverbs can be used to compare people or things. Special forms of these words are used to make comparisons.

▶ **Use the comparative form of an adjective or adverb when you compare a person or thing with one other person or thing.**

Mt. Rainier is higher than Mt. Hood.

Mountain climbing is more dangerous than skydiving.

▶ **Use the superlative form of an adjective or adverb when you compare someone or something with more than one other person or thing.**

Mt. Everest is the highest of the three mountains.

I think Mt. Fuji is the most beautiful mountain of all.

Regular Forms of Comparison

For most one-syllable modifiers, add -er to form the comparative. Add -est to form the superlative.

One-Syllable Modifiers			
	Base Form	**Comparative**	**Superlative**
Adjectives	thin	thinner	thinnest
	brave	braver	bravest
Adverbs	slow	slower	slowest
	soon	sooner	soonest

You can also add -er and -est to some two-syllable adjectives. With others, and with two-syllable adverbs, use *more* and *most*.

Two-Syllable Modifiers			
	Base Form	**Comparative**	**Superlative**
Adjectives	shallow	shallower	shallowest
	awful	more awful	most awful
Adverbs	calmly	more calmly	most calmly
	briskly	more briskly	most briskly

With adjectives and adverbs having three or more syllables, use *more* and *most*.

Modifiers with More than Two Syllables			
	Base Form	**Comparative**	**Superlative**
Adjectives	beautiful	**more** beautiful	**most** beautiful
	dangerous	**more** dangerous	**most** dangerous
Adverbs	gracefully	**more** gracefully	**most** gracefully
	dangerously	**more** dangerously	**most** dangerously

Use only one sign of comparison at a time. Don't use *more* and *-er* together or *most* and *-est* together.

INCORRECT: **That beach has the most whitest sand.**

CORRECT: **That beach has the whitest sand.**

Irregular Forms of Comparison

The comparative and superlative forms of some adjectives and adverbs are completely different words. You don't need to add *-er* or *-est* to an irregular comparison.

Irregular Modifiers			
	Base Form	**Comparative**	**Superlative**
Adjectives	good	better	best
	bad	worse	worst
Adverbs	well	better	best
	much	more	most
	little	less	least

❷ Why It Matters in Writing

Comparative and superlative forms are used to compare and contrast things with each other.

> STUDENT MODEL
>
> Last year I thought math was the **most difficult** subject. This year I think English is **more difficult** than math.

❸ Practice and Apply

A. CONCEPT CHECK: Making Comparisons

Choose the correct comparative or superlative form to complete each sentence.

World's Eighth Natural Wonder
1. Australia's Great Barrier Reef is the (larger, largest) coral reef in the world.
2. The reef is also the (richer, richest) of all marine resources.
3. Biologists can (better, more better) study sea life near a reef than in open water.
4. The (biggest, most biggest) of all polyps, the animals that form a coral reef, are a foot in diameter.
5. Coral grows (better, best) of all in warm, shallow water.
6. During cold weather, vacationers visit the reef's northern islands (less, least) frequently than the southern ones.
7. A scuba dive is (more daring, most daring) than a glass-bottom-boat tour of the reef.
8. The Great Barrier Reef is (more fragile, most fragile) than a large rock formation would be.
9. The crown-of-thorns starfish is the reef's (deadlier, deadliest) enemy.
10. These starfish can devour polyps (more, most) quickly than the average starfish.

→ **For a SELF-CHECK and more practice, see the EXERCISE BANK, p. 281.**

B. WRITING: Comparing and Contrasting

Study the three pictures of sharks. Write a paragraph in which you compare and contrast them. Use comparative and superlative forms in your writing.

Great white shark

Whale shark

Hammerhead shark

Adjective or Adverb?

LESSON 6

❶ Here's the Idea

Some pairs of adjectives and adverbs are often confused.

Good* and *Well *Good* is always an adjective; it modifies a noun or pronoun. *Well* is usually an adverb, modifying a verb, an adverb, or an adjective.

MODIFIES

That was a good documentary about Mt. Everest.
ADJECTIVE   NOUN

MODIFIES

The filmmaker presented the information well.
VERB   ADVERB

Well is an adjective when it refers to health.

MODIFIES

After the film, I didn't feel well.
PRONOUN   ADJECTIVE

Real* and *Really *Real* is always an adjective; it modifies a noun or pronoun. *Really* is always an adverb; it modifies a verb, an adverb, or an adjective.

MODIFIES

She prefers real mountains to paintings of mountains.
ADJECTIVE   NOUN

MODIFIES

The Grand Canyon is really beautiful in the morning.
ADVERB   ADJECTIVE

Bad* and *Badly *Bad* is always an adjective; it modifies a noun or pronoun. *Badly* is always an adverb; it modifies a verb, an adverb, or an adjective.

MODIFIES   *MODIFIES*

That wasn't a bad hike, even though we planned it badly.
ADJECTIVE   NOUN   VERB   ADVERB

MODIFIES

I often feel bad about staying indoors so much.
PRONOUN   ADJECTIVE

CHAPTER 5

❷ Why It Matters in Writing

People make many mistakes using *good, real,* and *bad.* In your writing, check the word being modified to see if you need an adjective or an adverb.

well
Hiking at night is not a good idea if you can't see ~~good~~ in

really
the dark. I had a ~~real~~ scary experience once doing that. It was

badly
a real nightmare. I saw so ~~bad~~ in the dark that I stumbled off

a hill and fell into a cactus patch.

❸ Practice and Apply

CONCEPT CHECK: Adjective or Adverb?

Choose the correct word in parentheses. Then identify it as an adjective or an adverb.

London's *Call of the Wild*
1. American author Jack London described nature (good, well).
2. Much of his fiction is based on (real, really) experiences.
3. In his teens, he had (real, really) adventures as a sailor.
4. In 1897 he was (real, really) curious about a gold rush.
5. In Canada's Yukon Territory, he lived in a tiny cabin and struggled to survive in (bad, badly) weather.
6. Unfortunately, London felt (bad, badly) because he had scurvy, a disease caused by a lack of vitamin C.
7. Although he never found gold, London discovered a (good, well) subject for his stories and novels.
8. His first Yukon tales were received (good, well).
9. London's novel, *The Call of the Wild*, is based on a (real, really) dog he had known in the Yukon.
10. In "To Build a Fire," London tells the story of a young man facing a (bad, badly) problem.

➡ **For a SELF-CHECK and more practice, see the EXERCISE BANK, p. 282.**

Avoiding Double Negatives

LESSON 7

CHAPTER 5

❶ Here's the Idea

A **negative word** is a word that says "no." Contractions that end in *n't* are negative words. Remember, *n't* means *not*. A word like *can't* means "cannot." Some common negative words are listed below.

Common Negative Words			
barely	neither	nobody	nothing
hardly	never	none	nowhere

If two negative words are used together, the result is a **double negative.** Avoid double negatives in speaking and writing.

INCORRECT

I don't want no slackers on this hike.

CORRECT

I don't want any slackers on this hike.

I want no slackers on this hike.

❷ Why It Matters in Writing

Some writers accidentally create a double negative when they try to make a strong negative statement. However, a double negative makes a writer sound careless.

STUDENT MODEL

The largest cactus in North America is the saguaro. It
doesn't grow ~~nowhere~~ *anywhere* but in the deserts of southern

Arizona, southeastern California, and northwestern Mexico.
Saguaros ~~don't hardly need no~~ *need hardly any* water to survive. It almost

~~doesn't~~ never rain_∧*s* where saguaros live, but these plants can

store water in their stems for a long time.

138 Grammar, Usage, and Mechanics

➌ Practice and Apply

A. CONCEPT CHECK: Avoiding Double Negatives

Write the word in parentheses that correctly completes each sentence.

Beat the Heat
1. Desert dwellers live where there's barely (no, any) relief from high temperatures.
2. Many (don't have, have) no air conditioning.
3. They can't build with (nothing, anything) that gets too hot.
4. Some North Africans live underground in rock houses that don't (ever, never) get hot.
5. Adobe keeps houses cool but (can, can't) never be used in a damp climate.
6. In Syria, mud houses shaped like beehives may not be uncomfortable (either, neither).
7. Nobody (would, wouldn't) mind using solar-powered air conditioning to keep cool.
8. In Fiji, people who live in houses with thatched roofs (could, couldn't) hardly find a better design.
9. Houses that have shutters and tile floors stay cooler than those that don't have (none, any).
10. If you scarcely (ever, never) suffer from the heat, a desert home might be comfortable after all.

➜ **For a SELF-CHECK and more practice, see the EXERCISE BANK, p. 283.**

B. PROOFREADING: Eliminating Double Negatives

Find and correct five double negatives in the paragraph below. (There is more than one way to correct each double negative.)

Sand, Sand Everywhere
    Without sand, no one couldn't build sandcastles or walk on a beach. Sand is made of fine pieces of rock and minerals that aren't barely larger than clay or silt. In a desert, sand doesn't lie nowhere near water but covers the land. On a beach, sand isn't never always soft and white. For example, tourists visiting Hawaii can't hardly believe they are seeing black sand, which comes from volcanic lava.

Grammar in Literature

Using Adjectives and Adverbs

When you write about the great outdoors—or about any other topic—use adjectives and adverbs to make your descriptions vivid and enjoyable for readers. You can also use nouns and pronouns as adjectives. Notice the words Armstrong Sperry uses to describe a boy paddling a canoe in a tropical lagoon.

from
Ghost of the Lagoon
by Armstrong Sperry

A school of fish swept by like silver arrows. He saw scarlet rock cod with ruby eyes and the head of a conger eel peering out from a cavern in the coral. The boy thought suddenly of Tupa, ghost of the lagoon. On such a bright

ADJECTIVES
ADVERBS

day it was hard to believe in ghosts of any sort. The fierce sunlight drove away all thought of them. Perhaps ghosts were only old men's stories, anyway! . . .

As the canoe drew away from shore, the boy saw the coral reef that, above all others, had always interested him. It was of white coral—a long slim shape that rose slightly above the surface of the water. It looked very much like a shark. There was a ridge on the back that the boy could pretend was a dorsal fin, while up near one end were two dark holes that looked like eyes!

© Cheryl Cooper, 1995.

140

Practice and Apply

Working with a partner, fill in the blanks in the following poem with an appropriate adjective or adverb. Save your poem in your 📁 **Working Portfolio.**

Because it was a *(adjective)* day,
And everything was *(adverb)* gray,
We were getting *(adverb)* *(adjective)*,
even though we're *(adverb)* lazy.

Just then all the lights went *(adverb)*
And everyone began to shout.
"Who is that?" "It's me; I'm *(adverb)*."
"I loudly shouted out in fear."

So, cautiously we crept outside
(Adverb), *(adverb)*, eyes open *(adverb)*.
And what we saw, did not seem *(adjective)*,
But it *(adverb)* was, we say to you.

(Adjective) penguins, an *(adjective)* duck,
(Adjective) socks, a hockey puck;
(Adjective) fish and *(adjective)* cats
(Adjective) balls and *(adjective)* bats.

Then the wind just died away.
The sun came *(adverb)*, a *(adjective)* ray.
We looked around, a *(adverb)* pale,
And went *(adverb)* to write this tale.

A. Using Adjectives and Adverbs Read this passage. Then write the answers to the questions below it.

> **LITERARY MODEL**
>
> **(1)** "Have you dressed yet?" their grandmother called. **(2)** "Once a month in the sun and they must almost be forced," she muttered. **(3)** "Well, poor things, they've forgotten the warmth of the sun on their little bodies, what it is to play in the sea, yes. . . ." **(4)** Mrs. Pavloff reached for her protective sun goggles that covered most of her face. **(5)** It screened all ultraviolet light from the once life-giving sun; now, it, the sun, scorched the Earth, killing whatever it touched.
>
> —Alma Luz Villanueva, "The Sand Castle"

1. In sentence 1, what possessive pronoun is used as an adjective?
2. In sentence 2, what adverb tells *to what extent?*
3. In sentence 3, what two adjectives help you better picture the children in the story?
4. In sentence 4, what noun is used as an adjective?
5. In the last sentence, name one adjective.

B. Choosing the Right Modifier Choose the correct words from those given in parentheses.

Clever Coyotes
1. Coyotes don't have (no, any) problem with survival.
2. The coyote is (most adaptable, more adaptable) than many other animals in North America.
3. In the past, coyotes didn't live (nowhere, anywhere) but in the western part of North America and in Mexico.
4. Today, coyotes live (good, well) in many different places.
5. According to some wildlife experts, coyote populations are (more, most) widespread now than during the pioneer days.
6. First of all, coyotes hunt (real, really) efficiently.
7. If they can't find (no, any) mice, then they'll eat nearly anything, including bugs, fish, berries, watermelon, and garbage.
8. Also, their (deadlier, deadliest) enemy of all, the wolf, has vanished in many areas.
9. The coyote behaves (more cleverly, most cleverly) than people imagine.
10. Although coyotes in stories often act (bad, badly), real ones just fight to survive.

For each underlined item, choose the letter of the term that correctly identifies it.

Rachel Carson, a marine biologist, <u>certainly</u> influenced people to
(1)
protect the environment. In 1962 she published *Silent Spring,* a
book about the <u>harmful</u> effects of pesticides. She agreed that <u>these</u>
(2)   (3)
chemicals killed insects and rodents. But they also <u>badly</u> poisoned
(4)
<u>our</u> food and wildlife. Carson's book woke up <u>ordinary</u> people.
(5)   (6)
Even President John F. Kennedy became very <u>anxious</u>. He called
(7)
for a <u>government</u> study of pesticide use. The pesticide DDT was
(8)
finally banned in 1972. *Silent Spring* helped make the world safer.
An <u>American</u> Supreme Court judge said that the book was "the
(9)
<u>most important</u> chronicle of this century for the human race."
(10)

1. A. adverb modifying *influenced*
   B. adverb modifying *biologist*
   C. adverb modifying *Carson*
   D. adverb modifying *people*

2. A. adjective telling what kind
   B. adjective telling which one
   C. adjective telling how many
   D. adjective telling how much

3. A. adverb
   B. possessive pronoun
   C. pronoun used as adjective
   D. noun used as adjective

4. A. adverb modifying *poisoned*
   B. adverb modifying *food*
   C. adverb modifying *also*
   D. adverb modifying *killed*

5. A. demonstrative pronoun
   B. possessive pronoun
   C. possessive noun
   D. noun used as adjective

6. A. adjective modifying *book*
   B. adjective modifying *people*
   C. adverb modifying *woke*
   D. predicate adjective

7. A. proper adjective
   B. adverb
   C. predicate adjective
   D. article

8. A. proper adjective
   B. adverb
   C. noun used as adjective
   D. article

9. A. proper adjective
   B. comparative adverb
   C. predicate adjective
   D. article

10. A. comparative adverb
    B. superlative adverb
    C. comparative adjective
    D. superlative adjective

ADJ. & ADV.

Student Help Desk

Adjectives and Adverbs at a Glance

Adjectives modify nouns and pronouns.

The wildlife walk was terrific. It was long, too.

Adverbs modify verbs, adjectives, and other adverbs.

The usually quiet tour guide chattered very excitedly.

Modifiers in Comparisons

zoom Lens

	Comparative	Superlative
steep	steeper	steepest
leafy	leafier	leafiest
valuable	more valuable	most valuable
rugged	more rugged	most rugged
bravely	more bravely	most bravely
good	better	best
bad	worse	worst

Double Forms

Double Take

Double Negative	Fix
we can't hardly	we can hardly we can't
we don't never	we never we don't ever

Double Comparison	Fix
more better	better
most likeliest	most likely, likeliest

Field Guide

Modifier Problems

Good and Well

That's a good book.
↑ ADJECTIVE

I feel good about that.
↑ PREDICATE ADJECTIVE

Did you perform well?
ADVERB ↗

Does she look well?
PREDICATE ADJECTIVE ↗

Real and Really

That's a real problem.
↑ ADJECTIVE

He's really tired.
ADVERB ↗

Bad and Badly

What bad luck!
↑ ADJECTIVE

Do you feel bad?
↑ PREDICATE ADJECTIVE

I sing badly.
ADVERB ↗

The Bottom Line

Checklist for Adjectives and Adverbs

Have I remembered to . . .

____ use adjectives to add detail to my nouns?

____ capitalize proper adjectives?

____ use adverbs to describe actions clearly?

____ use the correct comparative and superlative forms?

____ avoid using adjectives as adverbs?

____ avoid double negatives?

Prepositions, Conjunctions, Interjections

Theme: Dragons

The Tale of a Dragon

"Oh-Oh" is right. The man in the photo might follow this interjection with a warning to his neighbors. He'll need plenty of prepositions to describe where the dragon is and some conjunctions to join his thoughts. In this chapter, you will learn how to use prepositions, conjunctions, and interjections. Let's hope you don't have to use them to warn your neighbors about any dragons.

Write Away: If Dragons Could Talk

If dragons could talk, this one might be saying, "I want you in my belly!" What might the man reply? Write a few sentences answering the dragon's threat. Tell the dragon what you will do or where you will hide. Express your fear or your bravery! Save the response in your 🗂 **Working Portfolio.**

Choose the letter of the term that correctly identifies each underlined item.

A dragon is a monster of legends. Most dragons have the claws
<u>of</u> a lion and the tail <u>of</u> a serpent. Their character can be kind
  (1)   (2)
<u>and</u> generous <u>or</u> evil and greedy. <u>In Western myths</u>, a fierce fire-
 (3)   (4)   (5)
breathing dragon is common, <u>but</u> Asian myths usually portray a
                             (6)
kindly dragon. Chinese dragons have five toes on each <u>claw</u>.
                                         (7)
Dragons appear with different numbers of legs and with or
<u>without</u> wings. According to legend, you cannot always tell when
 (8)
you will meet a dragon. <u>Yikes</u>! Look <u>behind</u> you!
                   (9)   (10)

1. A. conjunction
   B. preposition
   C. prepositional phrase
   D. interjection

2. A. preposition
   B. object of a preposition
   C. prepositional phrase
   D. conjunction

3. A. conjunction
   B. preposition
   C. prepositional phrase
   D. interjection

4. A. conjunction
   B. preposition
   C. object of a preposition
   D. interjection

5. A. conjunction
   B. preposition
   C. prepositional phrase
   D. interjection

6. A. conjunction
   B. preposition
   C. object of a preposition
   D. interjection

7. A. conjunction
   B. object of a preposition
   C. prepositional phrase
   D. interjection

8. A. conjunction
   B. preposition
   C. prepositional phrase
   D. object of a preposition

9. A. conjunction
   B. preposition
   C. prepositional phrase
   D. interjection

10. A. conjunction
    B. preposition
    C. prepositional phrase
    D. interjection

PREPOSITIONS

What Is a Preposition?

❶ Here's the Idea

▶ **A preposition is a word that shows a relationship between a noun or pronoun and some other word in the sentence.**

> **The knight on the dragon called for help.**
>   ↑ PREPOSITION

Here, the preposition *on* shows the relationship between *knight* and *dragon*. In the sentences below, notice how each preposition expresses a different relationship between the knight and the dragon.

> **The knight is under the dragon.**
>
> **The knight is above the dragon.**
>
> **The knight is beside the dragon.**
>
> **The knight is in the dragon.**

Common Prepositions				
about	at	despite	like	to
above	before	down	near	toward
across	behind	during	of	under
after	below	except	off	until
against	beneath	for	on	up
along	beside	from	out	with
among	between	in	over	within
around	beyond	inside	past	without
as	by	into	through	

Prepositional Phrases

▶ **A prepositional phrase consists of a preposition, its object, and any modifiers of the object.** The object of the preposition is the noun or pronoun following the preposition.

PREPOSITIONAL PHRASE

A Chinese New Year dragon is a symbol of strength.
PREPOSITION ↗   ↖ OBJECT

People drape silk over a bamboo dragon.
PREPOSITION ↗   ↖ MODIFIER ↖ OBJECT

Fifty people walk under the enormous dragon.

Use *between* when the object of the preposition refers to two people or things. Use *among* when speaking of three or more.

The dragon weaved *between* two boys.

The dragon weaved *among* the crowd.

Preposition or Adverb?

Sometimes the same word can be used as a preposition or as an adverb. If the word has no object, then it is an adverb.

PREPOSITIONAL PHRASE

The bamboo dragon toppled over a curb.
PREPOSITION ↗   ↖ OBJECT

The bamboo dragon toppled over.
↖ ADVERB

For more on adverbs, see p. 130.

PREPOSITIONS

❷ Why It Matters in Writing

Writers often use prepositions to describe where characters and objects are located in relation to one another. Notice how the prepositions in this dialogue tell the location of the character, the doorstep, and the entrance.

> **LITERARY MODEL**
>
> **Bilbo** (*holding script off and reading it*). "...I am now sitting **on** the very doorstep **of** the secret entrance **to** the dragon's cave."
>
> —J. R. R. Tolkien, *The Hobbit,*
> dramatized by Patricia Gray

❸ Practice and Apply

A. CONCEPT CHECK: What Is a Preposition?

Write the preposition and its object for each sentence.

Dragon Tales
1. Dragons from different cultures have their own characteristics.
2. The Eastern female dragon holds a fan with her tail.
3. The Chinese show most dragons without wings.
4. Swallows are among the Chinese dragons' favorite foods.
5. In Chinese mythology, nine dragons keep the Kowloon waters safe from harm.
6. Japanese dragons have three toes on each claw.
7. Western dragons are usually associated with evil.
8. Many tales pit brave knights against fierce dragons.
9. Two batlike wings lift the dragon above its victim.
10. Some breeds of Western dragons can change their shapes.

→ For a SELF-CHECK and more practice, see the EXERCISE BANK, p. 284.

B. WRITING: Using Prepositions

Think back to the response you wrote to the dragon in your **Write Away** on page 146. Write the dragon's answer to your response using five prepositions from the following list:

at, behind, below, by, for, in, into, off, on, out, to, up, with, without

Using Prepositional Phrases

1 Here's the Idea

A prepositional phrase is always related to another word in a sentence. It modifies the word in the same way an adjective or adverb would.

Adjective Phrases

▶ **An adjective phrase is a prepositional phrase that modifies a noun or a pronoun.** Like an adjective, a prepositional phrase can tell which one, how many, or what kind.

WHICH ONE?

The "dragon" in the water is really a lizard.
NOUN   ADJECTIVE PHRASE

WHAT KIND?

The Komodo dragon is a type of monitor lizard.

Adverb Phrases

▶ **An adverb phrase is a prepositional phrase that modifies a verb, an adjective, or an adverb.** Like an adverb, a prepositional phrase can tell where, when, how, why, or to what extent.

WHERE?

Desert lizards lie under the sand.
VERB   ADVERB PHRASE

HOW?

Their body temperatures are lower without sunlight.
ADJECTIVE

HOW?

This cooling method works well for a simple system.
ADVERB

Several prepositional phrases can work together. Each phrase after the first often modifies the object of the phrase before it.

A flying dragon glides with flaps of skin like wings.

Placement of Prepositional Phrases

When you write, try to place each prepositional phrase as close as possible to the word it modifies. Otherwise, you may confuse—or unintentionally amuse—your readers.

CONFUSING

With fiery breath, we surprised a dragon.

(Who has fiery breath?)

CLEAR

We surprised a dragon with fiery breath.

(Now the reader knows who has fiery breath.)

❷ Why It Matters in Writing

When you write about science, you can use prepositional phrases to describe *which one* and *what kind.* Notice how the prepositional phrases in the model describe what kind of lizard.

> **PROFESSIONAL MODEL**
>
> The Komodo dragon is a lizard **of the species** *Varanus komodoensis*. It is a prehistoric relic **from an earlier era.**
>
> —Rudy J. Goldstein

What kind of lizard

What kind of relic

❸ Practice and Apply

A. CONCEPT CHECK: Using Prepositional Phrases

Write the prepositional phrase and the word it modifies for each of the following sentences.

The Largest Lizard
1. The Komodo dragon is the largest lizard in the world.
2. Komodos live on a few Indonesian islands.
3. The Komodo's yellow forked tongue, over a foot long, can taste the air.
4. Its saliva has bacteria with no known antidotes.
5. The Komodo's teeth are dangerous to everyone.
6. The Komodo's teeth can shred a large animal in 20 minutes.
7. The Komodo can run 12½ miles an hour, fast for its 300-pound weight.
8. The residents of Komodo Island call this creature the *ora*.
9. Villagers tell tall tales about the ora.
10. The ora does not interest poachers around the island.

➡ **For a SELF-CHECK and more practice, see the EXERCISE BANK, p. 284.**

B. PROOFREADING: What Kind? or Which One?

Choose the prepositional phrase that most likely belongs in the numbered blank in the paragraph below.

a. from an earlier era   **d.** in Indonesia

b. with picture maps   **e.** with iron jaws

c. about huge lizards

Touring Komodo Island

    We took a tour of Komodo Island ___**(1)**___. On the island, we found a tour guide ___**(2)**___. The guide told us a story ___**(3)**___ that live on Komodo Island. The Komodo dragons look like lizards ___**(4)**___. They are dangerous predators ___**(5)**___.

Conjunctions

LESSON 3

❶ Here's the Idea

▶ **A conjunction is a word used to join words or groups of words.**

Joining Words and Groups of Words

Conjunctions often join words used in the same way. The words joined by a conjunction can be subjects, predicates, or any other kind of sentence parts.

SUBJECTS
Alligators and crocodiles live mainly in the water.
CONJUNCTION

OBJECTS
Crocodiles live in **salt water or fresh water.**
CONJUNCTION

Common Conjunctions
and   but   or   nor

Use *and* to connect similar ideas. Use *but* to contrast ideas.

Crocodiles have a long jaw and sharp teeth.
(*And* connects two parts of a crocodile's mouth.)

A young crocodile is small but powerful.
(*But* contrasts this crocodile's small size with its great power.)

Use *or* and *nor* to show choices.

Some crocodiles can live in salt water or fresh water.
(*Or* connects the choices *salt water* and *fresh water.*)

Joining Whole Thoughts

Conjunctions also can join whole thoughts, such as two sentences that are closely related.

Crocodiles are aggressive. Alligators are passive.

Crocodiles are aggressive, and alligators are passive.
↑ CONJUNCTION

(*And* joins two sentences about personality.)

The crocodile's snout is narrow. It has biting power.

The crocodile's snout is narrow, but it has biting power.
↑ CONJUNCTION

Use a comma before the conjunction when joining two complete sentences. Do not use a comma when joining two subjects or two verbs.

Alligators can live in 65-degrees-Fahrenheit water, but crocodiles drown at that temperature.

In 65-degrees-Fahrenheit water, crocodiles sink and drown.

❷ Why It Matters in Writing

When you are writing science material, the right conjunctions can help the reader know how features and habits relate to each other. Notice how the conjunctions in the model show the relationship between the newborn crocodile and its mother.

STUDENT MODEL

Newborn crocodiles float in water with their eyes **and** snouts above the surface. They swim alone, **but** their mother is always nearby. The young crocodiles must stay warm, **or** they will die.

And connects two similar features.

But joins two whole thoughts that contrast.

Or joins two whole thoughts that contrast.

CONJUNCTIONS

❸ Practice and Apply

A. CONCEPT CHECK: Conjunctions

Write the conjunction in each sentence, along with the words or groups of words that it joins.

Crocodiles and Alligators

1. There are many ways to tell whether an animal is a crocodile or an alligator.
2. A crocodile's snout is pointy, and an alligator's snout is broad.
3. Both the upper and lower teeth show on the crocodile.
4. Crocodiles often lose their teeth, but they grow new ones.
5. Large crocodiles eat antelope and deer.
6. Cold weather may cause deformity or death to baby crocodiles.
7. The snout usually shows differences, but the Indian Mugger crocodile looks much like an alligator.
8. Alligators do not have an enlarged fourth tooth, nor do they need it.
9. Most crocodiles hunt at night, but hungry ones hunt any time.
10. Never go near an alligator, or you may be badly injured.

➜ For a SELF-CHECK and more practice, see the EXERCISE BANK, p. 285.

B. REVISING: Changing Conjunctions

Rewrite the conjunctions so that the following paragraph makes sense.

Crocodile Meals

(1) Newly hatched crocodiles feed on bugs like grasshoppers **but** beetles. **(2)** Some adult crocs eat mammals like deer **but** cattle. **(3)** Crocodile teeth are good for holding prey, **or** they are not so good at cutting it. **(4)** A good hunter, the crocodile blends into the background **but** stays completely still. **(5)** Suddenly, it pounces **but** surprises its prey.

Interjections

❶ Here's the Idea

▶ **An interjection is a word or a phrase used to express emotion.**

Wow, there's a monitor lizard.

It's so big! **Awesome!**

> It can stand alone or be set off by a comma.

❷ Why It Matters in Writing

Stupid worms.

Writers often use interjections to express strong emotions, such as anger, joy, concern, surprise, terror, and disgust. Read the cartoon. What emotion is the poor, misguided worm expressing?

INTERJECTIONS

❸ Practice and Apply

Working Portfolio: Find your **Write Away** from page 146 or a sample of your most recent work. Add to your writing three interjections that express emotions. Use the interjections in the Student Help Desk on page 163 for ideas.

Grammar in Social Studies

Using Prepositions to Show Location

When you write about specific places for social studies, you can use prepositions along with maps to indicate direction and location. Study the map below. Then read the accompanying description of some of the famous places in San Francisco's Chinatown. Notice how prepositions and prepositional phrases help you picture what the area looks like and where different sites are located.

The entrance to Chinatown is guarded by a fabulous dragon in the Chinatown Gateway. As you enter from Bush Street, you'll walk under the dragon's coiled body and beautiful, decorated head. From the gateway, you stroll down Grant Street past the shops, restaurants, and gift stores on both sides of the street.

Practice and Apply

A. USING PREPOSITIONS

Study this map of today's Chinatown. Then write answers to the questions that follow, using prepositions and prepositional phrases in each of your sentences.

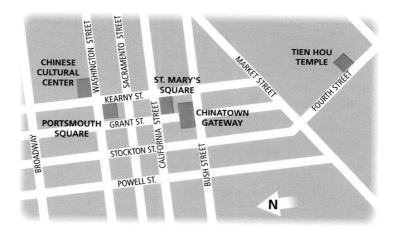

1. What route would you walk to go from the Chinatown Gateway to St. Mary's Square?
2. How would you get from St. Mary's Square to the Tien Hou Temple?
3. What is the best way to get from the Chinese Cultural Center to the Chinatown Gateway?

B. DRAWING A MAP

Draw a map of a park, a playground, or a gymnasium in your community or school. Then write a brief description, similar to the one on page 158, to accompany your map. Circle the prepositions that you use to explain the location of different landmarks. Finally, share your work with classmates.

Mixed Review

A. Prepositions, Conjunctions, Interjections Choose the correct word in parentheses to complete each sentence. Then identify the word as a preposition, a conjunction, or an interjection.

Famous Dragons

1. Dragons are famous (under, around) the world.
2. The Eastern Spiritual Dragon—Shen-Lung—controls the wind (but, and) the rain.
3. The Chinese Yellow Dragon gave the knowledge of writing (to, from) Emperor Fu Hsi.
4. People fear (but, or) respect European dragons.
5. The Vikings put dragon figureheads (to, on) their ships.
6. They believed the dragons would give them keen sight (and, or) skill.
7. Beowulf confronted a dragon in the epic poem *Beowulf*. (Wow! Out!)
8. The dragon has become an official part (by, of) the prince of Wales's armor.
9. Sea serpents are dragons (except, from) the seas.
10. "Nessie," the Loch Ness Monster, is a sea serpent, (or, but) she lives in a lake in Scotland.

B. Prepositional Phrases Read the passage and answer the questions below it.

A Komodo Ritual

(1) Dominant male Komodo dragons often compete for a female. (2) This ritual between two male Komodo dragons is typical. (3) The dragons wrestle in upright postures. (4) They use their tails for support. (5) They grab each other with their forelegs. (6) The loser of the battle may lie on the ground or run away.

1. What is the prepositional phrase in sentence 1?
2. What is the prepositional phrase in sentence 2?
3. Why is *between* used instead of *among* in sentence 2?
4. What is the prepositional phrase in sentence 3?
5. What is the object of the preposition in sentence 3?
6. What is the prepositional phrase in sentence 4?
7. What is the object of the preposition in sentence 4?
8. What is the prepositional phrase in sentence 5?
9. What is the object of the preposition in sentence 5?
10. Which prepositional phrase shows location in sentence 6?

Choose the letter of the term that correctly identifies each underlined item.

Eastern dragons have one obvious detail that makes them different <u>from one another</u>. Some Chinese people believe that
(1)
stories about <u>dragons</u> began <u>in China</u>. They say the dragon has
(2)   (3)
always had five toes. A wanderer <u>by</u> nature, the dragon traveled
(4)
the earth. Legend has it that the farther it wandered <u>from</u> China,
(5)
the more toes it lost. By the time it got <u>to Korea</u>, it had only four
(6)
toes, <u>and</u> after it reached Japan it had three. <u>Oh-oh</u>, will it
(7)   (8)
eventually lose all its toes? According to the Japanese, the dragon
began <u>in Japan</u>. Their story is the same <u>but</u> reversed. Their dragon
(9)   (10)
grew toes as it traveled.

---

1. A. conjunction
   B. preposition
   C. prepositional phrase
   D. interjection

2. A. object of a preposition
   B. prepositional phrase
   C. preposition
   D. interjection

3. A. conjunction
   B. preposition
   C. prepositional phrase
   D. object of a preposition

4. A. conjunction
   B. preposition
   C. prepositional phrase
   D. interjection

5. A. conjunction
   B. preposition
   C. prepositional phrase
   D. object of a preposition

6. A. conjunction
   B. preposition
   C. prepositional phrase
   D. object of a preposition

7. A. conjunction
   B. preposition
   C. prepositional phrase
   D. interjection

8. A. conjunction
   B. object of a preposition
   C. prepositional phrase
   D. interjection

9. A. conjunction
   B. preposition
   C. prepositional phrase
   D. interjection

10. A. conjunction
    B. preposition
    C. object of a preposition
    D. interjection

Student Help Desk

Prepositions, Conjunctions, Interjections at a Glance

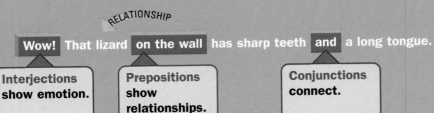

RELATIONSHIP

Wow! That lizard on the wall has sharp teeth and a long tongue.

Interjections show emotion.

Prepositions show relationships.

Conjunctions connect.

Prepositions, Conjunctions, Interjections   Summary

Preposition

Shows a relationship. Has an object.

RELATIONSHIP

lizard on the wall

PREPOSITION   OBJECT

Conjunction

Joins words or groups of words.
teeth and a tongue
with sharp teeth and with a long tongue

Joins whole thoughts.
Lizards have sharp teeth, but not all lizards are dangerous.

Interjection

Expresses emotion.
Eek! That lizard is huge!

CHAPTER 6

Prepositional Phrases — What Do They Do?

Adjective Phrases

Modify a noun or a pronoun.

Tell *which one*	That little lizard **on the wall**
Tell *what kind*	is a member **of the reptile family.**

Adverb Phrases

Modify a verb, an adjective, or another adverb.

Tell *when*	**In April** my little brother
Tell *where*	bought an iguana **at a store.** I was
Tell *why*	happy **for my brother.** This pet works
Tell *how* or *to what extent*	perfectly **for his age.**

Interjections! — Just a Few Ideas . . .

To express concern	oh-oh, oh no, oops
To express disgust	yuck, ick, gross
To express joy	awesome, hooray, yea
To express surprise	wow, what, whoops
To draw attention to	hey

The Bottom Line

Checklist for Prepositions, Conjunctions, and Interjections

Have I . . .

____ used prepositions to show relationships between two things?

____ placed prepositional phrases close to the words they modify?

____ used conjunctions to connect words or groups of words?

____ used conjunctions to connect whole thoughts?

____ used interjections to express strong emotion?

Chapter 7

Subject-Verb Agreement

He fly through the air with the greatest of ease!

Theme: Working Together

What's the Plan?

Timing means everything in a flying trapeze act. The flier and catcher must work carefully together. A mistake may lead to an embarrassing fall or even serious injury.

Agreement errors will not harm people, but they certainly can embarrass the writer. How would you correct the sentence on this photo? This chapter will help you learn to make subjects and verbs work together, or agree.

Write Away: Winning Teams

Think of some people you admire who need to work together to be successful. They can be a musical band, sports team, student organization, or some other group. Describe this group and explain what they are trying to do. Have they accomplished their goal? Save the writing in your 📁 **Working Portfolio.**

Diagnostic Test: What Do You Know?

Choose the letter of the best revision for each underlined group of words.

> What is a team? <u>Most of us immediately thinks</u> of sports. <u>Five</u>
> (1)
> <u>basketball players makes up one kind of team</u>. <u>Orchestras and</u>
> (2)
> <u>rock bands uses</u> teamwork. <u>At an accident scene are paramedics</u>
> (3)   (4)
> working as a team to save lives. <u>A team are not</u> just human
> (5)
> beings. <u>Either animals or humans makes</u> up a team. Animal teams
> (6)
> find missing people or assist disabled ones. <u>Many people works</u> as
> (7)
> a team to make a single movie. <u>Doesn't teams all unite</u> for a
> (8)
> common goal?

1. A. Most of us immediately
      think
   B. Most of us immediately is
      thinking
   C. Most of us will immediately
      thinks
   D. Correct as is

2. A. Five basketball players is
      making up one kind of team.
   B. Five basketball players
      make up one kind of team.
   C. Five basketball players has
      made up one kind of team.
   D. Correct as is

3. A. Orchestras and rock bands
      has to use
   B. Orchestras and rock bands
      use
   C. Orchestras and rock bands
      used
   D. Correct as is

4. A. At an accident scene is
      paramedics
   B. At an accident scene has
      been paramedics

C. At an accident scene was
   paramedics
D. Correct as is

5. A. A team were not
   B. A team is not
   C. A team cannot
   D. Correct as is

6. A. Either animals or humans
      is making
   B. Either animals or humans
      does make
   C. Either animals or humans
      make
   D. Correct as is

7. A. Many people was working
   B. Many people has worked
   C. Many people work
   D. Correct as is

8. A. Doesn't teams all unites
   B. Don't teams all unite
   C. Don't teams all unites
   D. Correct as is

S-V AGREEMENT

LESSON 1

Agreement in Number

CHAPTER 7

❶ Here's the Idea

▶ **A verb must agree with its subject in number.**

Number refers to whether a word is singular or plural. When a word refers to one person, place, thing, idea, action, or condition, it is singular. When a word refers to more than one, it is plural.

Singular and Plural Subjects

▶ **Singular subjects take singular verbs.**

<small>AGREE</small> <small>SINGULAR VERB</small>
Teamwork **is** **important in a jazz band.**
<small>SINGULAR SUBJECT</small>

Each musician listens to the others.

▶ **Plural subjects take plural verbs.**

<small>AGREE</small>
The musicians play without sheet music.
<small>PLURAL SUBJECT</small>   <small>PLURAL VERB</small>

They hear changes in each other's sounds.

Most nouns that end in *s* or *es* are plural. For example, *musicians* and *sounds* are plural nouns. However, most verbs that end in *s* are singular. *Listens* and *hears* are both singular verb forms.

Verb Phrases

▶ **In a verb phrase, it is the first helping verb that agrees with the subject.** A verb phrase is made up of a main verb and one or more helping verbs.

<small>AGREE</small>
Miles Davis has led groups in performance.
<small>SINGULAR VERB</small>

<small>AGREE</small>
His music is becoming legendary.

AGREE

All good groups have become **teams.**

↑ PLURAL VERB

AGREE

Even the soloists are playing **with a musical team.**

Doesn't and *Don't*

Two contractions we often use are *doesn't* and *don't*. Use *doesn't* with all singular subjects except *I* and *you*. Use *don't* with all plural subjects and with the pronouns *I* and *you*.

> **My mom doesn't like our band.**
> SINGULAR VERB:
> does+not=doesn't

> **My friends don't understand why.**
> PLURAL VERB: do+not=don't

I don't play **alone often.**

❷ Why It Matters in Writing

Errors in subject-verb agreement can occur when you revise your work. If you change a subject from singular to plural, or vice versa, make sure that the verb agrees with your revision.

STUDENT MODEL

DRAFT

Our band is always arguing. The guitar **player** wants to break up.

REVISION

Our band is always arguing. The guitar **players** want to break up.

❸ Practice and Apply

A. CONCEPT CHECK: Agreement in Number

For each sentence, write the verb form that agrees with the subject.

Meet the Beatles

1. Rock critics (considers, consider) the Beatles one of the most important groups in rock and roll history.
2. Their musical development (shows, show) constant growth and exploration.
3. In the late 1950s they (was, were) playing other people's songs in clubs.
4. However, their own compositions (was, were) changing popular music.
5. Beatles' songs (attracts, attract) listeners who like great melodies and clever lyrics.
6. By the mid-1960s they (was, were) performing to huge crowds in baseball stadiums.
7. Adults (remembers, remember) mobs of young fans screaming at Beatles' concerts.
8. The Beatles (was, were) considered wild in their day.
9. Such popular groups (affects, affect) clothing and hair styles.
10. Today their music still (plays, play) around the world.

➜ **For a SELF-CHECK and more practice, see the EXERCISE BANK, p. 285.**

B. PROOFREADING: Finding Agreement Errors

Proofread the following paragraph so that the verbs agree with the subjects. There are five errors.

STUDENT MODEL

Do you dislike order and discipline? Then you probably doesn't belong in a marching band. The band members must follow precise directions. A music director plan out every movement. Often the musicians forms words and patterns as they walk. Even their uniforms matches perfectly. Many schools has formed marching bands. The bands play at sporting events and other special occasions.

Compound Subjects

❶ Here's the Idea

A **compound subject** is made up of two or more subjects joined by a conjunction such as *and, or,* or *nor.*

Subjects Joined by *And*

▶ **A compound subject whose parts are joined by and usually takes a plural verb.**

A firefighter and a paramedic help save lives.

Subjects Joined by *Or* or *Nor*

▶ **When the parts of a compound subject are joined by *or* or *nor*, the verb should agree with the part closest to it.**

AGREES

A professional or volunteers serve on emergency teams.

AGREES

Volunteers or a professional serves on emergency teams.

❷ Why It Matters in Writing

When you revise your writing, you may decide to change the order of compound subjects to make a sentence sound more natural. If the subjects are joined by *or* or *nor*, make sure that the verb agrees with the new order.

Traffic problems or bad weather interferes with rescue operations.

Bad weather or traffic problems interfere with rescue operations.

❸ Practice and Apply

A. CONCEPT CHECK: Compound Subjects

Identify the sentences containing mistakes in subject-verb agreement and rewrite the verb correctly. If a sentence contains no error, write *Correct*.

Searching the Waters

1. Volunteer men and women composes the Larimer County Dive Rescue Team in Colorado.
2. Rescue and critical care are their goal.
3. Desperate calls and dispatches arrives at any hour.
4. Terrible storms and fog often confronts the team.
5. Terrified victims or darkness frustrate their efforts.
6. Ferocious whitewater or dangerous rapids slows them down.
7. These brave men and women often risk their own lives.
8. Donations and fund-raising events supports this important service.
9. Sometimes fatally injured victims or dead bodies is recovered from the rising waters.
10. But these brave men and women has also saved many lives.

→ For a SELF-CHECK and more practice, see the EXERCISE BANK, p. 286.

B. REVISING: Making Compound Subjects and Verbs Agree

A member of the Dive Rescue Team wrote these notes quickly, based on a frantic distress call. Rewrite the sentences for your report, making sure the verbs agree with their compound subjects. You may want to reverse the order of some compound subjects to make a sentence sound more natural.

Distress call, Oct. 15, 3:00 P.M.
A man and a woman has fallen into the Big Thompson River. Either two kayaks or one kayak are missing. Susan Brady and Juan Martinez is coordinating the rescue. Heavy rainstorms or fog are expected.

LESSON 3

❶ Here's the Idea

Many errors in subject-verb agreement occur when a prepositional phrase falls between the subject and verb.

▶ **The subject of a verb is never found in a prepositional phrase.** Don't be fooled by words that come between the subject and the verb. Mentally block out those words. Then decide whether the subject is singular or plural and match the verb to it.

AGREE

SINGULAR SUBJECT   SINGULAR VERB

A **team** ~~from several countries~~ **was working** on the Russian space station Mir.

PLURAL SUBJECT
Members ~~of the Russian and American space programs~~ **pose together aboard Mir.**
PLURAL VERB

Here's How **Choosing the Correct Verb**

Astronauts from Russia (has, have) abandoned Mir.

1. Mentally block out a prepositional phrase.
   Astronauts ~~from Russia~~ (has, have) abandoned Mir.
2. Decide if the subject is singular or plural.
   Astronauts = plural subject
3. Choose the verb that agrees with it. (have = plural verb)
   Astronauts from Russia have abandoned Mir.

❷ Why It Matters in Writing

Writers use prepositional phrases to tell more about the subject. When you do the same, make sure your verb goes with the subject, not the object of the preposition.

> **PROFESSIONAL MODEL**
>
> The international missions aboard Mir were a grand experiment. One result of these missions was the mutual respect that grew between Russian and U.S. astronauts.
>
> —Angel Morales

PLURAL SUBJECT, PLURAL VERB

SINGULAR SUBJECT, SINGULAR VERB

❸ Practice and Apply

CONCEPT CHECK: Phrases Between Subjects and Verbs

Choose the correct verb for each sentence below.

Teamwork in Space

1. The benefits from a space program (is, are) unpredictable.
2. Tension between the Soviet Union and the United States (was, were) a major reason for Mir's construction.
3. However, the result of this experiment (is, are) greater cooperation among nations.
4. The abandonment of Mir (has, have) become necessary due to mechanical problems.
5. Scientists and engineers from many nations (is, are) building Mir's replacement.
6. Space buffs throughout the world eagerly (awaits, await) its completion.
7. Labs within space stations (provides, provide) great places for science experiments.
8. The astronauts aboard a space station (depends, depend) heavily on their support team back home.
9. A ground crew at the mission control center (oversees, oversee) every mission.
10. Together, government agencies and private companies (makes, make) space flight possible.

→ **For a SELF-CHECK and more practice, see the EXERCISE BANK, p. 286.**

LESSON 4 Indefinite Pronouns as Subjects

❶ Here's the Idea

Some pronouns do not refer to a definite, or specific, person, place, thing, or idea. These pronouns are called **indefinite pronouns**.

▶ **When used as subjects, some indefinite pronouns are always singular. Some are always plural. Others can be singular or plural depending on how they're used.**

Indefinite Pronouns			
Singular	another	anybody	anyone
	anything	each	either
	everybody	everyone	everything
	neither	nobody	no one
	nothing	one	somebody
	someone	something	
Plural	both	few	many	several
Singular or Plural	all	any	most	none	some

Singular indefinite pronouns take singular verbs.

Everyone knows about camels in desert caravans.

Everything about them seems strange and exotic.

Plural indefinite pronouns take plural verbs.

Few of us realize their importance to desert people.

Many rely on the camel for everyday living.

Both of the camels in this photo are Bactrian camels.

Singular or Plural?

The indefinite pronouns *all, any, most, none,* and *some* can be either singular or plural. When you use one of these words as a subject, think about the noun it refers to. If the noun is singular, use a singular verb. If it is plural, use a plural verb.

REFERS TO

All of the camels carry supplies for humans on their humps.

REFERS TO

Some of the Mongolian desert still has wild Bactrian camels.

Sometimes an indefinite pronoun refers to a noun in a previous sentence.

PLURAL NOUN   INDEFINITE PRONOUN

The camels went eight days without water. All were healthy.   PLURAL VERB

❷ Why It Matters in Writing

When writing about people or animals, you'll often need indefinite pronouns as subjects. Correct subject-verb agreement helps readers know whether you're talking about one individual or several.

PROFESSIONAL MODEL

Sled dogs pull sleds across snow and ice in northern regions. **Many** of the dogs **are** purebred, but **some are** mixed breeds, especially in Alaska. **Each** of the dogs **has** a heavy coat and can sleep outside in temperatures as low as −70 degrees Fahrenheit.

—Lucy Armstrong

❸ Practice and Apply

A. CONCEPT CHECK: Indefinite Pronoun Subjects

Rewrite correctly each sentence in which the verb does not agree with the subject. If a sentence is correct, write *Correct*.

Guiding Lights
1. Everyone have heard of seeing-eye dogs.
2. Few knows the term *hearing dogs.*
3. All of these dogs alerts their owners to sounds of danger.
4. Several of the dog breeds is especially suited for work with visually challenged people.
5. Some of the best dogs includes German shepherds, Labrador retrievers, and golden retrievers.
6. Most of the states guarantees access rights to guide-dog users.
7. No one in these states is allowed to keep people with dog guides from public places.
8. Everyone recognizes a seeing-eye dog by its special harness and U-shaped handle.
9. Many knows that hearing dogs have a bright yellow or orange collar and leash.
10. Both of the canine helpers gives visually challenged and hearing-impaired people more independence.

➡ **For a SELF-CHECK and more practice, see the EXERCISE BANK, p. 287.**

B. WRITING: Using Indefinite Pronouns Correctly

For each sentence, choose the verb that agrees with the subject.

1. No one (seems, seem) neutral on the subject of dogs as pets.
2. Something about this topic (make, makes) people argue.
3. Many (praises, praise) dogs for their loyalty and obedience.
4. Few of the cat lovers (agrees, agree).
5. Some of them (thinks, think) dogs are just loud and stupid.
6. Somebody (accuses, accuse) a dog of having bad manners.
7. Others (blames, blame) the owner for bad training.
8. Some of the worst fights between neighbors (involves, involve) dogs.
9. Often neither of the sides (want, wants) to compromise.
10. Yet everybody (know, knows) pets are like family members.

Subjects in Unusual Positions

❶ Here's the Idea

In some sentences, the subject comes after the verb or between parts of the verb phrase. For these sentences, you have to find the subject first to make the verb agree.

Sentences that Begin with a Prepositional Phrase

Writers sometimes start a sentence with a prepositional phrase. In some of these sentences, the verb comes after the subject.

From his left hand comes Al's 90-mile-an-hour pitch.
SINGULAR VERB ⬆   SINGULAR SUBJECT ⬆

Sentences that Begin with *Here* or *There*

When a sentence begins with *here* or *there,* the subject often comes after the verb.

Here is a starting pitcher with a serious fastball.
⬆ SINGULAR VERB   ⬆ SINGULAR SUBJECT

There are several games on this field tonight.
⬆ PLURAL VERB   ⬆ PLURAL SUBJECT

Questions

In many questions, the subject follows the verb or comes between parts of the verb.

Does this goofball team ever win?
⬆ SINGULAR HELPING VERB   ⬆ SINGULAR SUBJECT

PLURAL HELPING VERB
Do both boys play on the team?
⬆ PLURAL SUBJECT

Here's How **Choosing the Correct Verb**

(Is, Are) the starting pitchers stronger than the relievers?

1. Turn the sentence around, putting the subject before the verb.
   The starting **pitchers** (is, are) stronger than the relievers.

2. Determine whether the subject is singular or plural.
   pitchers (plural)

3. Make sure the subject and verb agree.
   The starting **pitchers are** stronger than the relievers.

---

❷ Why It Matters in Writing

You can vary sentences by beginning with *here* or *there* or by beginning with a prepositional phrase. When you do so, make sure that the subjects and verbs agree.

Never in all my life **have I seen** such faith and friendship, such loyalty between men. There **are many** among you who call me harsh and cruel. But I cannot kill any man who proves such strong and true friendship for another.

—Fan Kissen, *Damon and Pythias*

❸ Practice and Apply

CONCEPT CHECK: Subjects in Unusual Positions

For each sentence below, first identify the subject and verb. If they agree, write *Correct.* If they don't agree, rewrite them.

World's Favorite Game
1. Does your friends like soccer?
2. There is no sport more popular in the world.
3. In the past, wasn't Americans big soccer fans?
4. Across this country is now thousands of youth soccer leagues.
5. Didn't 20 American soccer players win the Women's World Cup in 1999?
6. There was 12 nations competing in the 32 World Cup matches.
7. In front of their TV sets were one billion fans worldwide.
8. The final American match with China were the U.S.'s best-attended women's sports event.
9. Hasn't the women of Team USA become media favorites?
10. In addition to gymnasts and skaters, here is new heroines for teenaged girls.

➡ **For a SELF-CHECK and more practice, see the EXERCISE BANK, p. 288.**

Grammar in Literature

Subject-Verb Agreement

When you write, it's important to use correct subject-verb agreement. Like the members of the group of campers in the passage, subjects and verbs need to work together. When sentences are inverted, or when subjects and verbs are written as contractions, it's sometimes harder to choose correct subject-verb agreement. Notice the examples of subject-verb agreement in the inverted sentences in the passage below.

SCOUT'S
from
HONOR
by Avi

When we got off the bridge, we were in a small plaza. To the left was the roadway, full of roaring cars. In front of us, aside from the highway, there was nothing but buildings. Only to the right were there trees.

"North is that way," Max said, pointing toward the trees. We set off.

"How come you're limping?" Horse asked me. My foot *was* killing me. All I said, though, was, "How come you keep rubbing your arm?"

"I'm keeping the blood moving."

"We approached the grove of trees. "Wow," Horse exclaimed. "Country." ...

"Hey," Max cried, sounding relieved, "this is just like Brooklyn."

> In this sentence, the subject is the plural noun *trees.* So the verb, *were,* is also plural.

> Contraction *you're* is short for *you are.* Contraction *I'm* is short for *I am.* Both verbs agree with their subjects.

Practice and Apply

A. REVISING: Using Correct Subject-Verb Agreement

The following letter was written by a student during a camping trip with her scout troop. Because she dashed off the letter in a hurry, her subjects and verbs don't always agree. Rewrite her letter, correcting all errors in subject-verb agreement

Dear Folks,

What an experience! The rest of the girls and I am having the time of our lives. You wouldn't even recognize your daughter. She, along with the others, get up with the sun about 5:00 AM Then a team of us meet and decides what activities to do that day. There is swimming, hiking, horseback riding, and bird watching to choose from.

Ceramics are scheduled for tomorrow. I love using the potter's wheel.

My three weeks is almost over, so I may be home even before this message get there.

Love,

Deanna

P.S. Oops, I almost forgot. Several of my new friends is planning to come home and spend the rest of the summer with me.

B. WRITING: Journal

Write a journal entry describing an outdoor experience. Your experience can be real or imaginary. Write your journal entry as if the experience were in the present. Use correct subject-verb agreement. Save your writing in your ☐ **Working Portfolio.**

Mixed Review

A. Agreement in Number Write the verb form that agrees with the subject of each sentence.

1. Emergency Medical Technician-Paramedics (treats, treat) victims when a doctor isn't available.
2. All of the EMTs (is, are) trained medical workers.
3. Many (is, are) first at the scene of an accident or heart attack.
4. Drugs and medical equipment (is, are) carried in their special ambulance.
5. As a first step, paramedics on the scene immediately (contacts, contact) a doctor at a nearby hospital.
6. Any injuries or other important information (is, are) reported to the doctor.
7. A defibrillator (helps, help) correct an irregular heartbeat.
8. Another of the EMT's instruments (reports, report) heart activity.
9. In serious cases, heart attack victims or injured people (is, are) treated on the way to the hospital.
10. These brave men and women (has, have) saved many lives.

B. Additional Agreement Problems Read this report of a movie studio tour. Correct seven errors in subject-verb agreement and write the corrected sentences.

> **PROFESSIONAL MODEL**
>
> Are teamwork involved in making a movie? Yes! Here is some strange names for very important jobs. The lights and power distribution are set by the gaffer. Under the director of photography work the key grip. He is the chief builder of the lighting equipment. There is two assistants to the gaffer and the key grip. "Best boy electric" and "best boy grip" is their titles. These titles doesn't always describe the person. One of the best "boys" were about 50, and the other was a woman!

Lighting Technician

Camera Operator

Director

CHAPTER 7

Choose the letter of the best revision for each underlined section.

Search and rescue dogs is trained to find missing persons. There
(1)

are two different types of dogs. Some detects scent particles
(2)   (3)

carried by wind from the missing person's location. Other dogs on

a search team follow the trail of scent particles along the missing
(4)

person's path. The dogs smell the victim's clothing. A garment of
(5)

natural fibers are very helpful. Each of the dogs ignore all scents
(6)

except for the missing person's. Air scent dogs and trailing dogs
(7)

searches for victims in avalanches and in water. Doesn't dog and
(8)

handler teams train for two years for this job?

---

1. A. Search and rescue dogs are
      trained
   B. Search and rescue dogs is
      being trained
   C. Search and rescue dogs was
      being trained
   D. Correct as is

2. A. There is two different types
   B. There was two different
      types
   C. There has been two
      different types
   D. Correct as is

3. A. Some detect scent particles
   B. Some has detected scent
      particles
   C. Some is detecting scent
      particles
   D. Correct as is

4. A. dogs on a search team
      follows
   B. dogs on a search team is
      following
   C. dogs on a search team is to
      follow
   D. Correct as is

5. A. A garment of natural fibers
      were
   B. A garment of natural fibers
      have been
   C. A garment of natural fibers
      is
   D. Correct as is

6. A. Each of the dogs ignores
   B. Each of the dogs was
      ignoring
   C. Each of the dogs are ignoring
   D. Correct as is

7. A. Air scent dogs and trailing
      dogs searching
   B. Air scent dogs and trailing
      dogs was searching
   C. Air scent dogs and trailing
      dogs search
   D. Correct as is

8. A. Doesn't dog and handler
      teams trains
   B. Don't dog and handler
      teams trained
   C. Don't dog and handler
      teams train
   D. Correct as is

S-V AGREEMENT

Student Help Desk

Subject-Verb Agreement at a Glance

A singular subject takes a singular verb.

Our team wins the contest.

A plural subject takes a plural verb.

Many people share in the victory.

Indefinite Pronouns

If the indefinite pronoun is:	Make the verb:
Always singular everyone, anyone, everything, one, somebody	**Singular** **Everyone is** nervous.
Always plural both, few, many, several	**Plural** **Many come** to play.
Sometimes singular all, any, most, none, some	**Singular** **All** of our preparation **is** over.
Sometimes plural all, any, most, none, some	**Plural** **All** of the players **are** ready.

One for All

Compound Subjects

If the compound subject is:	Make the verb:
Joined by *and*	**Plural** The **winners and losers shake** hands.
Joined by *or* or *nor*	**Match the closest subject** Neither the **winners nor** the **loser looks** tired. Neither the **loser nor** the **winners look** tired.

All for One

Tricky Sentences — Make Them get Along

Kind of Sentence	Subject	Verb
Question		
Is the umpire ready?	umpire	is
Sentence Beginning with *Here* or *There*		
Here comes the pitch!	pitch	comes
Sentence Beginning with Prepositional Phrase		
Out of the park flies the ball!	ball	flies
Prepositional Phrase Between Subject and Verb		
The batter, in the fans' eyes, looks mighty.	batter	looks
Helping Verb		
Our players are winning.	players	are winning
The runner is scoring!	runner	is scoring

The Bottom Line

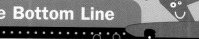

Checklist for Subject-Verb Agreement

Have I . . .

___ used a singular verb with a singular subject?

___ used a plural verb with a plural subject?

___ made the helping verb in a verb phrase agree with the subject?

___ used a plural verb with compound subjects joined by *and*?

___ made the verb agree with the closest part of a compound subject joined by *or* or *nor*?

___ checked whether indefinite pronoun subjects are singular or plural?

___ made verbs agree with subjects in unusual positions?

Capitalization

Watch out for big bear!
Find the cave at the base
of the mountain and fish
creek. Get the key from
the cave entrance and
follow fish creek
downstream to
shady road.

Theme: What's in a Name?

Follow That Bear!

These explorers carefully followed the directions, but they never found the meeting place. What happened? The person who wrote the directions didn't follow the rules of capitalization. The boys were on the lookout for a big bear instead of Big Bear Mountain. They thought they were supposed to go fishing in the creek instead of finding Fish Creek. They looked for a shady road instead of the road named Shady Road.

Write Away: Can You Get There from Here?
Write directions from where you are now to a particular place, such as your home. Include the names of landmarks, streets, and other places. Put your directions in your 🗂 **Working Portfolio.**

For each numbered item, choose the letter of the correct revision.

<u>can you think</u> of any weird place names? Imagine living in a
(1)
place called <u>peculiar, missouri,</u> or in other places like Diamond,
(2)
Zif, or Zig. In the book *Paris, Tightwad, and Peculiar: Missouri*
Place Names, <u>margot ford mcMillen</u> gives a history of place names
(3)
in Missouri. The writer states that <u>Tightwad, Missouri,</u> was
(4)
named after a merchant who cheated a mailman out of his
watermelon. The book covers humorous origins and places that
were named after the way they look, like <u>flat river</u>.
(5)
　　Another region with unusual place names is Newfoundland.
How would you like to travel to <u>bleak island, dead man's bay, or</u>
(6)
<u>breakheart point</u>? You can find these names in the book *<u>dictionary</u>*
<u>of Newfoundland english</u>. If you are interested in place names, you
(7)
can take a class to learn more about <u>Creative Names worldwide</u>.
(8)

1. A. can You think
   B. Can You think
   C. Can you think
   D. Correct as is

2. A. peculiar, Missouri,
   B. Peculiar, Missouri,
   C. Peculiar, missouri,
   D. Correct as is

3. A. Margot ford McMillen
   B. Margot ford mcMillen
   C. Margot Ford McMillen
   D. Correct as is

4. A. tightwad, missouri,
   B. tightwad, Missouri,
   C. Tightwad, missouri,
   D. Correct as is

5. A. Flat river
   B. Flat River
   C. flat River
   D. Correct as is

6. A. Bleak island, Dead man's
      bay, or Breakheart point
   B. Bleak Island, Dead Man's
      bay, or Breakheart point
   C. Bleak Island, Dead Man's
      Bay, or Breakheart Point
   D. Correct as is

7. A. *Dictionary Of Newfoundland*
      English
   B. *Dictionary of Newfoundland*
      English
   C. *Dictionary of Newfoundland*
      english
   D. Correct as is

8. A. Creative Names Worldwide
   B. creative Names worldwide
   C. creative names worldwide
   D. Correct as is

People and Cultures

LESSON 1

❶ Here's the Idea

Names and Initials

▶ **Capitalize people's names and initials.**

Sandra Cisneros   John F. Kennedy

Oprah Winfrey   Natsume Soseki

Personal Titles and Abbreviations

▶ **Capitalize titles and abbreviations of titles that are used before names or in direct address.**

Senator John Bullworth   Professor Henry Higgins

Capt. Kathryn Janeway   Rev. James L. Nash

Is my kitten going to be okay, Doctor?

Capitalize the abbreviations of some titles when they follow a name.

Jamie Crawford, M.D.   Fred Jones, Sr.

Angela Martinez, D.D.S.   George Collins, Ph.D.

▶ **Capitalize titles of heads of state, royalty, or nobility only when they are used before persons' names or in place of persons' names.**

Surgeon General David Satcher

Justice Sandra Day O'Connor

Queen Elizabeth

Czar Ivan IV was also known as Ivan the Terrible.

Do not capitalize titles when they are used without a proper name.

The duchess officially opened the ceremonies.

CHAPTER 8

Family Relationships

▶ **Capitalize words indicating family relationships only when they are used as names or before names.**

Aunt Laura   Cousin David   Uncle Al

Mom helped Aunt Sally choose the name for the new baby.

In general, do **not** capitalize a family relationship word when it follows the person's name or is used without a proper name.

I dreamed my uncle was King Arthur.

The Pronoun *I*

▶ **Always capitalize the pronoun *I*.**

Mother said that I was named after Uncle Henry.

Religious Terms

▶ **Capitalize the names of religions, sacred days, sacred writings, and deities.**

Religious Terms	
Religions	Judaism, Christianity, Islam
Sacred days	Rosh Hashanah, Good Friday
Sacred writings	Torah, Bible, Koran
Deities	God, Yahweh, Allah

Do not capitalize the words *god* and *goddess* when they refer to gods of ancient mythology.

The word *volcano* comes from the name of the Roman god of fire, Vulcan.

Nationalities, Languages, and Races

▶ **Capitalize the names of nationalities, languages, races, and most ethnic groups, and the adjectives formed from these names.**

German	Spanish	Korean
European	Asian American	Jewish

❷ Practice and Apply

CONCEPT CHECK: People and Cultures

Write the words and abbreviations that should be capitalized but are not in the paragraph below. Capitalize each correctly. If a sentence has no errors, write the word *correct*.

Middle Names
(1) Not long ago, i found a book of baby names in the attic that tells about how middle names originated. **(2)** It was written by jonathan p. algernon, jr. **(3)** Mom said it was the book she and Dad used to pick my name. **(4)** The book says that the spanish began using middle names about 1000 A.D. **(5)** Even though the early americans did not give their children middle names, by the mid-1800s german immigrants to the United States had made the practice popular. **(6)** president john quincy adams was the first president to use a middle name. **(7)** The most unusual middle name was chosen by a 13-year-old girl in 1965 who admired the folk song "Don't Ya Weep, Don't Ya Mourn." **(8)** Her name—mary dontyaweepdontyamourn schulz.

➡ For a **SELF-CHECK** and more practice, see the **EXERCISE BANK, p. 288.**

LESSON 2 — First Words and Titles

❶ Here's the Idea

Sentences and Poetry

▶ **Capitalize the first word of every sentence.**

My pen pal from Japan is named Suzu, which means "little bell."

▶ **In traditional poetry capitalize the first word of every line.**

> **LITERARY MODEL**
>
> All that is gold does not glitter,
> Not all those who wander are lost;
> The old that is strong does not wither,
> Deep roots are not reached by the frost.
>
> —J. R. R. Tolkien, "All That Is Gold"

Modern poets may choose not to begin each line of a poem with a capital letter. If you make this choice in your own writing, make sure the meaning of your work is still clear.

Quotations

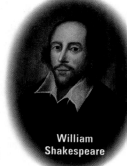

▶ **Capitalize the first word of a direct quotation if it is a complete sentence.**

Shakespeare was the first to write, "What's in a name?"

▶ **In a divided quotation, do not capitalize the first word of the second part unless it starts a new sentence.**

William
Shakespeare

"I have a name for my new kitten," said Sarah. "It's going to be Kitty!"

"Maybe you should think of another name," Mom said, "since that was the name of your last two cats."

CAPITALIZATION

Outlines

▶ **Capitalize the first word of each entry in an outline and the letters that introduce major subsections.**

I. Types of felines
   A. Domesticated cats
      1. Persian
      2. Tabby

Parts of a Letter

▶ **Capitalize the first word in the greeting and in the closing of a letter.**

Dear Mr. Macavity:

Dear Sir:

Sincerely yours,

Titles

▶ **Capitalize the first word, last word, and all important words in a title. Don't capitalize articles, conjunctions, or prepositions of fewer than five letters.**

Type of Media	Examples
Books	*Dogsong, Island of the Blue Dolphins*
Plays and musicals	*Annie, The Sound of Music*
Short stories	"Eleven," "Aaron's Gift"
Poems	"Ode to My Library," "Where the Sidewalk Ends"
Magazines and newspapers	*Highlights, TV Guide, The Washington Post*
Musical compositions	"The Star Spangled Banner"
Movies	*Tarzan, Prince of Egypt*
Television shows	*Seventh Heaven, Touched by an Angel*
Works of art	*Mona Lisa, Sunflowers*
Games	Space Genius, Name Game, Myths and Legends

❷ Practice and Apply

CONCEPT CHECK: First Words and Titles

Write the words that should be capitalized but are not in these sentences. Capitalize each correctly.

Popular Names

1. for centuries, one of the most common boys' names throughout the world has been *John*.
2. The name *John* can be found in many nursery rhymes, such as the following:

    deedle deedle dumpling, my son John
    went to bed with his stockings on.

John F. Kennedy

3. One form of the name *Johnny* is in the title of a famous early rock 'n' roll song by Chuck Berry, "Johnny b. goode."
4. The name *John Henry* might ring a bell, if you've read the legend, where he says, "before I let that steam drill beat me down, I'll die with my hammer in my hand."
5. The singer and composer John Lennon is often remembered for his song "imagine."

Jane Goodall

6. John F. Kennedy's famous words, "and so, my fellow Americans: ask not what your country can do for you; ask what you can do for your country," will endure for generations to come.
7. *jane* is the feminine form of *John,* and a famous woman with that name is Dr. Jane Goodall.
8. Another example of a famous Jane is the novelist Jane Austen, who wrote *Emma, Sense and sensibility,* and *persuasion.*
9. Jane Fonda, who starred in *Coming home,* has won two Oscars.
10. *John* and *Jane* can be found in a wide variety of forms in different countries and languages, as the following partial outline suggests:

    I. in France
       A. feminine
          1. Jeanne or Jeanette

➡ **For a SELF-CHECK and more practice, see the EXERCISE BANK, p. 289.**

CAPITALIZATION

Mixed Review

A. Capitalization in Outlining Rewrite the following portion of an outline, correcting the capitalization errors.

I. History of Names
- A. people's names
  - 1. first names
  - 2. middle names
  - 3. last names
- B. geographical names
  - 1. Land Names
  - 2. River and Mountain Names
  - 3. unusual names

B. Proofreading: Parts of a Letter Identify and correct the ten capitalization errors in the following letter.

Mr. John Little
510 N. Addison St.
Chicago, IL 60602

Dear mr. little,

I am writing about the puppy-naming contest that you advertised in the *Chicago tribune*. Your ad asked for the most creative names we could think of. I personally like Amadeus, after Wolfgang Amadeus Mozart, who composed *the marriage of Figaro*. Now, if you have a female pup, you might want to consider Greek mythology names like Calliope or Calypso, who entertained the Greek hero Odysseus in the long poem *The odyssey*. I recently read in an essay entitled "All about Pet names" that a person should consider the size, breed, and gender of the dog when choosing a name. You wouldn't want to name your male pit bull Muffy unless you have a very strong reason. Other names you might want to consider are Falstaff, Hercules, Lady, Venus, or Pluto.

Sincerely yours,

jemma roberts

LESSON 3

Places and Transportation

❶ Here's the Idea

Geographical Names

▶ In geographical names, capitalize each word except articles and prepositions.

Geographical Names	
Divisions of the world	Southern Hemisphere, International Date Line
Continents	Antarctica, Europe, South America
Bodies of water	Indian Ocean, Mississippi River, Lake Michigan
Islands	Guam, Prince Edward Island, Easter Island
Mountains	Appalachian Mountains, Himalayas, Adirondacks
Other landforms	Strait of Magellan, Sahara, Cape of Good Hope
Regions	Central America, Eurasia, Great Plains
Nations	Spain, Mexico, England
States	New York, Illinois, Florida
Cities and towns	Dallas, Springfield, Sacramento
Roads and streets	Route 66, Wall Street, Fifth Avenue

CAPITALIZATION

Bodies of the Universe

▶ Capitalize the names of planets and other specific objects in the universe.

Mercury   Tycho Brahe's Comet

Andromeda   Big Dipper   Ganymede

Saturn, Jupiter, and Mars were each named after mythical characters.

The planet closest to the sun is Mercury.

Regions and Sections

▶ **Capitalize the words *north, south, east,* and *west* when they name particular regions of the United States or the world or when they are parts of proper names.**

Some states in the Southeast, such as Virginia, Maryland, and North and South Carolina, were named after British royalty.

Do not capitalize these words when they indicate general directions or locations.

The state of Illinois is west of Indiana and south of Wisconsin.

Buildings, Bridges, and Other Landmarks

▶ **Capitalize the names of specific buildings, bridges, monuments, and other landmarks.**

Empire State Building	Washington Monument
Brooklyn Bridge	Mount Rushmore

The national monument in New Mexico known as the Gila Cliff Dwellings is the site of Pueblo Indian dwellings.

Planes, Trains, and Other Vehicles

▶ **Capitalize the names of specific airplanes, trains, ships, cars, and spacecraft.**

Names	Examples
Airplanes	*Enola Gay, Spruce Goose*
Trains	*City of New Orleans, Cannonball Express*
Ships	USS *Missouri,* *Titanic,* HMS *Bounty*
Cars	*Volkswagen, Camaro, Jaguar*
Spacecraft	*Discovery, Endeavor, Soyuz*

CHAPTER 8

❷ Practice and Apply

A. CONCEPT CHECK: Places and Transportation

For each sentence, write the words that should be capitalized. Do not write words that are already capitalized.

Naming the Land
1. In the early 1700s, French explorers began to colonize parts of what is now the south.
2. Near the gulf of mexico, the French founded a fort in an area settled by a Native American group called the Maubilian.
3. The French translated that name to mobile.
4. Around a nearby river, the French encountered the Alibamons (for whom the state of alabama is named).
5. Two centuries later, paddle wheel boats with names like the *delta queen* would travel the mississippi river, but in the 1700s French explorers made their way upriver in canoes.
6. Near the great plains, the French encountered a river called *ni* (river) *bthaska* (something flat and spread out).
7. The French called it the *rivière platte.*
8. *Ni bthaska* became the name of the state nebraska.
9. The French marveled at the beauty of the milky way.
10. Today, visitors can appreciate the breathtaking beauty of the land as they drive along interstate 80.

➡ **For a SELF-CHECK and more practice, see the EXERCISE BANK, p. 290.**

B. REVISING: Correcting Map Labels

Find and correct the capitalization errors in the map below. Notice that not all labels need to be changed.

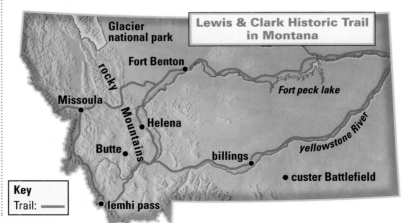

Glacier national park

Lewis & Clark Historic Trail in Montana

Fort Benton

rocky Mountains

Fort peck lake

Missoula

Helena

Butte

billings

yellowstone River

custer Battlefield

Key
Trail: ——

lemhi pass

CAPITALIZATION

Organizations and Other Subjects

LESSON 4

① Here's the Idea

Organizations and Institutions

▶ **Capitalize all important words in the names of organizations, institutions, stores, and companies.**

Summerville Middle School   Boston Public Library

Sarah's Beauty Shop   Oxford University

League of Nations   National Honor Society

Do not capitalize words such as *school, company, church, college,* and *hospital* when they are not used as parts of names.

We moved near the hospital.

Historical Events, Periods, and Documents

▶ **Capitalize the names of historical events, periods, and documents.**

Historical Events, Periods, and Documents	
Events	Harlem Renaissance, Revolutionary War
Periods	Space Age, Age of Exploration
Documents	Magna Carta, Constitution of the United States

The Declaration of Independence was adopted more than a year after the Revolutionary War began.

Time Abbreviations and Calendar Items

▶ **Capitalize the abbreviations B.C., A.D., A.M., and P.M.**

The ancient Egyptians developed history's first national government about 3000 B.C.

▶ **Capitalize the names of months, days, and holidays but not the seasons.**

October   Labor Day   fall

St. Valentine's Day   Monday   spring

The Thanksgiving holiday takes place every fall on the fourth Thursday of November.

Special Events, Awards, and Brand Names

▶ **Capitalize the names of special events and awards.**

the World Series   the Country Music Awards

the Stanley Cup   the Caldecott Medal

What runner will win the Boston Marathon this year?

▶ **Capitalize the brand name of a product but not a common noun that follows a brand name.**

Sun Safe sunscreen   Munchies potato chips

❷ Practice and Apply

CONCEPT CHECK: Organizations and Other Subjects

Identify and correct the words that should be capitalized in the following flyer.

Annual roller hockey Tournament

Where: Springdale middle school

When: saturday, October 17, through saturday, october 31. Games begin promptly at 7:00 p.m. each thursday, friday, and saturday of the tournament. The final game will be held on halloween. Come in costume and cheer for your favorite team!

Prizes: Third-place winners receive a case of zap cola and a $10 gift certificate to Jimmy's athletic warehouse. Second-place winners will get a gift certificate for a pair of air lite tennis shoes.

Grand Prize: First-place winners receive $500 and a team trophy, the Springdale silver puck.

Grammar in Math

Capitalization in Tables and Bar Graphs

When you write about statistics for math, you want to make sure your numbers are correct. But what about capitalization? You must pay attention to capitalization too; otherwise, people won't trust your numbers. Notice how proper names and important words are capitalized in the table and graph below.

Most Popular Dog Names	
Name	Number
Max	28
Sam	15
Lady	13
Rocky	9
Lucky	6
Missy	4

Capitalize all important words in titles

Capitalize proper names

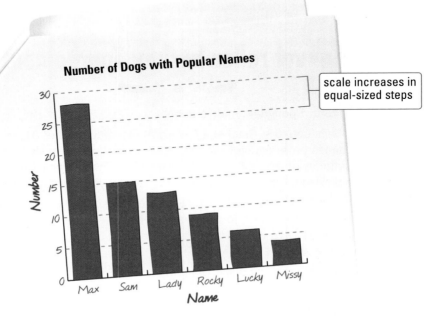

scale increases in equal-sized steps

Practice and Apply

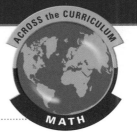

ACROSS the CURRICULUM

MATH

A. CONCEPT CHECK: Capitalization in Graphs and Tables

A student did some research into popular girls' names in the 1890s and quickly jotted down information. Correct the capitalization in the table. Use the following information to create your own bar graph like the one shown on the opposite page. Don't forget to include a title. Use equal-sized scale numbers that increase in steps of 10 (for example, 10, 20, 30, . . . and so on).

Most popular Names in the 1890s

Girl's Names	Number
Mary	59
anna	55
Elizabeth	46
emma	38
Margaret	32
rose	20

60
50
40
30
20
10
0
Mary

B. WRITING: Summarizing Information

Once you have created a bar graph, summarize the information in a short paragraph. Remember, when you summarize information, you explain the most important points. Be sure to check your capitalization. Save your paragraph in your **Working Portfolio.**

Capitalization **199**

A. Proofreading: Capitalization Identify and correct the capitalization errors in the following paragraph.

Imagine having to carry the name Minny vann the rest of your life because uncle Ed or grandma Vann thought it was cute! I admit that I've heard worse, though: Constance Noring, Jim Shortz, and Frank n. Stine, for example. Why do people inflict silly and embarrassing names on their children? My cousin's mother and father, whose last name is Tyme, named my cousin Justin because he was born at 11:59 p.m. on new year's eve. Not all silly names are intentional. When a man named E. Speaking entered the united states army and eventually reached the rank of general, he became general e. Speaking. When Claude Payne reached the rank of major, he became major Payne.

B. Editing and Proofreading Rewrite the business letter below using capitalization rules from this chapter.

U.S. Dept. of interior
National Park service
1849 c street
Washington, D.C. 20240

Dear sir:

I am a student at marietta junior high school in monroe, nebraska, and a member of mr. eric johnson's class Social Studies I. A class assignment is to plan a trip to visit some national monuments and parks. We will be traveling by tour bus and will travel west on interstate 80. We would like information on parks in Colorado and Wyoming, especially yellowstone national park and parks in the Teton mountains. We will probably make the trip in late may or early june of next year.

Please send us brochures about places that we might visit. Also, please send us any other suggestions you may have about our tour of the west.

sincerely,

amanda brady

For each numbered item, choose the letter of the correct revision.

> Sometime around <u>4000 b.c. and 3500 B.C.</u>, poets, astronomers,
> (1)
> and farmers began to create mythological names for constellations.
> The names of constellations varied, however, from <u>babylonia, to</u>
> (2)
> <u>Egypt, to Greece</u>. Most people are familiar with the <u>greek and</u>
> (3)
> <u>roman</u> names of stars after <u>myths, heroes, or Gods</u>. Take
> (4)
> <u>orion, the hunter</u>, for example. The story reminds people of a
> (5)
> great hunter holding his shield. In some cases, constellations were
> named after a figure in the sky. For example, a bear has been
> associated with the constellation <u>Ursa Major</u> <u>since the ice age</u>. In
> (6)   (7)
> 1930, the <u>International astronomical Union</u> set official boundaries
> (8)
> that defined the 88 constellations that exist today.

1. A. 4000 b.c. and 3500 b.c.
   B. 4000 B.c. and 3500 B.c.
   C. 4000 B.C. and 3500 B.C.
   D. Correct as is

2. A. babylonia, to egypt, to Greece
   B. Babylonia, to Egypt, to Greece
   C. babylonia, to egypt, to greece
   D. Correct as is

3. A. Greek and roman
   B. greek and Roman
   C. Greek and Roman
   D. Correct as is

4. A. myths, heroes, or gods
   B. Myths, Heroes, or Gods
   C. Myths, Heroes, or gods
   D. Correct as is

5. A. Orion, The Hunter
   B. orion, the Hunter
   C. Orion, the Hunter
   D. Correct as is

6. A. ursa major
   B. Ursa major
   C. ursa Major
   D. Correct as is

7. A. since the Ice age
   B. since the Ice Age
   C. Since the Ice Age
   D. Correct as is

8. A. international astronomical Union
   B. International Astronomical union
   C. International Astronomical Union
   D. Correct as is

Student Help Desk

Capitalization at a Glance

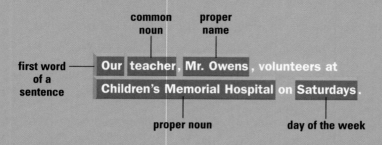

first word of a sentence

common noun

proper name

Our teacher, Mr. Owens, volunteers at
Children's Memorial Hospital on Saturdays.

proper noun

day of the week

Do Capitalize   Upper Case Ursula

Proper nouns that name people, places, and things:
Traditionally in **M**exico a firstborn daughter is named **M**aria.

Family words used as a name or part of a name:
Billy is **U**ncle William's nickname.

The first word of a sentence:
Do you know the origin of your name?

The first word in every line of traditional poetry:
The winter owl banked just in time to pass
And save herself from breaking window glass.
— Robert Frost, "Questioning Faces"

The first word, last word, and all important words in titles:
Across **F**ive **A**prils

Proper nouns that name a particular date, holiday, event, or award:
On **M**arch 17, **S**t. **P**atrick's **D**ay, people by the name of Pat, Patrick,
or Patricia can celebrate their saint's name.

Don't Capitalize   Lower Case Larry

Words after the first word of a closing of a letter:
Sincerely yours,   Yours truly,

Family words used as ordinary nouns:
I was named after my mom.

Calendar items if they name a season:
My name is Summer, but my favorite season is fall.

The common nouns that stand for people, places, or things:
My cousin enjoys riding her bike to school because she can stop at the store for some snacks.

Compass direction when indicating a general location:
I like to watch flocks of geese flying in formation, migrating south for the winter.

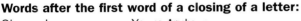
The Bottom Line

Checklist for Capitalization

Have I capitalized . . .

____ people's names and initials?

____ personal titles preceding names?

____ names of races, languages, and nationalities?

____ names of religions and religious terms?

____ names of bodies of the universe and other geographical terms?

____ names of monuments, bridges, and other landmarks?

____ names of particular planes, trains, and other vehicles?

____ names of organizations, institutions, and businesses?

____ names of historical events, eras, and documents?

____ names of special events, awards, and brand names?

Punctuation

- Mayor demands explanation, pg. A3.
- Power Company blames weather, pg. A5.
- Cost of disaster assessed, pg. B1.
- Propane sales skyrocket, pg. B9.

The Daily Tribune

Volume 36, issue 2,742

Tuesday, March 20, 2000

Emergency Power Lost in City

Theme: Great Mistakes and Disasters

Headline Headache

What event is the headline describing? It's hard to know without proper end marks in place. Is it "Emergency Power Lost in City!" in which the city has lost emergency backup power? Or is it "Emergency! Power Lost in City!" in which the city has lost all power? Punctuation helps make even simple messages easier to understand.

Write Away: Oops! News That's Unfit to Print
Write a headline describing a time you slipped up. It might describe when you forgot to study for a test, tripped over a neighbor's dog, or missed a bus. Be sure to punctuate your headline correctly. Save your work in your **Working Portfolio.**

For each numbered item, choose the letter of the best revision.

> Some mistakes are <u>tragic</u> Other mistakes have milder
> $\qquad$ (1)
> <u>consequences</u>; in fact, <u>theyre</u> just plain goofy. Take, for example,
> $\quad$ (2) $\qquad\qquad$ (3)
> the story <u>Cinderella.</u> Did you ever wonder why someone lucky
> $\qquad$ (4)
> enough to have a fairy godmother ended up with <u>glass shoes</u>! An
> $\qquad\qquad\qquad$ (5)
> older version of the story says that <u>Cinderellas'</u> slippers were
> $\qquad\qquad$ (6)
> made of *vair*, a type of fur. Charles <u>Perrault the writer</u>, mistakenly
> $\qquad\qquad$ (7)
> assumed that the word *vair* should have been <u>*verre*</u>. (*Verre* means
> $\qquad\qquad$ (8)
> "glass.") <u>Oh well?</u> Can you imagine a fancy prince exclaiming that
> $\quad$ (9)
> he would <u>"marry the owner of a fur slipper?"</u>
> $\qquad$ (10)

1. A. tragic.
   B. tragic,
   C. tragic —
   D. Correct as is

2. A. consequences.
   B. consequences,
   C. consequences?
   D. Correct as is

3. A. their
   B. they're
   C. theyr'e
   D. Correct as is

4. A. "Cinderella."
   B. *Cinderella.*
   C. CINDERELLA.
   D. Correct as is

5. A. glass shoes;
   B. glass shoes?
   C. glass shoes,
   D. Correct as is

6. A. Cinderella's
   B. Cinderellas
   C. Cinderella
   D. Correct as is

7. A. Perrault, the writer,
   B. Perrault the writer
   C. Perrault, the writer
   D. Correct as is

8. A. *verre*
   B. *verre,*
   C. *verre:*
   D. Correct as is

9. A. Oh well;
   B. Oh well,
   C. Oh well!
   D. Correct as is

10. A. he would marry the owner
       of a fur slipper?
    B. he would "marry the owner
       of a fur slipper.
    C. he would marry the owner
       of a "fur slipper."
    D. Correct as is

LESSON 1 Periods and Other End Marks

❶ Here's the Idea

Periods, question marks, and exclamation points are known as **end marks** because they indicate the end of a sentence. Periods have other uses as well.

Periods

▶ **Use a period at the end of a declarative sentence.** A declarative sentence makes a statement.

Not all blunders have bad results **.**

Some important discoveries have happened by accident **.**

▶ **Use a period at the end of almost every imperative sentence.** An imperative sentence gives a command. When these sentences express excitement or emotion, they end with exclamation points.

Tell us more about these great mistakes **.**

Don't stop **!** These stories are really interesting **.**

▶ **Use a period at the end of an indirect question.** An indirect question reports what a person asked without using the person's exact words.

DIRECT   Tracy asked, "Is this article about x-rays true **?** "

INDIRECT   Tracy asked whether the article about x-rays is true **.**

Question Marks

▶ **Use a question mark at the end of an interrogative sentence.** An interrogative sentence asks a question.

How were x-rays discovered **?**

Who first recognized them **?**

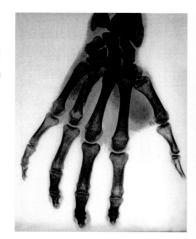

Exclamation Points

▶ **Use an exclamation point to end an exclamatory sentence.** An exclamatory sentence expresses strong feeling.

I can't believe it**!** That's an amazing bit of luck**!**

▶ **Use an exclamation point after an interjection or any other exclamatory expression.**

Hey**!** I bet the scientist who first saw them was surprised.

Wow**!** Strange things do happen in laboratories.

Other Uses for Periods

▶ **Use a period at the end of most abbreviations or after an initial.**

Common Abbreviations and Initials

Abbreviations

sec. second	**Dr.** Doctor	**Sr.** Senior	**tsp.** teaspoon
min. minute	**Nov.** November	**E.** East	**in.** inch
hr. hour	**Tues.** Tuesday	**St.** Street	**Prof.** Professor

Initials

R.R. railroad	**M.T.P.** Maria Theresa Parsons
P.O. post office	**P.M.** *post meridiem* (after noon)
M.D. doctor of medicine	**D.C.** District of Columbia

Abbreviations Without Periods

CD compact disc	**MVP** Most Valuable Player
UN United Nations	**mph** miles per hour
NY New York	**cm** centimeters

▶ **Use a period after each number or letter in an outline or a list.**

Outline

Uses for X-rays
I. Medical
  A. Pictures of bones and teeth
  B. Cancer treatments
II. Industrial
  A. Security devices
  B. Pest control

List

Parts of an X-Ray Machine
1. Glass tube
2. Negative electrode
3. Positive electrode
4. Electric current
5. Tube housing
6. Film compartment

❷ Practice and Apply

Write the words from the following paragraph that should be followed by periods, question marks, or exclamation points. Include these end marks in your answers.

X-rays Exposed

Did you know that x-rays were discovered by accident No kidding In 1895, Prof Wilhelm Roentgen, a German scientist, conducted a new experiment. He worked in a darkened room with a special vacuum tube. The tube used a bright electric current When Roentgen placed a sheet of black paper around the tube, he was surprised by the results Instead of seeing complete darkness, Roentgen noticed an eerie glow coming from a nearby screen How strange Roentgen soon realized that this glow was caused by mysterious invisible rays coming from the tube Can you guess why he called his discovery x-rays In science, the letter x means something unknown

➡ **For a SELF-CHECK and more practice, see the EXERCISE BANK, p. 291.**

Rewrite the announcement below, adding periods where they are needed.

Don't miss this year's
SCIENCE FAIR!

Date: Sat, Nov 13, 2004
Time: 10:00 AM–3:00 PM
Place: Girls' Gymnasium
Thomas A Edison Jr High
School
1120 N Red Robin Ln
Mt Vernon, OH

If you would like to participate,
please see Ms Walker.

Commas in Sentences

❶ Here's the Idea

Commas can be used to separate parts of a sentence.

Commas with Items in a Series

▶ **Use a comma after every item in a series except the last one.** A series consists of three or more items.

The story of Daedalus and his son Icarus teaches us about **cleverness , stubbornness ,** and **foolishness.**

Each man used **wax , feathers ,** and a **harness** to make a pair of wings.

Icarus and Daedalus **put on their wings , ran along the beach ,** and **flew toward the open sea.**

▶ **Use commas between two or more adjectives of equal rank that modify the same noun.**

Both father and son made a **quick , daring** escape.

> **Here's How** Adding Commas Between Adjectives
>
> To decide whether to use a comma between two adjectives modifying the same noun, try the following test.
>
> **Daedalus used large stiff feathers.**
>
> **1.** Place the word *and* between the adjectives.
> **Daedalus used large and stiff feathers.**
>
> **2.** If the sentence still makes sense, replace *and* with a comma.
> **Daedalus used large , stiff feathers.**

Do not use a comma between adjectives that together express a single idea.

Each pair of wings had many light feathers.

Commas with Introductory Words and Phrases

▶ **Use a comma after an introductory word or phrase to separate it from the rest of the sentence.**

Recklessly, Icarus flew too close to the sun.

According to Greek myth, Icarus fell when his wings melted.

Commas with Interrupters

▶ **Use commas to set off words or phrases that interrupt, or break, the flow of thought in a sentence.**

Daedalus , however, did fly to freedom.

This myth has been told , I am certain, by many authors.

Commas with Nouns of Direct Address

▶ **Use commas to set off nouns of direct address.** A noun of direct address names the person or group being spoken to.

Devon, explain why Daedalus warned Icarus about the sun.

Don't forget , class, that Icarus didn't listen to his father.

Commas with Appositives

An **appositive** is a word or phrase that identifies or renames a noun or pronoun that comes right before it. Use commas when the appositive adds extra information; do not use commas when the appositive is needed to make the meaning clear.

Olivia E. Coolidge , an English author, wrote about Greek myths. (The phrase *an English author* adds extra information.)

The English author Olivia E. Coolidge wrote about Greek myths. (The phrase *Olivia E. Coolidge* is needed information.)

Commas to Avoid Confusion

▶ **Use a comma whenever the reader might otherwise be confused.**

UNCLEAR   Soon after Icarus left Daedalus followed.

CLEAR   Soon after Icarus left , Daedalus followed.

② Practice and Apply

A. CONCEPT CHECK: Commas in Sentences

Write the words from the following passage that should be followed by commas.

Oil Takes Its Toll

In 1989, an oil tanker, the *Exxon Valdez,* went aground off the coast of Alaska. Eleven million gallons of smelly sticky oil spilled out of the tanker. Spread by the ocean current the oil slick soon coated 1,300 miles of Alaska's shoreline. The magnificent, sparkling beaches of Alaska turned oily and black. The spill killed approximately 2,800 otters 300 seals 250 bald eagles and 250,000 other birds.

Ten years later there were signs of recovery. A council was established after the spill to help restore wildlife. Molly McCammon its director indicated that things were looking better. The numbers of bald eagles and pink salmon were strong. She added however that more work needed to be done to improve the numbers of seals, herring, and ducks.

➡ **For a SELF-CHECK and more practice, see the EXERCISE BANK, p. 291.**

B. MIXED REVIEW: Using Punctuation Correctly

Write the words from the following passage that should be followed by end marks or commas. Include these punctuation marks in your answers.

The Great Caterpillar Catastrophe

In 1869, Leopold Trouvelot a French scientist imported caterpillars to Massachusetts. Why did he import them He hoped to crossbreed the adult form of these caterpillars, known as gypsy moths with the moths of silkworms He thought perhaps foolishly, that he could create a new American caterpillar, one that made valuable silk Unfortunately Trouvelot's experiment had a terrible outcome

One day a gust of wind knocked over a caterpillar cage in his house What a mess Crawling out an open window, the caterpillars escaped. Soon they grew into adult moths and migrated Over many years the moths spread to Virginia Maryland and New York Now they are pests that destroy healthy trees Who would believe that so much trouble could come from one mishap with caterpillars It's amazing

LESSON 3 # Commas: Dates, Addresses, and Letters

❶ Here's the Idea

See these rules in action in the letter below.

Commas in Dates, Addresses, and Letters	
Commas in dates	In dates, use a comma between the day and the year. (Use a comma after the year if the sentence continues.)
Commas in addresses	Use a comma between the city or town and the state or country. (Use a comma after the state or country if the sentence continues.)
Commas in letters	Use a comma after the greeting of a casual letter and after the closing of a casual or business letter.

CHAPTER 9

1   422 Fairfax Road

2   Milton , MA 02186

3   April 13 , 2000

4 Dear Jeri ,

5   Do you remember how we laughed

6 when we saw a picture of the Leaning

7 Tower of Pisa? Well, my grandma told me

8 that the tower tilts because of a terrible

9 mistake. Long ago, in Pisa , Italy , architects

10 planned to make a bell tower for the

11 town's cathedral. Everything went well in

12 the beginning. But during construction,

13 the tower started to lean. The builders

14 realized that the ground underneath the

15 tower was too soft. Unfortunately, the

16 tower leans a little bit more every year.

17   I'm planning to see the tower on

18 March 21 , 2001 , when I visit my grandma

19 in Italy. It will be her 90th birthday. I

20 hope the tower is still standing by then.

21   Your friend ,

22   Christa

Line 2: comma between city and state

Line 3: comma between day and year

Line 4: comma after greeting

Line 9: commas after city and country

Line 18: commas after day and year

Line 21: comma after closing

WATCH OUT Do not use a comma between the state and the ZIP code.

❷ Practice and Apply

A. CONCEPT CHECK: Commas: Dates, Addresses, and Letters

The letter below is a field trip proposal that a student has been asked to write for class. Write the words and numbers from the letter that should be followed by commas.

175 Green Street
Englewood CO 80110
May 6 2000

Dear Mr. Clayton

I think that our social studies class should visit the history museum on October 12 2000 our field trip day. We'd have fun seeing exhibits on the things we've studied. So far, we've learned about ancient people of Mesopotamia, Egypt, and China. I especially liked reading stories about the Great Pyramid in Giza Egypt and the Ch'in tomb near Sian China. Of course, if we go, we'll have to stop by my favorite place, the mummy room! It would be a mistake to miss it!

I hope that you will accept my proposal.

Sincerely

Malcolm

➡ For a SELF-CHECK and more practice, see the EXERCISE BANK, p. 292.

B. WRITING: Dear Friend

Put a letter together using these parts. Don't forget to add commas where they belong.

1300 Dearborn St.

As ever

Dear Matt

June 25, 2000

Chicago IL 60610

Sarah

I enjoyed your letter, especially the sandcastle story. My family is going to a party in Milwaukee Wisconsin next Saturday. Would you like to join us?

PUNCTUATION

Punctuating Quotations

❶ Here's the Idea

To punctuate quotations, you need to know where to put quotation marks, commas, and end marks.

Direct Quotations

A direct quotation is the exact words of a writer or a speaker.

▶ **Use quotation marks at the beginning and the end of a direct quotation.**

   "All passengers assemble on deck,**"** said the captain.

▶ **Use commas to set off explanatory words used with direct quotations (whether they occur at the beginning, in the middle, or at the ends of sentences).**

   The captain said, "All passengers assemble on deck."

   "All passengers," said the captain, "assemble on deck."

   "All passengers assemble on deck," said the captain.

▶ **If a quotation is a question or an exclamation, place the question mark or exclamation point inside the closing quotation marks.**

   "Have we hit an iceberg?" a crewman asked.

▶ **If quoted words are part of a quotation or exclamation of your own, place the question mark or exclamation point outside the closing quotation marks.**

   Did I hear him say, "I believe we're sinking"?

Commas and periods always go inside closing quotation marks. They're too little to stay outside.

CHAPTER 9

Indirect Quotations

▶ **Do not use quotation marks to set off an indirect quotation.**

An indirect quotation tells, in different words, what someone said. An indirect quotation is often introduced by the word *that*. It does not require a comma.

DIRECT   Captain Smith shouted to the radio operators, "You can do no more. Abandon your cabin."

INDIRECT   Finally, Captain Smith told the radio operators that they should abandon their cabin.

Divided Quotations

A divided quotation is a direct quotation that is separated into two parts. Explanatory words such as *he said* or *she said* come between the parts.

▶ **Use quotation marks to enclose both parts of a divided quotation.**

"The ship," the owner said, "is unsinkable."

▶ **Do not capitalize the first word of the second part of a divided quotation unless it begins a new sentence.**

"The ship is unsinkable," he said, "because of its double-bottomed hull."

"The ship is unsinkable," he said. "It has extra protection because of its double-bottomed hull."

▶ **Use commas to set off the explanatory words used with a divided quotation.**

"This ship," he explained, "has extra safety features."

PUNCTUATION

Quotation Marks in Dialogue

▶ **In dialogue, a new paragraph and a new set of quotation marks signal a change in speakers.**

A dialogue is a conversation between two or more speakers.

LITERARY MODEL

"Ready?"

"Ready."

"Now?"

"Soon."

"Do the scientists really know? Will it happen today, will it?"

"Look, look; see for yourself!"

The children pressed to each other like so many roses, so many weeds, intermixed, peering out for a look at the hidden sun.

—Ray Bradbury, "All Summer in a Day"

Using Quotation Marks

Use this model to review the punctuation in this lesson.

PROFESSIONAL MODEL

"Did you know that the *Titanic* was not the only large ship to be lost at sea?" Amanda asked.

"What other ship was lost?" replied Linda. ── Questions

"In 1840, the largest ship was the *President*," explained Amanda. "On its third trip across the Atlantic, it left New York and was never heard from again." │ Divided quotation

"If that's true," Linda questioned, "then why hasn't anyone made a movie about the *President?* Who knows about it?" ── Divided quotation

"Well, we do!" exclaimed Amanda. ── Exclamations

"Right!" shouted Linda. "Hey, let's use this idea for our social studies project."

❷ Practice and Apply

A. CONCEPT CHECK: Punctuating Quotations

Rewrite each sentence, adding quotation marks and other punctuation where needed. If a sentence is correct, write *Correct*.

A Bug in the Works!

"Why is the word *bug* used to describe a computer problem asked Steve.

Well, began Jessie. "In 1945, a computer scientist named Grace Murray Hopper was working in a computer lab."

"So far, this isn't a very exciting story, commented Steve.

"Let me continue shouted Jessie. "While trying to finish a project, Hopper noticed that the computer continued to have problems."

What happened next questioned Steve.

Jessie explained, "When Hopper looked closer at the inside of the computer, she found a moth messing up everything."

"You're making this up exclaimed Steve

"No, it's true, stated Jessie. "She glued the dead moth to the log book with a note explaining the accident." Jessie added, Ever since then, computer problems have been called bugs."

➜ For a SELF-CHECK and more practice, see the EXERCISE BANK, p. 293.

B. WRITING: He Said; She Said

Choose one frame from this cartoon and write it as a short dialogue. Add explanatory words such as *Calvin bragged* or *Susie explained* to make your work clearer. Be sure to punctuate your dialogue correctly.

Calvin and Hobbes by Bill Watterson

Semicolons and Colons

① Here's the Idea

A **semicolon** separates parts in a sentence. It is stronger than a comma but not as strong as a period. A **colon** shows that a list follows. Colons are also used after greetings in business letters and in expressions of time.

Semicolons in Compound Sentences

▶ **Use a semicolon to join parts of a compound sentence without a coordinating conjunction.**

The mistake was simple; the result was disastrous.

Semicolons with Items in a Series

▶ **When there are commas within parts of a series, use semicolons to separate the parts.**

Bodies within the solar system include the nine planets; about 50 satellites, such as Earth's moon; more than 1,000 comets, such as Halley's comet; and thousands of asteroids.

Colons

▶ **Use a colon to introduce a list of items.**

Planets revolve around the sun in this order: Mercury, Venus, Earth, Mars, Jupiter, Saturn, Uranus, Neptune, and Pluto.

Mars has these earthlike features: ice-covered poles, an atmosphere, and changing seasons.

Do not use a colon directly after a verb or a preposition.

INCORRECT Through the telescope he saw: Mars, the Red Planet.

▶ **Use a colon after the formal greeting in a business letter or letter of complaint.**

BUSINESS Dear Principal Jones: Dear Ms. Mark:

For a model, see the business letter in the Model Bank.

▶ **Use a colon between hours and minutes in expressions of time.**

The lecture starts at 7:30 P.M. A reception follows at 9:00 P.M.

❷ Practice and Apply

A. CONCEPT CHECK: Semicolons and Colons

Write the words from the following passage that should be followed by semicolons or colons. Include these punctuation marks in your answers.

A "Simple" Mistake

In December of 1998, NASA successfully launched the Mars Climate Orbiter. It was designed to get detailed information about Mars and its weather conditions. According to plan, it would record the following data atmospheric temperatures, dust levels, water vapor levels, and cloud cover.

On September 23, 1999, the Climate Orbiter was ready to go into orbit around Mars. At about 500 A.M. Eastern time, rocket firings began, and radio contact was lost. Contact was expected to be restored about 530 A.M. But instead the worst of sounds came from scientists' computers silence, silence, and more silence.

Hours later, NASA scientists were grim the mission had failed. One team of scientists had used *metric* measurements another team had used *English* measurements. This mix-up put the spacecraft off course by about 60 miles! Of course, NASA lost the orbiter and all of its contents an infrared temperature meter, a device for measuring moisture, communications instruments, and other specialized equipment. A $125-million craft had been lost due to a simple metric conversion mistake.

➡ For a SELF-CHECK and more practice, see the EXERCISE BANK, p. 293.

B. WRITING: Lost in Deep Space

It's easy to lose things, especially in the deep darkness of a closet or locker! Write about a time you misplaced something important, such as your lunch, your uniform, a CD, or a homework assignment. Include information about all the places you looked and the things you picked up while searching. Make sure to include semicolons and colons in your description.

Hyphens, Dashes, and Parentheses

❶ Here's the Idea

Hyphens, dashes, and parentheses help make your writing clear by separating or setting off words or parts of words.

Hyphens

▶ **Use a hyphen if part of a word must be carried over from one line to the next.**

1. Separate the word between syllables.
RIGHT: let-ter   WRONG: lette-r

2. The word must have at least two syllables to be broken.
RIGHT: num-ber   WRONG: ea-rth

3. You must leave at least two letters on each line.
RIGHT: twen-ty   WRONG: a-round

▶ **Use hyphens in certain compound words.**

self-confident   brother-in-law

▶ **Use hyphens in compound numbers from twenty-one through ninety-nine.**

twenty-three   seventy-two

▶ **Use hyphens in spelled-out fractions.**

one-half   three-fourths

Dashes

▶ **Use dashes to show an abrupt break in thought.**

Sojourner Truth—whose birth name was Isabella Baumfree— spent many years of her life speaking out against slavery.

Parentheses

▶ **Use parentheses to set off material that is loosely related to the rest of the sentence.**

Sojourner Truth met Harriet Tubman (a conductor of the Underground Railroad) during the Civil War.

CHAPTER 9

LESSON 6

❷ Practice and Apply

A. CONCEPT CHECK: Hyphens, Dashes, and Parentheses

Rewrite each sentence, adding hyphens, dashes, and parentheses where needed. If a sentence is correct, write *Correct*.

Breaking a Promise to the Wrong Woman

1. Isabella Baumfree was born into slavery in the late 1790s the exact date is unknown.
2. John Dumont, Baumfree's owner, promised to give her freedom if she worked extra hard.
3. However, Dumont scoundrel that he was refused to honor his word.
4. In a bold move, Baumfree walked off Dumont's farm in search of freedom.
5. She found safety in the home of neighbors they were peaceful Quakers who bought out the remainder of her time as a slave.
6. At the age of about forty six, Baumfree renamed herself Sojourner Truth and began to speak publicly about her suffering.

Sojourner Truth

7. Truth was an eloquent preacher, although she couldn't read or write she never had a formal education.
8. She traveled all over the country even to the White House speaking about abolishing slavery.
9. Truth was an extremely tall woman over six feet tall which helped her get an audience's attention quite easily.
10. Her quick wit and self confidence helped Sojourner Truth become one of the nation's most popular public figures.

→ For a SELF-CHECK and more practice, see the EXERCISE BANK, p. 294.

B. REVISING: Using Hyphens

Rewrite the following phrases, adding hyphens where needed. If a phrase is correct, write *Correct*.

1. seventy five days
2. thirty minutes
3. your sister in law
4. one fifth of a year
5. two thirds of an hour
6. your sister's law firm

Apostrophes

LESSON 7

❶ Here's the Idea

Apostrophes are used in possessive nouns, contractions, and some plurals.

Apostrophes in Possessives

▶ **Use an apostrophe to form the possessive of any noun, whether singular or plural.**

For a singular noun, add 's even if the word ends in s.

Sam**'s** baseball   Francis**'s** cap

For plural nouns that end in s, add only an apostrophe.

the spectator**s'** cheers   the player**s'** uniforms

For plural nouns that do not end in s, add 's.

women **'s** team   family **'s** plan

Apostrophes in Contractions

▶ **Use apostrophes in contractions.**

In a contraction, words are joined and letters are left out. An apostrophe replaces the letter or letters that are missing.

Commonly Used Contractions		
I am → I'm	you are → you're	you will → you'll
she is → she's	they have → they've	it is → it's
cannot → can't	they are → they're	was not → wasn't

Don't confuse contractions with possessive pronouns, which do not contain apostrophes.

Contractions Versus Possessive Pronouns	
Contraction	**Possessive Pronoun**
it's (*it is* or *it has*)	its (belonging to it – *its wing*)
who's (*who is*)	whose (belonging to whom – *whose glove*)
you're (*you are*)	your (belonging to you – *your arm*)
they're (*they are*)	their (belonging to them – *their yard*)

CHAPTER 9

WATCH OUT

Apostrophes in Plurals

▶ **Use an apostrophe and s to form the plural of a letter, a numeral, or a word referred to as a word.**

Your *i* 's look like *e* 's.   How many 6 's are in her uniform number?

The sportscaster's report was filled with *too bad's* and *next time's.*

❷ Practice and Apply

A. CONCEPT CHECK: Apostrophes

Find and correct the errors in the use of apostrophes.

Mistakes Turn to Triumph

A series of mistakes came just before the 1996 Olympic Games most memorable moment. It was July 23, the last night of team competition in womens gymnastics. Dominique Moceanu fell on both of her vaults. The U.S. teams chances for a gold medal looked bad. Kerri Strug's turn came next. Kerri fell too—badly. She thought maybe shed broken her ankle. She didnt know if she should take her second vault. Kerris coach, Bela Karolyi, left the decision up to her. Kerri didn't think her team would win if she didn't try again—so she did. Everyones gaze was fixed on her as she sprinted down the runway, vaulted—and landed perfectly. Seconds later, after gently lifting her aching foot, shed crumpled to the mat. Her courage lifted a nations heart. And the womens team won gold!

➡ For a SELF-CHECK and more practice, see the EXERCISE BANK, p. 294.

B. WRITING: Using Possessives and Contractions

Write the correct form from the choices in the parentheses.

(Whose/Who's) side are you on for tonight's game? I'm going to cheer for the Wolverines. (Their/They're) offense is incredible! I can't wait to see (Tess'/Tess's) amazing moves. Believe me, (your/you're) going to regret it if you don't support them. (Its/It's) going to be one terrific victory!

Punctuating Titles

① Here's the Idea

Use quotation marks and italics correctly in titles to show what kind of work or selection you are writing about.

Quotation Marks

▶ **Use quotation marks to set off the titles of short works.**

Quotation Marks for Titles	
Book chapter	"The Dream" from *Dogsong*
Short story	"Flowers and Freckle Cream"
Essay	"Bringing Home the Prairie"
Article	"Home on an Icy Planet"
Song	"The Star-Spangled Banner"
Poem	"Analysis of Baseball"

Italics and Underlining

▶ **Use italics for titles of longer works and for the names of ships, trains, spacecraft, and airplanes (but not the type of plane).** In handwriting, you show that something should be in italic type by **underlining** it.

Italics or Underlines for Titles			
Book	*The Lost Garden*	**Epic poem**	*The Odyssey*
Play	*The Hobbit*	**Painting**	*Mona Lisa*
Magazine	*World*	**Ship**	*Titanic*
Movie	*The Lion King*	**Train**	*City of New Orleans*
TV series	*Cosby*	**Spacecraft**	*Viking I*
Long musical work	*The Barber of Seville*	**Airplane**	*Air Force One*

❷ Practice and Apply

A. CONCEPT CHECK: Punctuating Titles

Correctly punctuate the titles in each sentence, using either quotation marks or underlining as appropriate.

Mistakes in the Media

1. You can read about real mistakes—big and small—in news magazines such as Newsweek.
2. In the classic film The Wizard of Oz, Dorothy makes the mistake of taking her home for granted until she loses it.
3. Mistakes That Worked is the title of a book that describes mistakes that have helped people.
4. Everyone can relate to the common human mistakes that family members make in the TV series Cosby.
5. In Homer's epic poem the Odyssey, the blinded Cyclops can't see Odysseus and his men escape under the bodies of sheep.
6. Many popular songs, such as You're Gonna Miss Me When I'm Gone, are about mistakes in love.
7. The short story Scout's Honor describes many funny mistakes made by a group of boy scouts on a camping trip.
8. In the poem Casey at the Bat, poor Casey strikes out.
9. The best-selling children's book of all time, The Tale of Peter Rabbit, has a main character who always gets into trouble.
10. Did you read the newspaper article with the blooper headline—Red Tape Holds Up New Bridge?

➡ For a SELF-CHECK and more practice, see the EXERCISE BANK on p. 295.

B. WRITING: Be the Judge

Write down the title of your favorite book, poem, movie, TV show, and song. Exchange your titles with a partner. Review your partner's list and check each title for underlining or quotation marks.

Grammar in Literature

Using Punctuation in Poetry

When you write poetry, punctuation is very important. The first word of each line of poetry is often capitalized even if it doesn't begin a sentence. Furthermore, sentences may not end when a line does. Notice how the punctuation in the following poem helps you understand its meaning.

The Quarrel
by Eleanor Farjeon

Two Birds, One Worm (1989), © William Wegman. Watercolor on paper, 11" x 14".

I quarreled with my brother,
I don't know what about,
One thing led to another
And somehow we fell out.
The start of it was slight,
The end of it was strong,
He said he was right,
I knew he was wrong!
We hated one another.
The afternoon turned black.
Then suddenly my brother
Thumped me on the back,
And said, "Oh, come along!
We can't go on all night—
I was in the wrong."
So he was in the right.

An apostrophe marks a contraction. This tells readers the language of the poem is informal.

Commas indicate that the sentence continues onto the next line.

An exclamation mark ends a strong emotional statement.

Quotation marks enclose the brother's exact words.

Practice and Apply

A. REVISING: Adding Punctuation to Poetry

A student wrote the following poem about an embarrassing moment he experienced. He got so caught up in describing what happened that he completely forgot to use punctuation. Rewrite the poem, adding necessary punctuation marks.

It started just like any day
I quickly dressed I grabbed my books
I got my bike and rode away

When I rode up to the school
An empty playground met my eyes
Which made me think Uh oh not cool
Whats the deal What a strange surprise

I saw my teacher walking by
Her goofy dog walked at her side
It seemed so strange I asked her why
She wasn't getting set inside

She smiled and then she said to me
Todays the day I take it slow
Because its Saturday you see
But I guess you didnt know

B. WRITING: Learning by Mistakes

Many people believe that making mistakes is the best way to learn. Write a poem about a mistake you made and the lesson you learned from it. Be sure to punctuate your poem correctly. Save your writing in your ▱ **Working Portfolio.**

Mixed Review

A. Commas, Semicolons, and Colons Write the words and numbers from the following passage that should be followed by commas, semicolons, or colons. Include these punctuation marks in your answers.

Kudzu—Love It or Hate It!

What's kudzu? It's a thick sturdy vine found in the southeastern United States. The plant was first brought to this country in 1876 for the Centennial Exposition in Philadelphia Pennsylvania. Many Southerners liked its large fragrant blooms. They began to use it in their gardens. For many years kudzu was grown to create shade in hot dry areas.

By the 1950s however people began to see that they made a big mistake when they planted kudzu. Its vines became uncontrollable. They overtook trees poles and abandoned buildings. Kudzu vines destroyed many gardens and forests they blocked out the sunlight.

Today, kudzu continues to be a nuisance to many Southerners. Yet some have tried to make the best of this bad situation by creating the following items from kudzu jellies, syrups, candy and baskets. In fact there are several kudzu recipe books they give instructions for those interested in cooking up the curious creeper. Though they may either love or hate kudzu, most Southerners agree that it's here to stay!

B. End Marks and Other Punctuation Put the letter together using these parts. Add the missing punctuation marks where they belong.

Dahlonega GA 30533

Sincerely

Can you please send me a company brochure Im interested in purchasing a copy of your documentary film The Amazing Story of Kudzu

January 10 2004

Dear Mr Shores

125 Mountain Laurel Circle

Sonia J Smith

For each numbered item, choose the letter of the best revision.

> Would you believe me if I told you the sky was <u>falling</u> More than
> (1)
> likely, <u>youll</u> say no. <u>However</u>—if a highly respected scientist were to
> (2)   (3)
> tell you that the most glorious comet was going to fly across the sky,
> you'd probably believe him or her. Perhaps this story will change
> your mind. <u>In January 1974</u> Harvard astronomer Fred Whipple
> (4)
> predicted that the comet Kohoutek would give the most spectacular
> show of the century. Other <u>astronomers</u> declared that Kohoutek had
> (5)
> a tail 50 million miles long. They said it would stretch <u>one sixth</u> of
> (6)
> the way across the sky. Hundreds of people began buying <u>telescopes</u>
> (7)
> <u>binoculars,</u> and even Kohoutek T-shirts as they waited for the
> comet. Finally, on the day of the show, the comet fizzled in <u>it's</u>
> (8)
> display. <u>Time</u> magazine described Kohoutek as <u>a disappointing dud.</u>
> (9)   (10)

1. A. falling.
   B. falling!
   C. falling?
   D. Correct as is

2. A. youll'
   B. you'll
   C. you-ll
   D. Correct as is

3. A. However,
   B. However
   C. However;
   D. Correct as is

4. A. In January, 1974,
   B. In January, 1974
   C. In January 1974,
   D. Correct as is

5. A. astronomer's
   B. astronomers'
   C. astronomers-
   D. Correct as is

6. A. one sixth-
   B. one-sixth
   C. one—sixth
   D. Correct as is

7. A. telescopes, binoculars,
   B. telescopes' binoculars,
   C. telescopes—binoculars,
   D. Correct as is

8. A. its'
   B. its
   C. it(s)
   D. Correct as is

9. A. "Time"
   B. *Time*
   C. Time,
   D. Correct as is

10. A. "a disappointing dud,"
    B. "a disappointing dud".
    C. "a disappointing dud."
    D. Correct as is

Student Help Desk

Punctuation at a Glance

Parentheses

Colon

Exclamation Point

Dash

Apostrophe

Hyphen

Comma

Question Mark

Period

Semicolon

Quotation Marks

Punctuating Titles   Long or Short

Italics (longer works)

Books, Movies, Magazines, Spacecraft, Airplanes,

Plays, Ships, Trains, TV series, Paintings,

Long musical works, Epic poems

Quotation Marks (shorter works)

Stories, Essays, Songs, Poems, Book chapters,

Episodes in a TV series, Magazine articles

Punctuation with Commas   Separating Ideas

	Use commas . . .	Examples
Items in a series	to separate a series of words	I want to find gold, silver, or jewels.
Adjectives	to separate adjectives	Let's look for old, deserted ships.
Introductory words	to separate introductory words	For centuries, grand ships crossed oceans.
Interrupters	to set off interrupters	Many, believe me, held riches.
Nouns of direct address	to set off nouns of direct address	Where should we hunt, Evan?

...nctuation with Quotation Marks In or Out

Always Inside no matter what

Periods Rob said, "Hey, let's go to the movies ."

Commas "That's a good idea ," replied Ann.

...ometimes Inside if they punctuate the part within the quotation marks

Question marks "Should we see a disaster movie ?" asked Rob.

...clamation points "I love disaster movies !" exclaimed Ann.

...metimes Outside if they punctuate the overall sentence, not just the quote

Question marks Did you enjoy reading the story "Shipwrecked "?

...clamation points No, but I liked "Castaway "! I think it's been made into a movie. Let's see if it's playing!

The Bottom Line

Checklist for Punctuation

Have I . . .

____ ended every sentence with the appropriate end mark?

____ used commas to separate items in a series?

____ used commas correctly in dates, addresses, and letters?

____ used quotation marks before and after a speaker's words?

____ used apostrophes to form contractions and possessives?

____ used italics and quotation marks correctly for titles?

Diagramming: Sentence Parts

Here's the Idea

Diagramming is a way of showing the structure of a sentence. Drawing a diagram can help you see how the parts of a sentence work together to form a complete thought.

Watch me for diagramming ti

Simple Subjects and Verbs

Write the simple subject and verb on one line. Separate them with a vertical line that crosses the main line.

Tigers growl.

Tigers	growl

Compound Subjects and Verbs

For a compound subject or verb, split the main line. Put the conjunction on a dotted line connecting the compound parts.

Compound Subject

Tigers and lions growl.

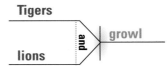

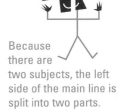

Because there are two subjects, the left side of the main line is split into two parts.

Compound Verb

Tigers growl and roar.

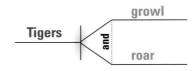

Compound Subject and Compound Verb

Tigers and lions growl and roar.

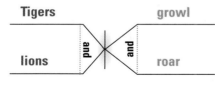

Because there are two subjects and two verbs, both sides of the main line are split into two parts.

A. CONCEPT CHECK: Subjects and Verbs

Diagram these sentences, using what you have learned.

1. Trainers shout.

2. Leopards pace and snarl.

3. Horses and riders circle and bow.

Adjectives and Adverbs

Write adjectives and adverbs on slanted lines below the words they modify.

Marvelous acrobats step quite nimbly overhead.

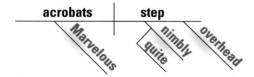

B. MIXED REVIEW: Diagramming

Diagram the following sentences.

1. Tiny Lucinda climbs carefully.

2. The strong young acrobat leaps skillfully.

3. She swings gracefully overhead.

4. Her powerful partner jumps and misses.

5. He plunges sharply downward.

6. The wide net waits below.

7. Lucinda and the other acrobats gasp.

8. The anxious audience fidgets and waits.

9. The lucky acrobat lands and smiles.

10. The audience claps wildly.

DIAGRAMMING

Diagramming: Complements

Subject Complements

- Write a predicate noun or a predicate adjective on the main line after the verb.
- Separate the subject complement from the verb with a slanted line that does not cross the main line.

Predicate Noun

Clowns are skillful performers.

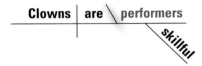

Predicate Adjective

Clowns quite often seem sad.

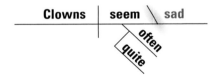

C. CONCEPT CHECK: Subject Complements

Diagram these sentences using what you have learned.

1. The smallest clown appears very serious.
2. His face is a sad mask.

Direct Objects

A direct object follows the verb on the main line.

One clown drives a tiny car.

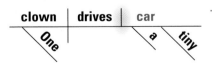

The vertical line between a verb and its direct object does not cross the main line.

Write compound direct objects on parallel lines that branch from the main line.

The driver wears a floppy hat and giant shoes.

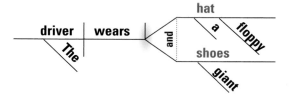

Indirect Objects

Write an indirect object below the verb, on a horizontal line connected to the verb by a slanted line.

The driver gives seven other clowns a ride.

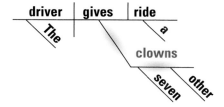

D. MIXED REVIEW: Diagramming

Diagram the following sentences.

1. The Zolanda Circus is very popular.
2. Muscular workers pitch the gigantic tent.
3. Flexible acrobats practice courageous leaps.
4. The lion tamer gives his giant beasts a large meal.
5. An elegant elephant eyes some delicious hay.
6. People gradually fill the empty bleachers.
7. They give the ringmaster their complete attention.
8. The ringmaster creates a hush.
9. The arena becomes a silent stage.
10. Six white horses carry six beautiful dancers.

Diagramming: Prepositional Phrases

Prepositional Phrases

- Write the preposition on a slanted line below the word the prepositional phrase modifies.
- Write the object of the preposition on a horizontal line after the preposition.
- Write any modifier of the object on a slanted line below the object.

Actors in plays need strength and coordination.

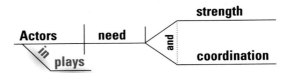

They sometimes leap over scenery on the stage.

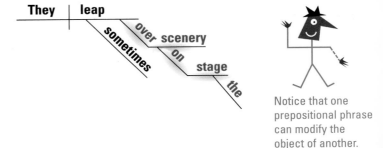

Notice that one prepositional phrase can modify the object of another.

E. CONCEPT CHECK: Prepositional Phrases

Diagram these sentences, using what you have learned.

1. The actor climbed to the top of the ladder.
2. The hat on her head swayed in the breeze.
3. She held tightly to the rungs of the ladder.
4. A gust of wind blew the hat off her head.
5. It fell through the air to the ground.

Diagramming: Compound Sentences

Compound Sentences

- Diagram the independent clauses on parallel horizontal lines.
- Connect the verbs in the two clauses by a dotted line with a solid step in it.
- Write the coordinating conjunction on the step.

The playwright writes the script, and the director chooses the actors.

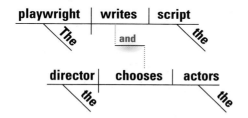

The conjunction goes on the step.

F. CONCEPT CHECK: Compound Sentences

Diagram these sentences using what you have learned.

1. The actors have come to the first rehearsal, but the writer is still making changes.
2. The actors study their parts, or they walk around nervously.
3. The director is ready, and the rehearsals can now begin.

G. MIXED REVIEW: Diagramming

Diagram the following sentences.

1. Rehearsals of the new play will start today.
2. The director is eager and the cast is ready.
3. Designers are making models of the stage sets.
4. Carpenters will construct the sets in the scene shop.
5. They will paint the scenery, but the stage crew will move it into place.
6. The role of the thief will be played by a well-known actor.
7. An unknown actor from a nearby town will play the detective.
8. The detective does not solve the case of the lost piano, but the audience does.
9. Everyone recognizes the thief by the end of the play.
10. The play will be a big hit with the audience.

Quick-Fix Editing Machine

You've worked hard on your assignment. Don't let misplaced commas, sentence fragments, and missing details lower your grade. Use this Quick-Fix Editing Guide to help you detect grammatical errors and make your writing more precise.

Fixing Errors

Improving Style

1 Sentence Fragments

What's the problem? Part of a sentence has been left out.

Why does it matter? A fragment can be confusing because it does not express a complete thought.

What should you do about it? Find out what is missing and add it.

What's the Problem?

Quick Fix

A. A subject is missing.
Tripped and broke his glasses.

Add a subject.
My dad tripped and broke his glasses.

B. A predicate is missing.
My skateboard in his way.

Add a predicate.
My skateboard **was** in his way.

C. Both a subject and a predicate are missing.
In real trouble now.

Add a subject and a predicate to make a complete sentence.
I am in real trouble now.

For more help, see Chapter 1, pp. 25–27.

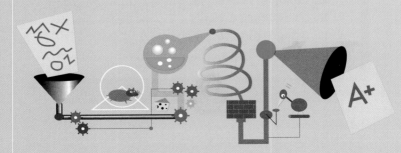

QUICK FIX

Run-On Sentences

What's the problem? Two or more sentences have been written as though they were a single sentence.

Why does it matter? A run-on sentence doesn't show where one idea ends and another begins.

What should you do about it? Find the best way to separate the ideas or to show the proper relationship between them.

What's the Problem?

Quick Fix

A. The end mark separating two complete sentences is missing.

Someone wrote a book about cats who painted with their paws people took it seriously.

Add an end mark to divide the run-on sentence into two sentences.

Someone wrote a book about cats who painted with their paws. People took it seriously.

B. Two complete thoughts are separated only by a comma.

Pictures showed the cats "painting," they were just clawing the canvas.

Add a conjunction.

Pictures showed the cats "painting," **but** they were just clawing the canvas.

OR

Replace the comma with an end mark and start a new sentence.

Pictures showed the cats "painting." **They** were just clawing the canvas.

For more help, see Chapter 1, pp. 25–27.

QUICK FIX

3 Subject-Verb Agreement

What's the problem? A verb does not agree with its subject in number.

Why does it matter? Readers may think your work is careless.

What should you do about it? Identify the subject and use a verb that matches it in number.

What's the Problem?

Quick Fix

What's the Problem?	Quick Fix
A. The first helping verb in a verb phrase does not agree with the subject. Some **friends has** been working on a class project.	Decide whether the subject is singular or plural, and make the helping verb agree with it. Some friends have been working on a class project.
B. The contraction doesn't agree with its subject. **They doesn't** agree on everything.	Use a contraction that agrees with the subject. They don't agree on everything.
C. A singular verb is used with a compound subject that contains *and*. **The actors and the director wants** the film to be good.	Use a plural verb. The actors and the director want the film to be good.
D. A verb doesn't agree with the nearer part of a compound subject containing *or* or *nor*. Either the twins or **Elena are** going to star in the film.	Make the verb agree with the nearer part. Either the twins or **Elena is** going to star in the film.

For more help, see Chapter 7, pp. 166–177.

What's the Problem?

Quick Fix

E. A verb doesn't agree with an indefinite-pronoun subject.

Decide whether the pronoun is singular or plural, and make the verb agree with it.

Everybody have an opinion about the subject of the film.

Everybody has an opinion about the subject of the film.

F. A verb agrees with the object of a preposition rather than with the subject.

Mentally block out the prepositional phrase, and make the verb agree with the subject.

The five students on the **team votes** on the final topic.

The five **students** on the team **vote** on the final topic.

G. A verb doesn't agree with the true subject of a sentence beginning with *here* or *there*.

Mentally turn the sentence around so that the subject comes first, and make the verb agree with it.

(Some old **costumes are** here.)

Here is some old costumes.

Here **are** some old **costumes.**

For more help, see Chapter 7, pp. 166–177.

4 Pronoun Reference Problems

What's the problem? A pronoun does not agree in number, person, or gender with its antecedent, or an antecedent is unclear.

What does it matter? Lack of agreement or unclear antecedents can confuse your readers.

What should you do about it? Find the antecedent and make the pronoun agree with it, or rewrite the sentence to make the antecedent clear.

What's the Problem?

Quick Fix

What's the Problem?	Quick Fix
A. A pronoun doesn't agree with its antecedent in number and gender. The **veterinarian** is coming to class with **their** animal "patients."	**Find the antecedent and make the pronoun agree in number and gender.** The **veterinarian** is coming to class with **her** animal "patients."
B. A pronoun doesn't agree with its antecedent in person or number. **Pet owners** can learn a lot if **you** listen to a vet.	**Change the pronoun to agree with the antecedent.** **Pet owners** can learn a lot if **they** listen to a vet.
C. A pronoun doesn't agree with an indefinite-pronoun antecedent. **Everyone** argued about **their** favorite pets.	**Decide whether the indefinite pronoun antecedent is singular or plural, and make the pronoun agree with it.** **Everyone** argued about **his or her** favorite pets.
D. A pronoun could refer to more than one noun. **Kay** and **Arnetta** love dogs, and **she** wants to work at a shelter.	**Substitute a noun for the pronoun to make the reference specific.** **Kay** and **Arnetta** love dogs, and **Arnetta** wants to work at a shelter.
E. A pronoun agrees with a noun in a phrase rather than with its antecedent. A German shepherd, along with the other **dogs,** did **their** tricks for us.	**Mentally block out the phrase and make the pronoun agree with its antecedent.** A **German shepherd,** ~~along with the other dogs,~~ did **his** tricks for us.

For more help, see Chapter 3, pp. 69–79.

5 Incorrect Pronoun Case

What's the problem? A pronoun is in the wrong case.

Why does it matter? Readers may think your work is sloppy and careless, especially if your writing is for a school assignment.

What should you do about it? Identify how the pronoun is being used, and replace it with the correct form.

What's the Problem?

What's the Problem?	Quick Fix
A. A pronoun following a linking verb is in the wrong case.	Always use the subject case after a linking verb.
The owner of the turtle **was him.**	The owner of the turtle **was he.**
B. A pronoun used as a direct object is in the wrong case.	Always use an object pronoun as a direct object.
Mom **told Ben and I** to keep the turtle in our room.	Mom **told Ben and me** to keep the turtle in our room.
C. *Who* or *whom* is used incorrectly.	Use *who* if the pronoun is a subject and *whom* if it is an object.
Whom let the turtle out of its box?	**Who** let the turtle out of its box?
Who did you see playing with it last?	**Whom** did you see playing with it last?
D. A pronoun in a compound subject is in the wrong case.	Always use the subject case for a pronoun used as part of a compound subject.
Ben and me looked everywhere for that turtle.	**Ben and I** looked everywhere for that turtle.
E. A pronoun followed by an identifying noun is in the wrong case.	Mentally block out the identifying noun to test for the correct case.
Us boys found it in the bathroom before Mom came in!	We ~~boys~~ found it in the bathroom before Mom came in!

For more help, see Chapter 3, pp. 57–79.

6 *Who* and *Whom*

What's the problem? The pronoun *who* or *whom* is used incorrectly.

Why does it matter? When writers use *who* and *whom* correctly, readers are more likely to take their ideas seriously.

What should you do about it? Decide how the pronoun functions in the sentence, and then use the correct form.

What's the Problem?

What's the Problem?	Quick Fix
A. *Whom* is incorrectly used as the subject pronoun. **Whom is going** to choose the holiday decorations this year?	Use *who* as the subject pronoun. **Who is going** to choose the holiday decorations this year?
B. *Who* is incorrectly used as the object of a preposition. You're going **with who** to the mall?	Use *whom* as the object of a preposition. You're going **with whom** to the mall?
C. *Who* is incorrectly used as a direct object. **Who do** you **trust** to get inexpensive ones?	Use *whom* as a direct object. **Whom do** you **trust** to get inexpensive ones?
D. *Who's* is incorrectly used as the possessive pronoun *whose*. These beautiful decorations are **who's?**	Use *whose* to show possession. These beautiful decorations are **whose?**

For more help, see Chapter 3, pp. 66–68.

QUICK FIX

Confusing Comparisons

What's the problem? The wrong form of an adjective or adverb is used in making a comparison.

Why does it matter? Comparisons that are not worded correctly can be confusing.

What should you do about it? Use a form that makes the comparison clear.

What's the Problem?

What's the Problem?	Quick Fix
A. **Both *-er* and *more* or *-est* and *most* are used in making a comparison.** There is nothing **more grosser** than stale pizza. Yesterday we had the **most stalest** pizza I have ever tasted.	Delete one of the two forms from the sentence. There is nothing ~~more~~ **grosser** than stale pizza. Yesterday we had the ~~most~~ **stalest** pizza I have ever tasted.
B. **A superlative form is used where a comparative form is needed.** I think it was **worst** than the lunch I had two days ago.	When comparing two things, always use the comparative form. I think it was **worse** than the lunch I had two days ago.
C. **A comparative form is used where a superlative form is needed.** In any case, it has to be the **more disgusting** lunch I have eaten this month.	When comparing more than two things, always use the superlative form. In any case, it has to be the **most disgusting** lunch I have eaten this month.

For more help, see Chapter 5, pp. 133–135.

QUICK FIX

8 Verb Forms and Tenses

What's the problem? The wrong form or tense of a verb is used.

Why does it matter? Readers may regard your work as careless or find it confusing.

What should you do about it? Change the verb to the correct form or tense.

What's the Problem?

Quick Fix

A. The wrong form of a verb is used with a helping verb.

Our family **had went** on several sightseeing tours before this one.

Always use a participle form with a helping verb.

Our family **had gone** on several sightseeing tours before this one.

B. A helping verb is missing.

We **been** to every famous place in three states.

Add a helping verb.

We **have been** to every famous place in three states.

C. A past participle is used incorrectly.

I **seen** the United Center, a popular arena, on a previous trip to Chicago.

To write about the past, use the past form of a verb.

I **saw** the United Center, a popular arena, on a previous trip to Chicago.

OR

Change the verb to the past perfect form by adding a helping verb.

I **had seen** the United Center, a popular sports arena, on a previous trip to Chicago.

D. Different tenses are used in the same sentence even though no change in time has occurred.

My dad **drove** for hours, and the road **seems** to go on forever.

Use the same tense throughout the sentence.

My dad **drove** for hours, and the road **seemed** to go on forever.

For more help, see Chapter 4, pp. 96–110.

Missing or Misplaced Commas

What's the problem? Commas are missing or are used incorrectly.

Why does it matter? Incorrect use of commas can make sentences difficult to follow.

What should you do about it? Determine where commas are needed, and add them or take them out.

QUICK FIX

What's the Problem?

Quick Fix

A. A comma is missing from a compound sentence.

Our town has a skateboard park and we use it nearly every day.

Add a comma before the conjunction.

Our town has a skateboard park, and we use it nearly every day.

B. A comma is missing before the conjunction in a series.

The park includes a ramp, a half-pipe and a jumping track.

Add a comma.

The park includes a ramp, a half-pipe, and a jumping track.

C. A comma is incorrectly placed after a closing quotation mark.

"We didn't want kids skateboarding in the streets", the mayor said.

Always put a comma before a closing quotation mark.

"We didn't want kids skateboarding in the streets," the mayor said.

D. A comma is missing after an introductory word or phrase.

After the grand opening all of us skateboarders tried it out.

Add a comma at the end of the word or phrase.

After the grand opening, all of us skateboarders tried it out.

E. Commas are missing around an appositive that is not essential to the meaning of the sentence.

Mom says I live in the skateboard park my second home.

Add commas to set off the appositive.

Mom says I live in the skateboard park, my second home.

For more help, see Chapter 9, pp. 209–211.

10 Improving Weak Sentences

What's the problem? A sentence repeats ideas or contains too many ideas.

Why does it matter? Sentences that are repetitive or too long can confuse and bore readers.

What should you do about it? Make sure each sentence is complete and contains a clearly focused idea.

What's the Problem?

Quick Fix

A. A group of words does not express a complete thought.

The poet Emily Dickinson a very private person.

Add a subject or predicate to make a complete sentence.

The poet Emily Dickinson **was** a very private person.

B. A sentence doesn't give any new information or repeats an idea that has already been stated.

Emily Dickinson is my favorite poet. **I really like her a lot.**

Get rid of words and phrases that repeat an idea, and add more details.

Emily Dickinson is my favorite poet, **because her poems tell a lot about everyday life.**

C. A single sentence contains too many loosely connected ideas.

She didn't intend for most of her poetry to be published, and after her death, Emily's sister found many of the poems and she had them published.

Divide the sentence into two or more sentences. Decide which ideas can be combined and which ideas should be kept separate.

She didn't intend for most of her poetry to be published. After Emily's death, her sister found many of the poems and had them published.

⑪ Avoiding Wordiness

What's the problem? A sentence contains unnecessary words.

Why does it matter? Wordy sentences can confuse and bore readers.

What should you do about it? Use words that are more precise and get rid of any unnecessary words.

What's the Problem?

Quick-Fix

A. An idea is needlessly expressed in two ways.

Emergency room doctors treat everything from broken bones to severe bleeding **and all sorts of cases** at a moment's notice.

Delete words and phrases that repeat an idea.

Emergency room doctors treat everything from broken bones to severe bleeding ~~and all sorts of cases~~ at a moment's notice.

B. A sentence is overloaded with modifiers.

The doctor uses **a small gray battery-operated** computer to take notes.

Substitute a more precise word for a string of modifiers.

The doctor uses a **laptop** computer to take notes.

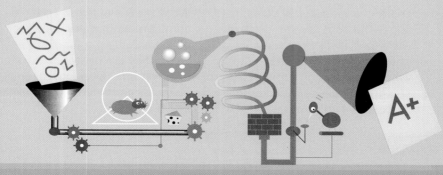

12 Varying Sentence Structure

What's the problem? Too many sentences begin in the same way.

Why does it matter? Lack of variety in sentences makes writing dull and choppy.

What should you do about it? Rearrange the phrases in some of your sentences. Use different types of sentences, such as questions and commands, for more variety and impact.

What's the Problem?

Quick Fix

A. Too many sentences in a paragraph begin the same way.

Have you ever wondered what's inside a baseball? **I took** one apart to find out. **I took** off some pieces of leather in the first layer. They were stitched together with thick red thread. **I then unwrapped** yards and yards of yarn wound very tightly. **I found** two layers of rubber under the wool. **I discovered** a small ball of cork at the center. Now you won't have to destroy your own baseball to see what's inside.

Rearrange the words or phrases in some of the sentences.

Have you ever wondered what's inside a baseball? I took one apart to find out. **The first layer** I took off was made of some pieces of leather. They were stitched together with thick red thread. **Then** I unwrapped yards and yards of yarn wound very tightly. **Under the yarn,** I found two layers of rubber. **At the center,** I discovered a small ball of cork. Now you won't have to destroy your own baseball to see what's inside.

B. Too many declarative sentences are used.

There is a reason why popcorn pops. The corn kernels that are used for popcorn contain a lot of water. When they are heated, the water expands and turns into steam. This causes the kernels to explode into a mass.

Add variety by rewriting one sentence as a command, question, or exclamation.

What makes popcorn pop? The corn kernels that are used for popcorn contain a lot of water. When they are heated, the water expands and turns into steam. This causes the kernels to explode into a mass.

Varying Sentence Length

What's the problem? A piece of writing contains too many short sentences.

Why does it matter? Choppy sentences without many details can bore readers.

What should you do about it? Combine or reword sentences to create sentences of different lengths.

What's the Problem?

Too many short sentences are used.

My friend Gabriela competed in a race. It was a bicycle race. The race was yesterday. The weather was hard on the racers. The day was hot and humid.

Gabriela easily rode up the mountain trail. It was difficult to steer on the way down. Gabriela won the race. The crowd cheered.

Quick Fix

Get rid of sentences that add only one detail about the subject. Insert those details into other sentences.

Yesterday my friend Gabriela competed in a **bicycle** race. The **hot and humid** weather was hard on the racers.

OR

Use conjunctions such as *or, and,* or *but* to combine related ideas or sentences.

Gabriela easily rode up the mountain trail, **but** it was difficult to steer on the way down. Gabriela won the race, **and** the crowd cheered.

QUICK FIX

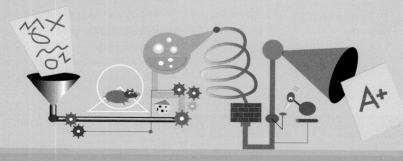

14 Adding Supporting Details

What's the problem? Not enough details are given for readers to fully understand the topic.

Why does it matter? Unanswered questions or unsupported opinions weaken writing.

What should you do about it? Add information and details that will make statements clear.

What's the Problem?	Quick Fix
A. Questions are not answered.	Add details that tell who, what, when, where, why, and how.
Wolves communicate.	Wolves communicate by using different types of howls.
B. No explanation is given.	Add definitions and facts to help readers understand the topic.
Each howl matches a certain situation.	Each howl, or **call,** matches a certain situation. **One kind of howl signals that a wolf wants to "talk." Another warns of danger. When wolves gather to hunt, they howl to greet each other.**
C. No reason is given for an opinion.	Add a reason.
My new guitar is great.	My new guitar is great **because it makes me look as cool as my favorite musician.**
D. No details are given.	Add details describing how the topic looks, sounds, feels, tastes, or smells.
In fact, everyone is impressed with my guitar.	In fact, everyone is impressed with my guitar. **The wood is as golden as a maple leaf in autumn. There's a fancy design around the sound hole. The nylon strings shine like silvery threads.**

15 **Avoiding Clichés and Slang**

What's the problem? A piece of formal writing contains clichés or slang expressions.

Why does it matter? Clichés have been used so often that they no longer mean anything to readers. Slang is not appropriate in formal writing.

What should you do about it? Reword sentences to replace clichés and slang with clear, fresh expressions.

What's the Problem?

Quick Fix

A. A sentence contains a cliché.

Replace the cliché with a fresh description or explanation.

The icicles were **as sharp as needles.**

The icicles were **like crystal daggers.**

B. A sentence contains inappropriate slang.

Replace the slang with more appropriate language.

The store owner is unpopular because he will often **dis the kids who hang around** his store.

The store owner is unpopular because he will **often yell at the teens who meet in** his store.

QUICK FIX

16 Using Precise Words

What's the problem? Nouns, modifiers, or verbs are not specific.

Why does it matter? Writers who use words that are too general do not give readers a clear picture of their topic.

What should you do about it? Replace general words with precise ones.

What's the Problem?

Quick Fix

A. Nouns are too general.

If you use your **head,** cleaning your room won't be an unpleasant **thing.**

Use specific nouns.

If you use some **creativity,** cleaning your room won't be an unpleasant **task.**

B. Modifiers are too general.

You can **really** whisk away dirt with **some different** objects.

Use vivid adjectives and adverbs.

You can **expertly** whisk away dirt with **three common household** objects.

C. A sentence tells about an action instead of showing it with exact verbs.

First **use** a blow dryer set on high to dust furniture. Next, **get rid of** dirt on the ceiling **using** an old T-shirt and a baseball bat. Then **put** your dirty clothes away.

Use vivid verbs to show action.

First, **blast** away furniture dust with a blow dryer set on high. Then make those nasty cobwebs **vanish** by draping an old T-shirt over the end of a baseball bat and **swiping** it around the ceiling. Make your dirty clothes **disappear** by **stuffing** them into a laundry bag, or **shoving** them under your bed.

Using Figurative Language

What's the problem? A piece of writing is dull or unimaginative.

Why does it matter? Dull writing bores readers because it doesn't help them form mental pictures of what is being described.

What should you do about it? Add figures of speech to make writing lively and to create pictures in readers' minds.

What's the Problem?

A description is dull and lifeless.

The other runner was gaining on me. I heard her breathing as she tried to pass me.

I relaxed for a moment as I ran a few feet ahead. Then I heard her footsteps on the track.

Quick Fix

Add a simile.

The other runner was gaining on me. Her powerful breathing was **like an ocean wave** as she tried to pass me.

OR

Rewrite the sentence, adding a metaphor.

I relaxed for a moment as I ran a few feet ahead. As I rounded the last bend, **her footsteps on the cinder track were pesky mosquitoes.**

18 Paragraphing

What's the problem? A paragraph contains too many ideas.

Why does it matter? A long paragraph discourages readers from continuing.

What should you do about it? Break the paragraph into shorter paragraphs. Start a new paragraph whenever a new idea is presented or the time, place, or speaker changes.

What's the Problem?

My great-grandfather told me how his family from Poland traveled to the United States. He was only 12 years old at the time. When their ship arrived in New York, his mother was ill. An immigration official put a cross on her jacket with chalk. The official said that anyone with a cross on his or her clothing could not enter the United States. "What did you do?" I asked eagerly. Grandpa smiled as he said, "When nobody was looking, I wiped the chalk mark off my mother's jacket. The family stayed together!" Later as we ate lunch, Grandpa gave me a wink. I knew that he thought I was just as clever as he was.

Quick Fix

My great-grandfather told me how his family from Poland traveled to the United States. He was only 12 years old at the time. When their ship arrived in New York, his mother was ill.

Start a new paragraph to introduce a new idea.

An immigration official put a cross on her jacket with chalk. The official said that anyone with a cross on his or her clothing could not enter the United States.

Start a new paragraph whenever the speaker changes.

"What did you do?" I asked.

Grandpa smiled as he said, "When nobody was looking, I wiped the chalk mark off my mother's jacket. The family stayed together!"

Start a new paragraph to change the time or the place.

Later as we ate lunch, Grandpa gave me a wink. I knew that he thought I was just as clever as he was.

What's the Problem?

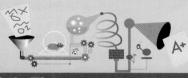

An essay is treated as one long paragraph.

In the Old West, mail service was unbelievably slow. Until 1858 California had very irregular mail service. It often took two to three months for a letter to arrive. When the Overland Mail Service began that year, it used stage-coaches to carry mail and passengers as well. Now, imagine a trip to California in 1858. You eagerly board a train in St. Louis, Missouri. After riding nearly 150 miles, you transfer to a stagecoach. Hold on tight, because the ride is really rough. The stage coach speeds wildly downhill at five miles per hour. You and the mail travel almost constantly day and night. Sleep is practically impossible. Don't worry. The coach eventually jolts to a stop in San Francisco. Shaking and exhausted, you climb down. Just think, though, your trip took only 24 days. Now that's service!

Quick Fix

In the Old West, mail service was unbelievably slow. Until 1858 California had very irregular mail service. It often took two to three months for a letter to arrive. When the Overland Mail Service began that year, it used stagecoaches to carry mail and passengers as well.

Start a new paragraph to introduce another main idea.

Now, imagine a trip to California in 1858. You eagerly board a train in St. Louis, Missouri. After riding nearly 150 miles, you transfer to a stagecoach. Hold on tight, because the ride is really rough. The stagecoach speeds wildly downhill at five miles per hour. You and the mail travel almost constantly day and night. Sleep is practically impossible.

Set the conclusion off in its own paragraph.

Don't worry. The coach eventually jolts to a stop in San Francisco. Shaking and exhausted, you climb down. Just think, though, your trip took only 24 days. Now that's service!

Student Resources

Exercise Bank

Boost your grammar fitness! Use the Exercise Bank to find the answers to the Self-Check items that are circled in yellow ➡. In addition, you can complete exercises in this section to get extra practice in a skill you've just learned.

1 The Sentence and Its Parts

1. Complete Subjects and Predicates (links to exercise on p. 7)

➡ **1.** CS: People around the world; CP: tell Cinderella stories.
2. CS: The oldest version of all; CP: comes from China.

On a sheet of paper, label one column "Complete Subjects" and a second column "Complete Predicates." Write the complete subject and the complete predicate in each sentence below.

1. "Cinderella" is one of the best-known folktales.
2. Similar stories exist in many cultures.
3. The main characters go by different names.
4. An ancient Egyptian story tells of Rhodopis.
5. The poor young woman is sold into slavery.
6. Her master gives her a pair of slippers.
7. A great falcon carries off one of the slippers.
8. The bird drops it in the Pharaoh's lap.
9. This powerful ruler searches for the slipper's owner.
10. Rhodopis marries the Pharaoh at the end of the story.

2. Simple Subjects (links to exercise A, p. 9)

➡ **1.** tortoise   **2.** rabbit

On a separate sheet of paper, write the simple subject in each sentence.

1. A poor woodcutter lived with his wife in a humble cottage.
2. One day, a fairy granted him three wishes.
3. The excited couple discussed their good fortune at dinner.
4. The hungry husband carelessly wished for a sausage.
5. A huge sausage fell onto the table.
6. The wife complained about his wasteful wish.
7. Her spouse made another wish.
8. Now the sausage hung from the wife's nose.
9. The startled man wished for the disappearance of the sausage.
10. Three wishes brought him nothing but regret!

3. Simple Predicates, or Verbs (links to exercise A, p. 11)

➡ **1.** is   **2.** served

On a separate sheet of paper, write the simple predicate, or verb, in each sentence.

1. Diane Wolkstein is a distinguished storyteller, writer, and teacher.
2. After college, this New York City native studied pantomime in Paris.
3. She returned to New York City in 1967.
4. The city's Department of Parks and Recreation offered her a job as a recreational director.
5. In the city's parks, Wolkstein told stories from around the world.
6. She hosted the radio program *Stories from Many Lands with Diane Wolkstein* for 12 years.
7. One writer described her as New York City's official storyteller.
8. Wolkstein travels to many lands in search of folktales.
9. Her seven trips to Haiti provided material for three books.
10. Students eagerly attend Wolkstein's classes and workshops on storytelling.

4. Verb Phrases (links to exercise on p. 13)

➡ **1.** was searching   **2.** should be

Write the verb phrase in each sentence. Be sure to include all the helping verbs.

1. Perhaps you have heard some stories by Hans Christian Andersen.
2. People have been enjoying this Danish writer's tales for more than 150 years.
3. A statue of Andersen was built in New York City's Central Park.
4. You may have read Andersen's tale "The Ugly Duckling."
5. The main character is hatched from an unusually large egg.
6. He does experience cruelty and rejection because of his appearance.
7. Of course, a surprise is awaiting him at the end of the story.
8. He has been a swan and not a duckling all along.
9. Andersen's stories probably will be popular for years to come.
10. You might know some of his other tales as well.

5. Compound Sentence Parts (links to exercise A, p. 15)

➡ **1.** ant *and* grasshopper   **2.** hopped *and* sang

On a separate sheet of paper, write the compound subject or compound verb in each sentence.

1. Homer composed and recited epic poems in ancient Greece.
2. The *Odyssey* and the *Iliad* are his two great works.
3. Odysseus, the hero of the *Odyssey*, travels home after a war and experiences difficulties along the way.
4. Many different characters and events delay him.
5. Scheming goddesses and horrible monsters set traps for him.
6. Cyclops, a giant one-eyed monster, captures and threatens Odysseus.
7. Odysseus thinks fast and invents a clever trick.
8. He and some of his companions blind the monster.
9. They race to the shore and sail away.
10. The furious Cyclops curses them and vows revenge.

6. Kinds of Sentences (links to exercise A, p. 17)

➡ **1.** D   **2.** INT

Identify each of the following sentences as declarative (D), interrogative (INT), exclamatory (E), or imperative (IMP).

1. Have you read the Chinese folktale "A Grain of Rice"?
2. Pong Lo, a poor young man, asks to marry the Emperor's daughter.
3. How dare he make such a request!
4. The Emperor threatens to have Pong Lo beheaded.
5. Instead, Pong Lo works hard for the Emperor and proves his worth.
6. Didn't the Emperor's daughter become sick?
7. Tell me how Pong Lo saves her life.
8. The grateful Emperor offers Pong Lo anything except his daughter's hand in marriage.
9. Pong Lo cleverly asks for one grain of rice, to be doubled each day for 100 days.
10. Explain how Pong Lo grows rich and marries the Emperor's daughter.

7. Subjects in Unusual Order (links to exercise A, p. 20)

➡ **1.** Subject: *friends;* verb: *are* **2.** Subject: (*You*); verb: *Tell*

In two columns on a separate sheet of paper, write the simple subject and the verb (or verb phrase) in each sentence.

1. Listen to the tale of Alfred Bulltop Stormalong.
2. Across the ocean sailed this enormous ship's captain.
3. There goes his unbelievably large ship.
4. Did the crew ride across the colossal deck on horses?
5. To the top of an extremely tall mast climbs a young sailor.
6. Here comes the most incredible part!
7. Years later, down climbs the same fellow with a long, gray beard!
8. Do you know any more tall tales?
9. Tell me another.
10. Use plenty of exaggeration.

8. Complements: Subject Complements (links to exercise A, p. 22)

➡ **1.** legendary PA   **4.** storytellers PN

Write the underlined word in each sentence, and identify it as either a predicate noun (PN) or a predicate adjective (PA).

1. John Henry is an American folk <u>hero</u>.
2. Maybe this African-American man was a real <u>person</u>.
3. According to some, he was a <u>worker</u> on a railroad-building project in the 1870s.
4. His life is the <u>subject</u> of a famous ballad.
5. In the ballad, his strength is <u>extraordinary</u>.
6. He is the <u>winner</u> in a contest with a powerful new steam drill.
7. His determination is <u>remarkable</u>, although the strain of winning kills him.
8. The victorious steel-driving man became a <u>legend</u>.
9. The legend grew more <u>famous</u> with each passing year.
10. John Henry is a <u>symbol</u> of the unbeatable human spirit.

9. Complements: Objects of Verbs (links to exercise on p. 24)

➡ **1.** beans (DO)   **4.** Jack (IO), breakfast (DO)

Write each object of a verb, and identify it as a direct object (DO) or an indirect object (IO).

1. Our class is planning a storytelling festival.
2. We called a professional storyteller.
3. She taught us her secrets.
4. We will invite students from other classes to our festival.
5. We can send them flyers a week before the big event.
6. At the library, Ms. Leung showed me several collections of folktales.
7. I must find just the right story.
8. Perhaps my grandmother can give me some advice.
9. The drama department lent our class a video camera.
10. Now we can film our performances.

10. Fragments and Run-Ons (links to exercise A, p. 27)

➡ **1.** CS   **2.** RO

Identify each of the following sentences as a fragment (F), a run-on (RO), or a complete sentence (CS).

1. Are cartoons that tell a story.
2. The boxes containing the scenes are called panels, the spaces containing the dialogue are called speech balloons.
3. Comic strips first appeared in newspapers in the 1890s.
4. Early comic strips featured humorous characters and situations, many people called them "funnies."
5. Some people still use that word to refer to comic strips.
6. Cartoonists of the 1930s.
7. Created dramatic and adventurous comic strips.
8. Today's audiences will recognize several comic-strip characters from the 1920s and 1930s.
9. Include Superman, Dick Tracy, and Little Orphan Annie.
10. Two of these characters have appeared in both movies and television shows, and one has appeared in a play.

2 Nouns

1. What Is a Noun? (links to exercise on p. 37)

➡ **1.** *place:* common   **2.** *Pompeii, Italy:* proper

Write each noun and identify it as common or proper.

1. In 1879, a father and his young daughter, Maria, explored a cave in Spain.
2. The cave was near their castle.
3. Maria held her candle up and saw paintings on the ceiling.
4. Each painting of an animal had been made by an artist more than 12,000 years ago.
5. In 1947, a young boy named Muhammad ed-dhib lost a goat near his village in Palestine.
6. While searching for the goat, Muhammad discovered a cave.
7. Later, Muhammad and a friend went back to the cave and found ancient biblical scrolls more than 2,000 years old.
8. The important writings are called the Dead Sea Scrolls.
9. In about 1871, Heinrich Schliemann found the lost city of Troy in what is now Turkey.
10. He had dreamed of finding the city since his days as a student.

2. Singular and Plural Nouns (links to exercise A, p. 39)

➡ **1.** priests; bodies   **2.** Egyptians

Rewrite the nouns in parentheses in their plural forms.

1. The ancient Egyptians buried precious (object) with their dead rulers.
2. Some ancient (Sumerian) buried other people with their royalty.
3. (Archaeologist) found many tombs in Ur, one of the ancient (city) of the Sumerians.
4. (Search) uncovered as many as 74 skeletons in one tomb.
5. Some skeletons were (man) clutching spears.
6. Others were (woman) wearing fancy gold (headdress).
7. (Photo) of the tombs show gold helmets and jewelry.
8. Also found in the tombs were the (remain) of (donkey) and oxen but no (sheep).
9. The Sumerians apparently believed that some people should take their (journey) to the afterlife with their king.
10. Did they agree to die so that their (life) could continue along with their king?

3. Possessive Nouns (links to exercise A, p. 42)

➡ **1.** England's; singular   **2.** Harbor's; singular

Write the possessive form of each noun in parentheses. Then identify each possessive noun as singular or plural.

1. Until recently, (archaeologists) discoveries were made without the help of technology.
2. Explorers hacking through a jungle stumbled upon a (temple) remains.
3. Farmers opened a huge mound in their fields and found an ancient (peoples) burial site.
4. (Today) aerial photos can reveal unusual sites to explore.
5. Vegetation, for example, grows lush in (Guatemala) deep soil.
6. A bare site may signal that something solid lies underneath the (soil) surface.
7. Satellite photos can show a (ruin) outlines.
8. A (technician) discovery of the faint outlines of forgotten roads has led to the finding of lost cities.
9. (Explorers) use of radar has located objects buried in the earth.
10. Computers have been used to improve a (document) image.

4. Nouns and Their Jobs (links to exercise A, p. 44)

➡ **1.** Inca: subject   **2.** Cuzco: subject; capital: complement

Identify each underlined noun as a subject, a complement, or an object of a preposition.

1. John Lloyd Stephens was an American lawyer.
2. In 1836, he researched ancient ruins in Central America.
3. Stephens was interested in lost civilizations.
4. He planned an expedition to find the ruins.
5. Stephens gave artist Frederick Catherwood a chance to go along on the trip.
6. In 1839, the two men explored a humid jungle in Honduras.
7. As they hacked through the thick vegetation, they came upon a tall stone pillar.
8. They also uncovered buildings overgrown with lush vines.
9. Their discovery was an ancient city.
10. Catherwood's drawings sparked interest in Mayan cities.

3 Pronouns

1. What Is a Pronoun? (links to exercise A, p. 55)

➡ **1.** you   **4.** they

List the personal pronoun(s) in each sentence.

1. Sheila is my best friend, but she makes really bad puns.
2. Once I told her that our family flew to Los Angeles.
3. "Did your arms get tired?" she asked. *Ha, ha,* I thought.
4. Reggie made the mistake of saying he ate a can of soup for his lunch.
5. What did Sheila say? "I hope you got the lead out."
6. My cousin Judith once complained to her, "This pencil needs sharpening."
7. Sheila fired back, "So, what's your point?"
8. We just groan at some of her jokes and how bad they are.
9. One day, I told her, "Don't punish us like this."
10. "Good one!" she said. "I will write it down."

2. Subject Pronouns (links to exercise on p. 58)

➡ **1.** They   **2.** she

Choose the correct pronoun in parentheses to complete each sentence.

1. Who reads books about childhood friends of famous people? That reader is (I, me).
2. (I, Me) read a story about the architect Frank Lloyd Wright.
3. (He, Him) designed many famous buildings in the United States.
4. One day, when Frank was 14, (he, him) noticed a group of bullies across the street.
5. (They, Them) had pulled crutches away from a classmate.
6. Was their victim Robie Lamp, a boy who had had polio? Yes, it was definitely (he, him).
7. Frank stood up to the bullies, and (they, them) backed off.
8. After that, Frank and Robie became good friends. Full of ideas, (they, them) often drew sketches of their inventions.
9. In one article, (I, me) read that they designed fantastic kites.
10. Lifelong friends and creators were (they, them)!

3. Subject and Object Pronouns (links to exercise on p. 60)

→ **1.** us (object)   **3.** He (subject)

Choose the correct pronoun(s) in parentheses. Identify each correct pronoun as a subject or an object.

1. (I, Me) just started going to a new middle school.
2. Rosa gave (I, me) advice about making friends.
3. (She, Her) said to smile and act friendly.
4. Let people know you're interested in (they, them).
5. (They, Them) want to make friends too, you know.
6. Do you like someone's new outfit? Tell (he or she, him or her) that.
7. I told (she, her) that one of the boys looked friendly.
8. She told me, "Ask (he, him) questions to find out if you like some of the same things."
9. I followed her advice, and guess what? (We, Us) both happen to like diving.
10. Between you and (I, me), making new friends is easier than I expected.

4. Possessive Pronouns (links to exercise A, p. 63)

→ **2.** its   **4.** Your

Choose the correct word in parentheses.

1. (Your, You're) not going to believe this story about a loyal friend.
2. (Its, It's) main character is a real dog named Hachi, who lived in Japan years ago.
3. Imagine this: (it's, its) 5:00 P.M. at a railroad station in Tokyo.
4. Every night at this time, Hachi goes to the station to greet his master. (It's, Its) no different this night.
5. City workers are getting off the train. (They're, their) tired after a long day's work.
6. Hachi searches (they're, their) faces. He doesn't see his master.
7. How could the dog know that his master died in the city that day? (You're, Your) probably thinking that's the end of the story, but it isn't.
8. Every evening for the rest of his life, Hachi comes to the station at 5:00 to wait for his master. You could set (your, you're) watch by him.

9. Each night, Hachi returns home alone. (Its, It's) a sad story but true.

10. The Japanese showed (their, they're) respect for Hachi's loyalty. After he died, they erected a statue of him on the spot where he used to wait for his master.

5. Reflexive and Intensive Pronouns (links to exercise on p. 65)

➡ **1.** herself—reflexive   **3.** themselves—reflexive

Write the reflexive or intensive pronoun in each sentence. Then identify it as reflexive or intensive.

1. Have you ever found yourself going a little crazy during a sporting event?

2. I myself went wild when the U.S. women's soccer team won the World Cup in 1999.

3. More than 90,000 fans in the Rose Bowl cheered themselves into a frenzy.

4. President Clinton himself was there to see the thrilling triumph.

5. The game itself was long and grueling: 120 minutes of play without a score.

6. Then both teams—the United States and China—found themselves playing in sudden-death overtime and facing a final shootout.

7. Brandi Chastain herself scored the winning penalty kick.

8. The 1999 event didn't mark the first time that the young women proved themselves champions.

9. The team had set a high standard for itself by winning the World Cup in 1991 and an Olympic gold medal in 1996.

10. Today, more than 7 million girls in the United States challenge themselves by playing on soccer teams.

6. Interrogatives and Demonstratives (links to exercise A, p. 68)

➡ **1.** Who; Int. **4.** who, Int.

Choose the correct word in parentheses to complete each sentence.

1. This Bugs Bunny video is (who's, whose)?

2. Bugs Bunny has starred in 263 short films, 10 long movies, 11 TV movies, and 6 TV series. (That, Those) would be big numbers for a human actor!

3. (Whose, Who's) always saying, "You're disss-picable!"
4. (That, Those) is Daffy Duck, who always loses out to Bugs.
5. (Who, Whom) is the guy called "Doc"?
6. I know to (who, whom) you're referring. It's Elmer Fudd.
7. (Whose, Who's) often grumbling "that rackin' frackin' varmint"?
8. Yosemite Sam—that's (who, whom)!
9. Your favorite character on Bugs Bunny is (who, whom)?
10. (Who, Whom) do you think of first?

7. Pronoun-Antecedent Agreement (links to exercise on p. 71)

➡ **2.** her—Annemarie Johansen   **5.** their—Nazis

Write the pronoun and its antecedent in each sentence or pair of sentences.

1. Chimpanzees raised in captivity cannot survive on their own in the wild.
2. People have donated their time and money to build chimpanzee shelters in Africa.
3. Jane Goodall, a famous wildlife expert, said she would help set up the shelters.
4. In the wild, a baby chimp might nurse from its mother for as long as five years.
5. At the shelters, baby chimps receive their milk from bottles.
6. Each caretaker, as part of his or her job, must teach the chimps new survival skills.
7. One female chimp had lived for years in a cage. She had to learn how to climb trees and pick berries.
8. One orphan had become sick and had lost all his hair.
9. The orphan was named Uruhara. It means "bald" in an African language.
10. In the sanctuary, Uruhara received lots of love and good care. Now he has hair again!

8. Indefinite Pronoun Agreement (links to exercise A, p. 74)

➡ **1.** their   **2.** his

Choose the correct pronoun(s) to complete the sentences.

1. All of the early Pilgrims owed (his or her, their) survival to the Wampanoag Indians.
2. Because nobody knew what to eat, (he or she, they) had to learn from the Wampanoags what foods to plant and harvest.

3. In 1621, many of the Pilgrims asked the Wampanoags to join (them, him or her) in a feast of thanksgiving.

4. At the feast, everyone could eat (his or her, their) fill of venison stew.

5. If someone preferred other food, (he or she, they) could have wild turkey or oysters.

6. All of the oysters were baked in (its, their) shells over an open fire.

7. Pumpkins were baked also. Each simmered in (its, their) maple syrup flavoring.

8. All could fill (his or her, their) wooden plates with sweet corn baked in the husk.

9. At least one of the Wampanoags brought venison as (his, their) contribution to the feast.

10. All of the Wampanoag and Pilgrim leaders ate (his or her, their) meal at a special table.

9. Pronoun Problems (links to exercise A, p. 76)

➡ **2.** us

Write the correct word in parentheses to complete each sentence.

1. (We, Us) tennis players are impressed by the champion sisters Venus and Serena Williams.

2. Our tennis coach gave (we, us) players tickets for the 1999 U.S. Open.

3. Serena Williams stunned (we, us) viewers at the final by defeating No. 1–ranked Martina Hingis.

4. In the semifinals, (we, us) spectators had seen Martina defeat Venus Williams, Serena's older sister.

5. Serena's victory even surprised (we, us) fans since this was her first appearance in a Grand Slam final.

6. (We, Us) sports historians know that she is the first African-American woman to win a major tennis title since 1958.

7. Serena and Martina competed fiercely for the trophy. When the match finally ended, (Serena, she) had won!

8. Both Venus and Serena are coached by their father. (Venus, She) and her sister have played together since childhood.

9. I wonder what that's like for (her, Serena).

10. Serena and Venus practice tennis on their home courts. (Serena, She) always gets a good workout!

10. More Pronoun Problems (links to exercise A, p. 78)

➡ **1.** me   **4.** her

Write the correct pronoun to complete each sentence.

1. Natalie and (me, I) surveyed kids who were best friends.
2. Both (she, her) and (me, I) reported the answers in our school newspaper.
3. Between you and (I, me), we thought our questions were pretty good.
4. We interviewed several people. Natalie asked (them, they) all, "Is it okay for friends to fight?"
5. Dominic, unlike most of the kids, wanted (his, their) answers kept private.
6. Richard, who has lots of friends, brought (his, their) oldest friend, Greg, to the interview.
7. We asked (he, him) and Greg, "How much time do you think friends should spend together?"
8. Hillary and Ming-Jie had (their, her) turn next.
9. We asked Hillary and (her, she), "Would you lie to a friend to save her feelings?"
10. Ming-Jie and (she, her) agreed that friends should be honest, even if sometimes the truth hurts!

4 Verbs

1. What Is a Verb? (links to exercise A, p. 90)

➡ **1.** developed   **2.** traveled

Write the verb or verb phrase in each of the following sentences.

1. Submarines float easily.
2. They also can dive all the way to the ocean floor.
3. They may stay underwater for months.
4. They operate underwater with the help of double-hull construction.
5. Between the inner and outer hulls are ballast tanks.
6. The sailors flood these tanks with seawater.
7. The seawater increases the ship's weight.
8. Horizontal rudders, or hydroplanes, steer the ship downward.
9. While underwater, the sailors navigate with radar, sonar, and periscopes.
10. The ship rises to the surface with the removal of the seawater from its ballast tanks.

2. Action Verbs and Objects (links to exercise A, p. 93)

➡ **1.** us (indirect object); risks (direct object)
   2. world (indirect object); automobile (direct object)

Write the 15 complements in these sentences. If the sentence contains no complements, write *None.*

1. Motorcycle-type engines give snowmobiles power.
2. The vehicles' handlebars connect to a pair of skis up front.
3. This connection gives drivers steering ability.
4. Instead of a rear wheel, a continuous rubber track propels them.
5. A throttle lends drivers a means of acceleration.
6. A brake lever enables drivers to stop.
7. Snowmobiles can achieve speeds exceeding 85 miles an hour.
8. They can climb slopes of 65 degrees.
9. Snowmobiles take people groceries in inaccessible areas.
10. They also can give their riders a thrill.

3. Linking Verbs and Predicate Words (links to exercise on p. 95)

➡ **1.** was (linking verb); woman (predicate noun)
   4. seemed (linking verb); candidate (predicate noun)

Identify each linking verb, predicate noun, and predicate adjective in the sentences below.

1. Bangladesh is a small country between India and Myanmar, on the Bay of Bengal.
2. It has become a very densely populated country.
3. Its capital, Dacca, has grown large.
4. The main mode of transportation in Dacca is the rickshaw.
5. These rickshaws are three-wheeled vehicles powered by humans.
6. They are completely dependent on human power, with no motor of any kind.
7. There must be about 400,000 rickshaws in Dacca.
8. Many people appear dependent on them for transport.
9. Rickshaw transport looks convenient for riders.
10. Yet the job of powering them seems very hard on the drivers.

4. Principal Parts of Verbs (links to exercise on p. 97)

➡ **1.** past participle   **3.** past

Identify the form of each underlined verb as the present, the present participle, the past, or the past participle.

If you **(1)** walked somewhere today, you **(2)** used the most healthful form of transportation. Walking **(3)** gives you a sense of well-being and energy. It **(4)** helps you beat stress. Walking two miles a day **(5)** protects your heart. A person who **(6)** is running down the road is also protecting his or her heart. But running eventually **(7)** causes wear and tear on the body, especially knee joints. However, walking **(8)** benefits your health for a lifetime. And if you **(9)** have gone for a walk in the woods on a beautiful day, you **(10)** have discovered another good reason to walk: it's fun.

5. Irregular Verbs (links to exercise on p. 100)

➡ **1.** began   **2.** ran

Choose the correct form of the verb to complete each sentence.
  1. People around the world have always (made, maked) use of rivers and oceans for transportation.
  2. In the 19th century, it (costed, cost) a fortune to transport goods to California from the east coast.
  3. Ships (goed, went) all the way around South America—nearly 8,000 additional miles—to get there.
  4. Sometimes ships (sank, sinked) at sea, which killed passengers and destroyed cargo.
  5. Eventually, people (thought, thinked) of a way to shorten the trip.
  6. They (digged, dug) a canal across the Isthmus of Panama.
  7. They (spent, spended) ten years working on the canal.
  8. It (runned, ran) more than 40 miles between the Caribbean Sea and the Pacific Ocean.
  9. Many of the canal workers (fell, falled) ill with malaria.
  10. The Panama Canal (became, becomed) a much-needed shortcut for cargo ships carrying such important goods as fuel and food.

6. Simple Tenses (links to exercise A, p. 103)

➡ **1.** past   **5.** present

Identify the tense of each underlined verb as present, past, or future.
  1. In the middle of the 19th century, the Oregon Trail served as the route to the West for 80,000 to 200,000 pioneers.

2. The 2,000-mile journey <u>attracted</u> gold hunters, fur traders, missionaries, and especially farmers.
3. To this day, their destination, the Pacific Northwest, <u>has</u> some of the most fertile farmland in the world.
4. During much of 1986, pilot and history buff Maurice Brett <u>was retracing</u> the settlers' trip in his airplane.
5. He <u>documented</u> the journey with photographs and movies.
6. In rocky sections of the trail, the ruts from heavy wagons <u>are</u> still three feet deep.
7. In grassy sections, the tracks from the wagon wheels <u>are</u> still <u>showing</u> in the soil.
8. It <u>took</u> the pioneers four to six months to make the journey Brett completed in 12 days by plane.
9. Brett <u>will write</u> a book about the experience.
10. He <u>will enjoy</u> the memory of his experience for many years to come.

7. Perfect Tenses (links to exercise A, p. 106)

➡ **1**. Past. Perf.　　**3**. Pres. Perf.

Write the verb in each sentence, and identify its tense as present perfect, past perfect, or future perfect.

1. For centuries, navigation has been a challenge.
2. At the end of their journeys sailors in ancient times often had ended up continents away from their destinations.
3. By the late 1950s, scientists had invented artificial satellites.
4. Satellites have been a huge help to navigation.
5. They have led to the development of the Global Positioning System (GPS).
6. This navigation system has used signals from at least three satellites at any one time.
7. People in trackless wilderness have found their way with portable GPS receivers, accurate to within 10 meters.
8. People also have used GPS successfully from cars, ships, and planes.
9. Perhaps someday, every car will have acquired a GPS receiver.
10. By then, global positioning will have rescued millions of lost travelers.

8. Using Verb Tenses (links to exercise A, p. 110)

➜ **1.** have used   **2.** opened

Choose the correct verb form from the choices in parentheses to complete each sentence.

1. One of the biggest drawbacks of cars always (has been, had been) pollution.
2. Early cars were so few in number that they (have done, did) little damage to the air.
3. The petroleum-based fuels used in automobiles (produce, will have produced) toxic emissions, such as carbon monoxide.
4. Petroleum-based engine oils (stay, had stayed) dangerous to the environment for a long time—they aren't biodegradable.
5. Now, scientists (had developed, are developing) new car fuels and lubricants from plants.
6. One of these new plant sources (is, was) sunflowers.
7. Sunflower oil (will create, creates) fewer particles than petroleum-based oils.
8. Therefore, sunflower oil (can keep, will have kept) a car's exhaust system cleaner than petroleum-based oils.
9. Some scientists predict that plant-based fuels and oils (will replace, have replaced) petroleum in the not-too-distant future.
10. They (reduce, will reduce) air pollution in years to come.

9. Troublesome Verb Pairs (links to exercise A, p. 113)

➜ **1.** lies   **3.** learned

Choose the correct word in parentheses in each of the following sentences.

1. Isle Royale (lies, lays) in the northwest section of Lake Superior.
2. When the state of Michigan was (laid, lay) out, Isle Royale became part of it.
3. This island first (rose, raised) to fame thousands of years ago when Indians mined its copper deposits.
4. Now it (teaches, learns) backpackers to appreciate the beauty of nature.
5. Rock ridges (raise, rise) hundreds of feet along the island's spine.
6. Moose and wolves (lay, lie) hidden in the pine forests.

7. Isle Royale is unspoiled partly because of the barriers nature has (raised, risen) around it.
8. Park rangers (taught, learned) us that the island became Isle Royale National Park in 1931.
9. To get to the island, pilots (sit, set) down seaplanes on the lake regularly.
10. The only other way to get to Isle Royale from the mainland is by (sitting, setting) for hours on a ferryboat.

5 Adjectives and Adverbs

1. What Is an Adjective? (links to exercise on p. 124)

➡ 1. American, landmark
2. dirty, swamp; ugly, shacks; much, garbage

Write each adjective and the noun or pronoun it modifies. Do not include articles.

1. Camping during a cold winter has numerous advantages.
2. Ordinary insects cannot live in the extreme cold.
3. Wild animals can be spotted easily against the white snow.
4. Knowledgeable campers appreciate the natural beauty of the wintry wilderness.
5. Winter camping provides a great opportunity to have the whole campsite to yourself.
6. On the other hand, slippery ice can complicate outdoor activities.
7. The variable temperatures of North American winters can create a variety of dangerous conditions.
8. If you have snowy weather and can't use your stove, you can't just order fast food.
9. Wet woolen sweaters take a long time to dry.
10. Even normal winter temperatures may cause serious discomfort.

2. Predicate Adjectives (links to exercise A, p. 126)

➡ **1.** inactive, Mount St. Helens   **2.** dangerous, volcano

Write the predicate adjective in each sentence, along with the noun it modifies.

1. On August 26, 1883, the island of Krakatoa looked frightful.
2. The island's volcano became active.
3. The ground felt shaky.
4. Explosions, which happened every ten minutes, sounded loud.
5. Because of thick smoke, the entire area seemed foggy.
6. As a result of the volcanic activity, waves in the sea grew gigantic.
7. For months after the eruptions, the atmosphere remained dusty.
8. The sky felt dark because thick clouds blocked the sun's light.
9. Following the eruptions, the sun sometimes appeared green.
10. Most of Krakatoa collapsed into the sea; the island was lost forever.

3. Other Words Used as Adjectives (links to exercise A, p. 129)

➡ **1.** most, climbers; mountain, formations   **2.** city, buildings

Write each noun or pronoun that is used as an adjective in these sentences, along with the word it modifies.

1. Would you crawl on your belly in a dark cave?
2. That activity appeals to many people known as cavers.
3. A cave adventure is nearly irresistible to them.
4. Cavers crawl through limestone passages, climb over rock bridges, and explore unusual formations.
5. These adventurers wear a helmet lamp, knee pads, warm clothes, and safety boots.
6. A cave guide helps cavers find their way.
7. One South Dakota cave is famous for its length of hundreds of miles.
8. Its temperature is always the same, no matter what the weather situation aboveground.
9. This cave has never been completely explored.
10. In some caves, you can see popcorn formations and soda straws, an unusual cavern feature.

4. What Is an Adverb? (links to exercise A, p. 132)

➡ **1.** *very, curious,* adjective
2. *studied, quite, often,* V, Adv.

Write each adverb and the word it modifies. Then identify the modified word as a verb, an adjective, or an adverb. There may be more than one adverb in a sentence.

1. Sacajawea played a very valuable role in the Lewis and Clark expedition.
2. Initially, Lewis and Clark hired a French-Canadian trader to help them understand the Native Americans they encountered.
3. They realized that the trader's wife was a more suitable interpreter.
4. Sacajawea, a Shoshone Indian, was just barely 17 or 18 when she joined the expedition.
5. She was obviously quite familiar with Native American culture.
6. As the expedition traveled west, her presence helped reassure wary tribes.
7. Patiently, Sacajawea showed the explorers how to find food.
8. She once bravely rescued scientific instruments from a sinking boat.
9. Sacajawea's son, Jean Baptiste, later became a translator himself for western travelers.
10. Today, many monuments honor Sacajawea's extremely important contributions.

5. Making Comparisons (links to exercise A, p. 135)

➡ **1.** largest   **2.** richest

Choose the word in parentheses that correctly completes each sentence.

1. Growing only about 13 feet long, a pygmy sperm whale is the (smaller/smallest) of all sperm whales.
2. A sei whale swims (more rapidly/most rapidly) than a blue whale.
3. The gray whale makes one of the (longest/more longest) migrations of any mammal, a journey of about 12,000 miles per year.
4. Sperm whales are the (better/best) divers of all.
5. A male humpback sings (more distinctively/most distinctively) than a female.
6. Humpbacks produce (more varied/most varied) sounds than gray whales.

7. Humpbacks sing (less/least) frequently than usual when they are feeding.
8. Whales can breathe (more efficiently/most efficiently) than humans because they can store and transport more oxygen.
9. Right whales are (more easily/most easily) hunted than other whales because right whales are slow swimmers.
10. Because they use technology to hunt whales, humans pose the (worse/worst) of all threats to whale populations.

6. Adjective or Adverb? (links to exercise on p. 137)

➡ 1. *well,* adverb   2. *real,* adjective

Choose the correct modifier in parentheses, then identify it as an adjective or an adverb.

1. When John James Audubon was a young adult, his business ventures turned out (bad/badly).
2. Because he could paint (good/well) and had a great love of nature, he eventually became an artist and a naturalist.
3. In the early 1800s, he had roamed the countryside and studied birds (real/really) closely.
4. Usually, he sketched (real/really) specimens of birds.
5. His paintings capture birds very (good/well) in their natural settings.
6. In Pennsylvania, Audubon took a (bad/badly) fall into a frozen creek.
7. While in the South, he felt (bad/badly) after he got yellow fever.
8. Despite such risks, Audubon conducted a (good/well) search for many different species of birds.
9. *The Birds of America* is a (real/really) beautiful collection of his paintings.
10. Audubon made a (real/really) contribution to natural history as well as to art.

7. Avoiding Double Negatives (links to exercise A, p. 139)

➔ **1**. any   **2**. have

Write the word in parentheses that correctly completes each sentence.

1. There hasn't (ever/never) been a higher temperature recorded in the world than 136°F.
2. This temperature couldn't occur (anywhere/nowhere) but in a desert—in this case, the Sahara, in northern Africa.
3. Much of the Sahara isn't (nothing/anything) but empty plateaus and plains.
4. Most plants and animals can't thrive (nowhere/anywhere) but near an oasis.
5. Grasses, shrubs, and trees (can/can't) scarcely get by in some parts of the Sahara.
6. Some short-lived plants there don't (ever/never) live for more than six to eight weeks.
7. Lizards, some gazelles, and foxes that inhabit the Sahara can live for long periods without (no/any) water to drink.
8. Many human residents don't live (nowhere/anywhere) permanently but travel seasonally to find available water.
9. Typically, these nomads don't have (no/any) cars.
10. Because the roads in the Sahara are so poor, these people couldn't go (nowhere/anywhere) without a camel.

6 Prepositions, Conjunctions, and Interjections

1. What Is a Preposition? (links to exercise A, p. 150)

➡ **1.** from (preposition); cultures (object)
   2. with (preposition); tail (object)

Write the preposition in each sentence, along with its object.

1. The helmeted iguana is a lizard that reminds people of a small dragon.
2. This iguana has a tall crest on the nape of its neck.
3. The crest shortens and tapers at its back.
4. A shorter crest runs the length of the iguana's body.
5. The helmeted iguana has a slender body with long legs.
6. Casque-headed iguanas are green or brown with darker crossbands.
7. Like all iguanas, they are covered with scales.
8. Pet casque-headed iguanas need water but rarely bathe in it.
9. Some pet-store iguanas come from southern Mexico.
10. Generally, they live in areas where leafy plants grow.

2. Using Prepositional Phrases (links to exercise A, p. 153)

➡ **1.** in the world (prepositional phrase), lizard (word modified)
   2. on a few Indonesian islands (prepositional phrase), live (word modified)

Write the prepositional phrase in each sentence, along with the word or words it modifies.

1. From a distance, salamanders may resemble small lizards.
2. Salamanders are amphibians with long bodies and long tails.
3. Many salamanders have glands in their skin that secrete a slimy substance.
4. When they are under attack, they ooze this slime.
5. Some salamanders live in water.
6. Others live on land.
7. Still others divide their time between land and water.
8. In very hot weather, salamanders find damp places.
9. All salamanders require exposure to water.
10. Without it, they will die.

3. Conjunctions (links to exercise A, p. 156)

➜ **1.** or (conjunction); crocodile, an alligator (words joined)
    2. and (conjunction); A crocodile's snout is pointy, an
        alligator's snout is broad (groups of words joined)

Write the conjunction in each sentence, along with the words or groups of words that it joins.

1. Lizards and crocodiles are different types of reptiles.
2. Most crocodiles spend much of their time in water, but many lizards are land lovers.
3. Lizards come in all shapes and sizes.
4. Most lizards are found in the tropics or in deserts.
5. Typically they lay eggs, but some lizards have live young.
6. Lizards eat small animals or plants.
7. A few lizards have small legs or none at all.
8. Usually a lizard has four legs and its body is scaly.
9. The slow-worm is a lizard, but it doesn't have legs.
10. Most lizards are harmless, but the Gila monster is poisonous.

7 Subject-Verb Agreement

1. Agreement in Number (links to exercise A, p. 168)

➜ **1.** consider   **2.** shows

Write the form of the verb that agrees with the subject of each sentence.

1. A medical worker (is, are) also known as a health care provider.
2. Nurses (forms, form) an important part of the health care team in every hospital.
3. These health care providers (cooperates, cooperate) closely with doctors.
4. A nurse also (need, needs) to work well with patients and their families.
5. Nurses (completes, complete) one to four years in a certification program.
6. A nurse's responsibilities (includes, include) the observation and treatment of patients.
7. However, a nurse (doesn't, don't) prescribe medication for patients.
8. One type of specially trained nurse (has, have) the title of nurse practitioner.

9. Nurse practitioners (performs, perform) some tasks formerly assigned to doctors.
10. Today, more men (is, are) becoming nurses than in the past.

2. Compound Subjects (links to exercise A, p. 170)

➡ **1.** Volunteer men and women compose the Larimer County Dive Rescue Team in Colorado. **5.** Terrified victims or darkness frustrates their efforts.

Proofread these sentences for errors in subject-verb agreement. If a sentence contains an error, rewrite the sentence correctly. If a sentence contains no error, write *Correct.*

1. Humans and dogs works together all over the world to raise sheep.
2. Herding dogs and their puppies move sheep from one pasture to another.
3. The border collie and the Australian kelpie is two popular herding breeds.
4. Neither rain nor snow prevent a good herding dog from doing its job.
5. Whistles or spoken commands are two ways the shepherd communicates with the dog.
6. "Come by" and "That'll do" has special meanings to the shepherding dog.
7. The skill and ability of the dog makes the shepherd's job much easier.
8. A well-trained herding dog or puppy sometimes cost hundreds of dollars!
9. Shepherds and farmers agrees, however, that the cost is worth every penny.
10. The love and affection of a herding dog for its owner are marvelous to see.

3. Phrases Between Subject and Verb (links to exercise on p. 172)

➡ **1.** are   **2.** was

Write the correct verb to complete each sentence. Choose from the verbs in parentheses.

1. The world under the seas (is, are) explored in the films of Jacques Cousteau and his sons, Philippe and Jean-Michel.
2. But the story of their lives (is, are) worth filming also.
3. Many important events in the history of their work (is, are)

good possibilities for scenes, for example, the events below.

4. Jacques Cousteau, with the help of an engineer, (is, are) responsible for the invention of the Aqua-Lung, which allowed humans to breathe underwater.

5. Cousteau, with a crew, (renovate, renovates) a minesweeper which he names the *Calypso,* to use in exploring the ocean.

6. Perhaps Cousteau, in his free time, (write, writes) about sea exploration.

7. Philippe, under his father's guidance, (film, films) ocean life for the Cousteau Society.

8. Jean-Michel, Philippe, and Jacques (build, builds) a miniature submarine, the Diving Saucer.

9. Jacques and Jean-Michel, throughout the world, (publicize, publicizes) the threat of ocean pollution.

10. Their movies, without fail, (make, makes) the public aware of limited water resources.

4. Indefinite Pronoun Subjects (links to exercise A, p. 175)

➡ 1. Everyone has heard of seeing-eye dogs.
2. Few know the term *hearing dogs.*

Proofread these sentences for errors in subject-verb agreement. If a sentence contains an error, rewrite the sentence correctly. If a sentence contains no error, write *Correct.*

1. Almost everyone has seen a rowboat on a lake or river.

2. But not many has seen a shell, the sleek, pencil-thin boat used in rowing races.

3. Both is propelled through the water by pulling on oars, long wooden poles with a blade on one end.

4. Everything on a racing shell has been designed for speed.

5. Each of the eight rowers need to pull the oars in perfect rhythm with the other members of the team.

6. Many admires the strength and stamina of the rowers.

7. Some lifts weights to improve their strength and stamina.

8. None train harder than the members of the U.S. Olympic rowing team.

9. All of the rowers' special skills is needed to make the boat glide straight.

10. One is the ability to follow the orders of the coxswain, or leader of the rowing team.

5. Subjects in Unusual Positions (links to exercise on p. 177)

➡ **1.** subject, friends; verb phrase, does like; Do your friends like soccer?

2. subject, sports; verb, is correct

Identify the subject and the verb in each sentence below. If they agree, write *Correct.* If they don't agree, write the form of the verb that goes with the subject.

1. Would you enjoy an adventure under the surface of the sea?

2. Under the waves are just the place for me.

3. There is no noisy crowds and traffic.

4. Before your eye appears all the wonders of the ocean.

5. Can you imagine the many varieties of colorful fish?

6. Just think of the brilliant corals and shells!

7. There is no more beautiful sights anywhere.

8. Here is another thing to think about.

9. In the oceans swims some of the most intelligent creatures on the planet—dolphins and whales.

10. Give me a job like Jacques Cousteau's anytime!

8 Capitalization

1. People and Cultures (links to exercise A, p. 188)

➡ **1.** I   **4.** Spanish

Write the word or initial that should be capitalized in each sentence. If a sentence contains correct capitalization, write *Correct.*

1. When I was born, my parents nicknamed me "hooper."

2. As a kid, i hated the name.

3. My family kept the name because aunt Ellen thought it was cute.

4. In elementary school, my best friend was named Alfred e. Zee.

5. Naturally, he was nicknamed "Easy," and by fourth grade even principal Johnson called him by that name.

6. Most people in the british Isles where I live object to insulting nicknames, like "Stinky."

7. Researchers, headed by professor Rom Harre, found that nicknames were common in all cultures.
8. A nickname can be a shortened form of a person's birth name.
9. For example, princess Diana was nicknamed "Di."
10. Whether you are american, german, or some other nationality, chances are you have a nickname, though you may not like it.

2. First Words and Titles (links to exercise on p. 191)

→ **1.** For   **2.** Deedle, Went

Write the word that should be capitalized in each sentence. (Do not write the words that are already capitalized.)

1. both first and last names have special meanings and origins.
2. When I wrote a letter to the local genealogical society about last names, I did not know the name of the director, so I began my letter, "dear sir or madam."
3. I found out that English last names often are related to occupations, such as miller, a word used in this nursery rhyme:
   there was a jolly miller,
   lived on the river Dee.
4. You may be asking, "what is a miller?" A miller is "someone who grinds grain into flour."
5. According to the *encyclopaedia britannica,* most cultures use names that refer to the occupation of one's father.
6. some names have very specific meanings, such as the Hawaiian name Kanani, which means "the beauty."
7. I asked my mom, "does my name have a special meaning?"
8. Names of characters in books and movies often have particular meanings, such as the name of the character Luke Skywalker in *star wars.*
9. Some writers choose names not for meaning but for the sound, as T. S. Eliot did for his poem "macavity: The Mystery cat."
10. I used the following outline section to research the origin of names:
   I. Names
      A. arabic
         1. occupational
         2. titles

3. Places and Transportation (links to exercise A, p. 195)

➡ **2.** Gulf, Mexico **3.** Mobile

Write the word or words that should be capitalized in each sentence. (Do not write the words that are already capitalized.)

1. In 1579, the English explorer Sir Francis Drake anchored his ship, the *golden hind,* near the western coast of North America.
2. Drake claimed land we now know as part of the Pacific northwest.
3. Almost exactly 200 years later, another ship from england, piloted by the famous Captain Cook, reached the area.
4. Cook encountered foul weather soon after he reached land, and so he gave the name cape foulweather to the first land he saw.
5. The pacific ocean continued to fascinate explorers; from 1791 to 1794, Captain George Vancouver sailed the northern pacific coast.
6. Vancouver left his name on many landmarks in the region, including Vancouver island.
7. In addition to leaving his own name on landmarks, Vancouver named a mountain in the area mount rainier, after a friend of his.
8. Today, the region explored by these men can be viewed by traveling north on interstate 5.
9. One of the largest cities along the interstate is seattle.
10. The interstate ends at the northern border of washington.

4. Organizations and Other Subjects (links to exercise A, p. 197)

➡ Where: Middle School Grand Prize: Silver Puck

Write the word or words that should be capitalized in each sentence. (Do not write the words that are already capitalized.)

1. At the fall meeting of the senior class of Stockingdale high school, we decided we would hold a special sports event.
2. We named the event the spring sports festival.
3. It was planned for the month of may, which gave us plenty of time to prepare the games and to get sponsors lined up.
4. Getting sponsors was my job, and the first company I approached was flyrite sporting goods.
5. The company agreed to deliver an assortment of sporting goods on the friday before the games started.
6. When Mr. Hawkins, who teaches world history II, heard about our plans, he suggested that we expand the festival.

7. He thought we should name it after the golden age of greece and that it should include other events, such as debates and art exhibits.
8. We decided to invite representatives from Bradford university and other local colleges.
9. A lot of university representatives came, and even a scout from the nfl showed up at the exhibition football game.
10. The festival was to have ended by 10 p.m. on saturday, but the last group of people left at midnight.

9 Punctuation

1. Periods and Other End Marks (links to exercise A, p. 208)

→ accident?   kidding!

Write the words in the passage that should be followed by periods, question marks, or exclamation points. Include these end marks in your answers.

How many symbols of the United States can you name In addition to the American flag and the Statue of Liberty, you might mention the Liberty Bell But did you know that this famous bell was flawed from its very beginning No kidding Commissioned by the Pennsylvania Provincial Assembly, the bell was completed in 1752 Can you believe that the bell cracked the first time it was tested It's true In fact, the bell was so poorly made that it needed to be recast twice before it was hung in the Pennsylvania statehouse Unfortunately, the bell cracked again, in 1835

In 1846, on the anniversary of George Washington's birthday, the bell cracked so badly that it could not be fixed Today, the Liberty Bell rests in a pavilion close to Independence Hall in Philadelphia, but it cannot be rung. How sad

2. Commas in Sentences (links to exercise A, p. 211)

→ smelly   current

Write the words in the passage that should be followed by commas.

In 1928, Sir Alexander Fleming a British scientist accidentally discovered a solution to a serious medical problem. While working at a London hospital, Fleming had begun to study staphylococci, a strain of bacteria. His research involved preparing bacteria cultures examining any changes in the cultures, and recording any important findings.

One day Fleming noticed something strange while cleaning his laboratory equipment. Inside one dish, a small patch of mold grew. Fleming wondered how this could be. After all, the bacteria were known to harm most living things. He realized almost instantly that this mold held the answer to the great medical problem. In time Fleming and other scientists used the mold to develop penicillin the world's first antibiotic drug. Today, when patients recover from pneumonia, spinal meningitis and other serious infections treated with penicillin, they have Fleming to thank.

3. Commas: Dates, Addresses, and Letters (links to exercise A, p. 213)

➡ Englewood   6

Write the words in the letter that should be followed by commas.

222 Green Street
New York NY 10010
May 3 2000

Dear Harry,

How are you? I'm sure you're looking forward to the big race. I'll be arriving in Phoenix Arizona on May 10 2001 the day before you compete. I can't wait to see you!

Speaking of races, I heard a story you might appreciate about a man named Wim Esajas. In 1960, he was scheduled to run in the 800-meter event at the Summer Olympics in Rome Italy. On the morning of the race, Esajas decided to rest at the Olympic Village. Later that afternoon at the track, he discovered that he had made a terrible mistake. To his horror, Esajas learned that heats for the race had already been held, and that he had been withdrawn from the event! Sadly, he returned to his home in Surinam Dutch Guiana never having competed in the Olympics.

I hope you don't repeat Esajas's mistake! Remember to set your alarm clock. I'll be cheering for you!

Your big sis

Elsie

4. Punctuating Quotations (links to exercise A, p. 217)

→ **1.** "Why is the word *bug* used to describe a computer problem?" asked Steve.
    3. Correct

Rewrite each incorrect sentence, adding quotation marks and other punctuation where needed.

"Did you know that people today are still trying to straighten the Leaning Tower of Pisa?" asked Rosemary.

"No, I didn't," replied Kayla. What have they done so far to fix it

"The tower's foundation was strengthened with concrete in 1934, explained Rosemary, but that didn't seem to help.

Kayla asked, Have they done anything else to straighten it

"Well, steel cables were added to support the tower in 1992," Rosemary stated.

I'm sure it's all fixed by now said Kayla.

"Not yet," sighed Rosemary. "In 1999, engineers began a project to straighten the tower by removing soil under its base." Rosemary added They think this approach will correct the monument's famous tilt and save it from toppling over.

I sure hope it works! exclaimed Kayla.

5. Semicolons and Colons (links to exercise A, p. 219)

→ data: 5:00

Write the words in the paragraph that should be followed by semicolons and colons. Include these punctuation marks in your answers.

In 1609, Galileo Galilei built his own telescope to study the night sky. Using this device, he made the following observations spots on the sun, crags on the Earth's moon, and moons circling Jupiter. Galileo's discoveries were remarkable they eventually lead to greater advances in astronomy and physics. At the time, however, his work was widely criticized by authorities.

Leaders were particularly upset by Galileo's view of the Earth and its relationship to the sun. They believed that the Earth was the center of the universe. Galileo, however, supported an entirely different opinion it caused him a great deal of trouble. Galileo observed scientifically that the planets, including the Earth, all revolved around the sun. Galileo published his theory in 1632 as a result, he was punished. Galileo experienced many hardships at the hands of his enemies trials, isolation, and house arrest. Through it all, he remained true to his beliefs and to science.

6. Hyphens, Dashes, and Parentheses (links to exercise A, p. 221)

➜ **1.** Isabella Baumfree was born into slavery in the late 1790s (the exact date is unknown).

2. Correct

Read the following passage. Insert hyphens, dashes, and parentheses in the underlined portions where necessary. If the underlined text is correct, write *Correct.*

Have you ever wondered why the **(1)** <u>twenty six</u> letters on a computer keyboard are arranged the way they are? It's because of the invention of the typewriter **(2)** <u>first introduced in 1874</u>. Christopher Latham Sholes, an American printer, had been working on typewriting devices in the 1860s. After reading an article about a typewriting machine **(3)** <u>an article from an issue of *Scientific American*</u>, Sholes made a **(4)** <u>primitive</u> typewriter from **(5)** <u>a telegraph key, piano wire, carbon paper, and glass</u>. Though this machine could type only one letter **(6)** <u>the letter w</u> it caught the attention of financial investors. Sholes improved the machine and patented it in 1868.

Sholes found a problem, though, with **(7)** <u>the alphabetical arrangement of letters on the keys</u>. If he typed too quickly, the keys would jam. To solve this problem, Sholes invented QWERTY **(8)** <u>a new way of organizing letters on the keyboard</u>. By keeping the keys of frequently used letters apart from each other, Sholes **(9)** <u>discovered</u> that he could type without jamming the keys. Although another letter arrangement **(10)** <u>one that was faster and more accurate</u> was invented by August Dvorak in the 1930s, we continue to use the QWERTY system invented by Sholes.

7. Apostrophes (links to exercise A, p. 223)

➜ Games'   women's

Find and correct the errors in the use of apostrophes.

Have you ever wondered how some places were named? Well, theres an amusing story behind Greenlands' name. Contrary to what you might think, Greenland, the largest island in the world, was not named for it's rich green fields. In fact, only the coasts of Greenland turn green, and this change occurs only during the islands summers. No, the name comes from an ancient trick.

According to historians, the Vikings interest in settling new areas prompted the naming of Greenland. The Vikings are said to have called this frigid place Greenland in order to entice people to move there, far away from their homes. Apparently, the Vikings trick was successful in attracting some families to Greenland.

Today, Greenland is populated almost entirely by Inuit and European people. Though theyr'e able to farm in the countrys southwestern coastal areas, Greenlanders spend more time fishing, hunting, or sheep herding.

8. Punctuating Titles (links to exercise A, p. 225)

➡ **1.** *Newsweek*   **3.** *Mistakes That Worked*

Write the 10 titles in this passage, setting them off correctly with either quotation marks or underlining.

The 1977 movie Close Encounters of the Third Kind was first shown in a sneak preview. Business reporter William Flanagan from New York magazine attended. In his review, Flanagan gave the film poor marks and said that it lacked the spark of Star Wars. Eventually, the later movie was appreciated as a groundbreaking science fiction film, but certainly not because of this critic!

Of course, other critics are known to have made mistakes too. Walter Kerr, an esteemed drama critic for the New York Times, attended a performance of the musical West Side Story when it opened on Broadway. Kerr is said to have openly yawned and declared the production a bore. However, the musical, based on William Shakespeare's tragedy Romeo and Juliet, went on to enjoy success on Broadway for many years. Its music was also popular, with chart-topping songs such as Tonight and Maria.

Though it may seem surprising today, many critics did not appreciate the work of John Keats in his day. Author of the classic poems Ode to a Nightingale and Ode on a Grecian Urn, Keats was told by one critic to give up writing and to go back to working in a pharmacy.

Quick-Fix Spelling Machine

QUICK–FIX SPELLING MACHINE: PLURALS OF NOUNS

SINGULAR	RULE	PLURAL
skateboard painting ticket	Add -s to most nouns.	skateboards paintings tickets
	WATCH OUT! The exceptions to this rule are nouns whose plurals are formed in special ways, such as *man (men), woman (women),* and *child (children).*	
hiss dish ditch box buzz	Add -es to nouns that end in *s, sh, ch, x,* or *z.*	hisses dishes ditches boxes buzzes
auto igloo radio	Add -s to most nouns that end in *o.*	autos igloos radios
potato tomato mosquito	Add -es to a few nouns that end in *o.*	potatoes tomatoes mosquitoes
flurry deputy battery dairy	For most nouns ending in *y,* change the *y* to *i* and add -es.	flurries deputies batteries dairies
alley play turkey	Just add -s when a vowel comes before the *y.*	alleys plays turkeys
calf thief wife leaf knife	For most nouns ending in *f* or *fe,* change the *f* to *v* and add -es or -s.	calves thieves wives leaves knives
belief muff safe	Just add -s to a few nouns that end in *f* or *fe.*	beliefs muffs safes
series sheep species aircraft	Keep the same spelling for some nouns.	series sheep species aircraft

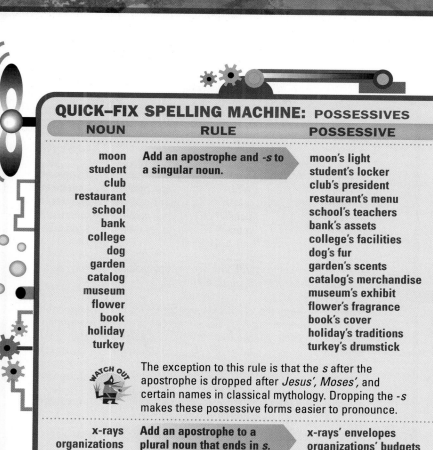

QUICK–FIX SPELLING MACHINE: POSSESSIVES

NOUN	RULE	POSSESSIVE
moon	Add an apostrophe and *-s* to a singular noun.	moon's light
student		student's locker
club		club's president
restaurant		restaurant's menu
school		school's teachers
bank		bank's assets
college		college's facilities
dog		dog's fur
garden		garden's scents
catalog		catalog's merchandise
museum		museum's exhibit
flower		flower's fragrance
book		book's cover
holiday		holiday's traditions
turkey		turkey's drumstick

WATCH OUT The exception to this rule is that the *s* after the apostrophe is dropped after *Jesus'*, *Moses'*, and certain names in classical mythology. Dropping the *-s* makes these possessive forms easier to pronounce.

NOUN	RULE	POSSESSIVE
x-rays	Add an apostrophe to a plural noun that ends in *s*.	x-rays' envelopes
organizations		organizations' budgets
teams		teams' coaches
buildings		buildings' windows
cities		cities' mayors
airports		airports' schedules
babies		babies' toys
groceries		groceries' prices
violets		violets' buds
necklaces		necklaces' clasps
butterflies		butterflies' wings

NOUN	RULE	POSSESSIVE
deer	Add an apostrophe and *-s* to a plural noun not ending in *s*.	deer's hoofs
oxen		oxen's load
salmon		salmon's gills
stepchildren		stepchildren's names
sheep		sheep's wool
mice		mice's nests
people		people's languages

SPELLING

QUICK-FIX SPELLING MACHINE: WORDS ENDING IN SILENT e

WORD	RULE	CHANGE
home engage hope tune shame state	Keep the silent *e* when a suffix beginning with a consonant is added to a word that ends in a silent *e*.	homeless engagement hopeful tuneless shameful statement

 Some words that are exceptions include *truly, awful, argument, ninth,* and *wholly.*

peace courage manage salvage outrage charge	Keep the silent *e* when a suffix beginning with *a* or *o* is added to a silent *e* word if the *e* follows a soft *c* or *g*.	peaceable courageous manageably salvageable outrageous chargeable
agree woe	Keep the silent *e* when a suffix beginning with a vowel is added to a word ending in *ee* or *oe*.	agreeable woeful
flake elevate haze institute shake create	Drop the silent *e* from the base word when you add a suffix beginning with *y* or a vowel.	flaky elevation hazy institution shaky creative

 Exceptions to this rule are such words as *changeable* and *courageous.*

QUICK–FIX SPELLING MACHINE: WORDS ENDING IN y

WORD	RULE	CHANGE
happy thirty merry greedy sneaky deputy	Change the *y* to *i* to add a suffix to a word ending in *y* if the *y* follows a consonant.	happiness thirtieth merriest greedily sneakier deputies
rally marry tally fry	Keep the *y* when adding *-ing* to a word ending in *y* if the *y* follows a consonant.	rallying marrying tallying frying
joy pay boy	Keep the *y* when adding a suffix to a word ending in a vowel and *y*.	joyous payable boyish

QUICK–FIX SPELLING MACHINE: WORDS ENDING IN A CONSONANT

WORD	RULE	CHANGE
mat slip hit dim	If a one-syllable word ends in a consonant preceded by a vowel, double the final consonant before adding a suffix beginning with a vowel.	matting slipped hitter dimmest
heap steal scoot meat	If a one-syllable word ends in a consonant preceded by two vowels, do not double the final consonant.	heaped stealing scooted meaty
transfer admit allot permit	Double the final consonant in a word of more than one syllable only if the word is accented on the last syllable.	transferring admitted allotting permitting

SPELLING

QUICK-FIX SPELLING MACHINE: ADVERBS

ADJECTIVE	RULE	ADVERB
sudden bad rapid	Add -*ly*.	suddenly badly rapidly
true	Drop *e*, add -*ly*.	truly
angry heavy steady	Change *y* to *i*, add -*ly*.	angrily heavily steadily

QUICK-FIX SPELLING MACHINE: COMPOUNDS

	SINGULAR	RULE	PLURAL
One word	dishcloth supermarket airport	Add -*s* to most words.	dishcloths supermarkets airports
Two or more words	feather bed atomic bomb attorney general	Make the main noun plural. The main noun is the noun that is modified.	feather beds atomic bombs attorneys general
Hyphenated words	son-in-law half-dollar vice-president	Make the main noun plural.	sons-in-law half-dollars vice-presidents

QUICK-FIX SPELLING MACHINE: OPEN AND CLOSED SYLLABLES

An *open syllable* ends in one vowel and has a long vowel sound.	baby labor fable cedar	ba by la bor fa ble ce dar
A *closed syllable* ends in a consonant and has a short vowel sound.	ladder mischief problem plunder	lad der mis chief prob lem plun der

QUICK-FIX SPELLING MACHINE: CONTRACTIONS

WORDS	RULE	CONTRACTION
I am	Combine a personal pronoun with a verb by adding an apostrophe in place of the missing letters.	I'm
you are		you're
he is		he's
she is		she's
it is		it's
we are		we're
they are		they're
I would		I'd
you would		you'd
he would		he'd
she would		she'd
we would		we'd
they would		they'd
I will		I'll
you will		you'll
he will		he'll
she will		she'll
it will		it'll
we will		we'll
they will		they'll
I have		I've
you have		you've
we have		we've
they have		they've
I had		I'd
you had		you'd
he had		he'd
she had		she'd
we had		we'd
they had		they'd
do not	Otherwise, combine two words into one by adding an apostrophe in place of the missing letters.	don't
where is		where's
there is		there's
could not		couldn't
would not		wouldn't
should not		shouldn't
is not		isn't
was not		wasn't
who is		who's

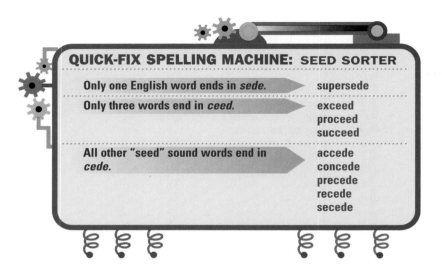

QUICK-FIX SPELLING MACHINE: SEED SORTER

Only one English word ends in *sede*.	supersede
Only three words end in *ceed*.	exceed proceed succeed
All other "seed" sound words end in *cede*.	accede concede precede recede secede

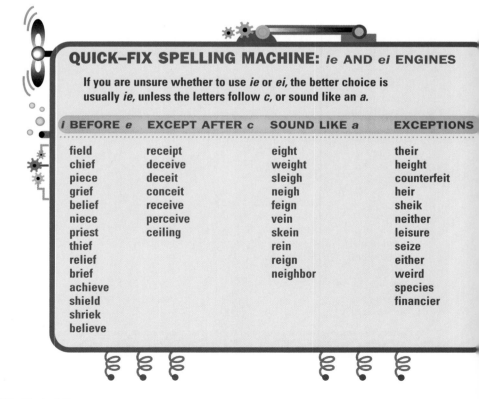

QUICK-FIX SPELLING MACHINE: *ie* AND *ei* ENGINES

If you are unsure whether to use *ie* or *ei*, the better choice is usually *ie*, unless the letters follow *c*, or sound like an *a*.

i BEFORE *e*	EXCEPT AFTER *c*	SOUND LIKE *a*	EXCEPTIONS
field	receipt	eight	their
chief	deceive	weight	height
piece	deceit	sleigh	counterfeit
grief	conceit	neigh	heir
belief	receive	feign	sheik
niece	perceive	vein	neither
priest	ceiling	skein	leisure
thief		rein	seize
relief		reign	either
brief		neighbor	weird
achieve			species
shield			financier
shriek			
believe			

QUICK-FIX SPELLING MACHINE: BORROWED WORDS

Over the centuries, as English speakers increased their contact with people from other lands, English speakers "borrowed" words from other languages. The English language began to grow in new directions and acquired new richness and flavor.

Spelling follows certain patterns in every language. For example, some letter patterns in French, Spanish, and Italian appear in words commonly used in English.

PATTERN	WORD

Some borrowed words keep their original spellings and pronunciations.

PATTERN	WORD
In many words taken from French, a final *t* is silent.	ballet beret buffet
In both English and French, a soft *g* is usually followed by *e*, *i*, or *y*.	mirage region energy
A hard *g* is followed by *a*, *o*, or *u*.	vague
Many words taken from the Dutch language have *oo* in their spellings.	cookie snoop hook caboose
Many words borrowed from Spanish end in *o*.	taco tornado rodeo bronco
Many words that were plural in Italian end in *i*.	spaghetti macaroni ravioli

Some words from other languages were changed to fit English rules of pronunciation and spelling.

PATTERN	WORD
Many words in Native American languages contain sound combinations unlike those in English words. English speakers found these words useful but difficult to pronounce, so they used more familiar sounds and letter combinations.	topaghan = toboggan tamahaac = tomahawk pakani = pecan squa = squaw wampumpeag = wampum qajaq = kayak

Commonly Misspelled Words

A
abbreviate
accidentally
achievement
analyze
anonymous
answer
apologize
appearance
appreciate
appropriate
argument
awkward

B
beautiful
because
beginning
believe
bicycle
brief
bulletin
business

C
calendar
campaign
candidate
caught
certain
changeable
characteristic
clothes
column

committee
courageous
courteous
criticize
curiosity

D
decision
definitely
dependent
description
desirable
despair
desperate
development
dictionary
different
disappear
disappoint
discipline
dissatisfied

E
eighth
eligible
eliminate
embarrass
enthusiastic
especially
essay
exaggerate
exceed
existence
experience

F
familiar
fascinating
favorite
February
foreign
fourth
fragile

G
generally
government
grammar
guarantee
guard

H
height
humorous

I
immediately
independent
irritable

J, K, L
judgment
knowledge
laboratory
library
license
lightning

literature
loneliness

M
mathematics
minimum
mischievous

N
necessary
nickel
ninety
noticeable
nuclear
nuisance

O
obstacle
occasionally
once
opinion
opportunity
outrageous

P
parallel
particularly
people
permanent
persuade
pleasant
pneumonia

possess
possibility
prejudice
principal
privilege
probably
psychology
pursue

R
realize
receipt
receive
recognize
recommend
reference
rehearse
repetition
restaurant
rhythm
ridiculous

S
sandwich
schedule
scissors
separate
sergeant
similar
sincerely
souvenir
specifically
strategy
success
surprise
syllable
sympathy
symptom

T
temperature
thorough
throughout
tomorrow
traffic
tragedy
transferred
truly
Tuesday
twelfth

U
unnecessary
usable

V
vacuum
vicinity
village

W
weird

Commonly Confused Words

Good writers master words that are easy to misuse and misspell. Study the following words, noting how their meanings differ.

accept, except   *Accept* means "to agree to something" or "to receive something willingly." *Except* usually means "not including."
Did the teacher *accept* **your report?**
Everyone smiled for the photographer *except* **Jody.**

advice, advise   *Advice* is a noun that means "counsel given to someone." *Advise* is a verb that means "to give counsel."
Jim should take some of his own *advice.*
The mechanic *advised* **me to get new brakes for my car.**

affect, effect   *Affect* means "to move or influence" or "to wear or to pretend to have." *Effect* as a verb means "to bring about." As a noun, *effect* means "the result of an action."
The news from South Africa *affected* **him deeply.**
The band's singer *affects* **a British accent.**
The students tried to *effect* **a change in school policy.**
What *effect* **did the acidic soil produce in the plants?**

all ready, already   *All ready* means "all are ready" or "completely prepared." *Already* means "previously."
The students were *all ready* **for the field trip.**
We had *already* **pitched our tent before it started raining.**

all right   *All right* is the correct spelling. *Alright* is nonstandard and should not be used.

a lot   *A lot* may be used in informal writing. *Alot* is incorrect.

borrow, lend   *Borrow* means "to receive something on loan." *Lend* means "to give out temporarily."
Please *lend* **me your book.**
He *borrowed* **five dollars from his sister.**

bring, take   *Bring* refers to movement toward or with. *Take* refers to movement away from.
I'll *bring* **you a glass of water.**
Would you please *take* **these apples to Pam and John?**

can, may   *Can* means "to be able," or "to have the power to." *May* means "to have permission to." *May* can also mean "possibly will."

We *may* **not use pesticides on our community garden.**
Pesticides *may* **not be necessary, anyway.**
Vegetables *can* **grow nicely without pesticides.**

capital, capitol, the Capitol	*Capital* means "excellent," "most serious," or "most important." It also means "seat of government." A *capitol* is a building in which a state legislature meets. *The Capitol* is the building in Washington, D.C., in which the U.S. Congress meets. **Going to the beach is a** *capital* **idea.** **Is Madison the** *capital* **of Wisconsin?** **Protesters rallied at the state** *capitol.* **A subway connects the Senate and the House in** *the Capitol.*
desert, dessert	*Desert* (des´ ert) means "a dry, sandy, barren region." *Desert* (de sert´) means "to abandon." *Dessert* (des sert´) is a sweet, such as cake. **The Sahara in North Africa is the world's largest** *desert.* **The night guard did not** *desert* **his post.** **Alison's favorite** *dessert* **is chocolate cake.**
fewer, less	*Fewer* refers to numbers of things that can be counted. *Less* refers to amount, degree, or value. *Fewer* **than ten students camped out.** **We made** *less* **money this year on the walkathon than last year.**
good, well	*Good* is always an adjective. *Well* is usually an adverb that modifies an action verb. *Well* can also be an adjective meaning "in good health." **Dana felt** *good* **when she finished painting her room.** **Angela ran** *well* **in yesterday's race.** **I felt** *well* **when I left my house.**
its, it's	*Its* is a possessive pronoun. *It's* is a contraction for *it is* or *it has.* **Sanibel Island is known for** *its* **beautiful beaches.** *It's* **great weather for a picnic.**
lay, lie	*Lay* is a verb that means "to place." It takes a direct object. *Lie* is a verb that means "to be in a certain place." *Lie,* or its past form *lay,* never takes a direct object. **The carpenter will** *lay* **the planks on the bench.** **My cat likes to** *lie* **under the bed.**

lead, led	*Lead* can be a noun that means "a heavy metal" or a verb that means "to show the way." *Led* is the past tense form of the verb. **Lead is used in nuclear reactors.** **Raul always *leads* his team onto the field.** **She *led* the class as president of the student council.**
learn, teach	*Learn* means "to gain knowledge." *Teach* means "to instruct." **Enrique is *learning* about black holes in space.** **Marva *teaches* astronomy at a college in the city.**
leave, let	*Leave* means "to go away from" or "to allow to remain." *Leave* can be transitive or intransitive. *Let* is usually used with another verb. It means "to allow to." **Don't *leave* the refrigerator open.** **She *leaves* for Scotland tomorrow.** **Cyclops wouldn't *let* Odysseus' men *leave* the cave.**
like	*Like* used as a conjunction before a clause is incorrect. Use *as* or *as if*. **Ramon talked *as if* he had a cold.**
lose, loose	*Lose* means "to mislay or suffer the loss of something." *Loose* means "free" or "not fastened." **That tire will *lose* air unless you patch it.** **My little brother has three *loose* teeth.**
passed, past	*Passed* is the past tense of *pass* and means "went by." *Past* is an adjective that means "of a former time." *Past* is also a noun that means "time gone by." **We *passed* through the Florida Keys during our vacation.** **My *past* experiences have taught me to set my alarm.** **Ebenezer Scrooge is a character who relives his *past*.**
peace, piece	*Peace* means "a state of calm or quiet." *Piece* means "a section or part of something." **Sitting still can bring a sense of *peace*.** **Here's another *piece* of the puzzle.**
principal, principle	*Principal* means "of chief or central importance" or refers to the head of a school. *Principle* means "a basic truth, standard, or rule of behavior." **Lack of customers is the *principal* reason for closing the store.** **The *principal* of our school awarded the trophy.** **One of my *principles* is to be honest with others.**

raise, rise | *Raise* means "to lift" or "to make something go up." It takes a direct object. *Rise* means "to go upward." It does not take a direct object.
The maintenance workers *raise* the flag each morning.
The city's population is expected to *rise* steadily.

set, sit | *Set* means "to place" and takes a direct object. *Sit* means "to occupy a seat or a place" and does not take a direct object.
He *set* the box down outside the shed.
We *sit* in the last row of the upper balcony.

stationary, stationery | *Stationary* means "fixed or unmoving." *Stationery* means "fine paper for writing letters."
The wheel pivots, but the seat is *stationary*.
Rex wrote on special *stationery* imprinted with his name.

than, then | *Than* is used to introduce the second part of a comparison. *Then* means "next in order."
Ramon is stronger *than* Mark.
Cut the grass and *then* trim the hedges.

their, there, they're | *Their* means "belonging to them." *There* means "in that place." *They're* is the contraction for *they are.*
All the campers returned to *their* cabins.
I keep my card collection *there* in those folders.
Lisa and Beth run daily; *they're* on the track team.

to, too, two | *To* means "toward" or "in the direction of." *Too* means "also" or "very." *Two* is the number 2.
We went *to* the mall.
It's *too* risky riding without a helmet.
***Two* amusement parks are offering reduced rates for admission.**

whose, who's | *Whose* is the possessive form of *who. Who's* is a contraction of *who is* or *who has.*
***Whose* parents will drive us to the movies?**
***Who's* going to the recycling center?**

your, you're | *Your* is the possessive form of *you. You're* is a contraction of *you are.*
What was *your* record in the fifty-yard dash?
***You're* one of the winners of the essay contest.**

Index

as helping verb, 89
  predicate adjectives and, 125
Become, 88, 125
Been, 12, 21, 57, 88, 89
Before, 148
Behind, 148
Being, 21, 88, 89
Being (verbs expressing), 88
Below, 148
Beneath, 148
Beside, 148
Better, 144
Between, 59, 78, 148, 149
Beyond, 148
Books, titles of, 190, 224
  titles of chapters in, 224
Both, 72, 127, 173
Brand names, capitalization of, 194, 197
Bring, 91
Building names, capitalization of, 194
Business letters, greetings in, 218
But, 14, 154–155
By, 59, 148

C

Calendar items, capitalization of, 196, 202, 203
Can, 12, 89
Can be, 57
Can't, 138, 144
Capitalization, 184–203
  of A.D. and B.C., 196
  of airplane names, 194
  of A.M. and P.M., 196
  of award names, 197, 202
  in bar graphs, 198–199
  of brand names, 194, 197
  of building names, 194
  of calendar items, 196, 202, 203
  of car names, 194
  checklist for, 203
  of deities, 187
  of first word of sentences, 189
  of geographical names, 193
  of historical items, 196
  of holidays, 196, 197, 202
  of languages, 188
  in letters, 190, 192, 200, 203
  of nationalities, 188
  of objects of the universe, 193
  of organization names, 196–197
  in outlines, 190, 192
  of people's names and initials, 186, 202
  of place names, 184, 193–195, 202

  of plane names, 194
  in poetry, 189, 202, 226
  of proper adjectives, 123
  of proper nouns, 36
  in quotations, 189, 215
  of races, 188
  of religious terms, 187
  rules for, 202–203
  of seasons, 196, 197, 203
  of ship names, 194
  of spacecraft names, 194
  of special events, 197
  in tables, 198–199
  of time abbreviations, 196
  of titles, 186–187, 190, 202
  of train names, 194
  of vehicle names, 194
  when not to use, 203
Captions, 45
Car names, capitalization of, 194
Cartoons, 217
Case, of pronoun, 54, 69, 77–79, 84, 245
CDs
  titles of, 224
Chapter titles, 225
Cities, capitalization of, 193
Clarification, writing to ask for, 20
Clarity. *See* Sentences, clear; Writing, clear.
Clauses, independent, 237
Clichés, avoiding, 255
Closing of a letter, 190
Colons, 218–219
Combining sentences, 14, 15, 155
  commas in, 26
Commands, sentences giving. *See* Imperative sentences.
Commas, 209–215, 230–231, 249
  in addresses, 212–213
  between adjectives, 209, 230
  with appositives, 210
  to avoid confusion, 210
  between city and state, 212
  in combining sentences, 26
  with conjunctions, 26, 155
  in dates, 212–213
  with interrupters, 210, 230
  with introductory words or phrases, 210, 230
  with items in series, 209
  in letters, 212–213
  misplaced or missing, 249
  with nouns of direct address, 210
  with quotation marks, 214–217, 231
  in sentences, 209–211
Common nouns, 36, 50

Herself, 64, 84
Him, 54–55, 59, 84
  problems with, 77
Himself, 64, 84
His, 54–55, 61, 84, 127
Historical items, capitalization of, 196
History, 131
Holidays, capitalization of, 196, 197, 202
Hyphens, 220–221

I

I, 54–55, 57, 84, 167, 187
  problems with, 77
Ideas.
  demonstrative pronouns and, 67
  joining, 154
  nouns for, 34, 36, 38, 43
  pronouns for, 54
  sentences with too many, 250
  sharing, 6–7
  similar, 33
Identifying nouns, pronouns with, 85
Imperative sentences, 16–17, 18, 28, 33, 206
In, 148
Indefinite articles, 123
Indefinite pronouns, 72–74, 80, 84, 127
  singular and plural, 72–74
  as subjects, 173–175
  subject-verb agreement and, 182–183
Independent clauses, diagramming of, 237
Indirect objects, 23–24, 43, 51, 91–93, 119
  diagramming of, 235
  objects of prepositions confused with, 91
  personal pronouns as, 59
  pronouns as, 84
  whom as one, 66
Indirect questions, punctuation for, 206
Indirect quotations, 214
Information. *See also* Media.
  sentences giving, 20
  sharing, 6–7
  writing to ask for, 20
Informative sentences, 20
Initials, periods with, 207
Inside, 148
Institution names, capitalization of, 196
Intensifiers, 130–131
Intensive pronouns, 64–65, 84
Interjections, 146, 157, 162–163

checklist for, 163
punctuation for, 207
Interrogative pronouns, 64, 80, 84
Interrogative sentences, 16–17, 18, 20, 28, 33, 206
Interrupters, 210, 230
Into, 148
Intransitive verbs, 92
Introduction.
  paragraphing for, 258
Introductory words or phrases, 210
  colons following, 218
  commas with, 230
Inverted sentences, 18–19
Irregular verbs, 97, 98–100, 116, 119
Is, 12, 21, 57, 88, 89
Islands, capitalization of, 193
It, 55, 57, 59, 84
Italics, 224, 230
It's, 61, 222
Its, 55, 61, 84, 127, 222
Itself, 64, 84

J

Joining words and thoughts, 154–155, 162–163. *See also* Connecting words.
Journal writing, 179
Just, 131

L

Labels, 42
Laid, 111
Lain, 111
Lakes, capitalization of, 193
Languages, capitalization of, 188
Lay, 111, 119
Learn, 112, 119
Learned, 112
Lend, 91
Letters, 272
  business, 218
  capitalization in, 190, 192, 200, 203
  commas in, 212–213
  greetings and closings in, 190
Lie, 111, 119
Like, 148
Linking verbs, 10, 12, 21, 88–89, 114, 115
  predicate adjectives with, 21, 33, 94–95, 125
  predicate nouns with, 21, 33
  subject pronouns with, 57
Lists
  periods in, 207

as objects of prepositions, 44
personal pronouns with, 75–79
possessive, 41–42, 50, 51, 222–223
predicate, 21, 22, 33, 43, 51, 94–95
prepositions and, 148
pronouns substituted for, 56
proper, 36, 50
in science, 46–47
specific, 256
spelling of possessive, 41, 51
Nowhere, 138
Number (of pronoun), 54, 69, 85. *See also*
        Plural pronouns; Singular pronouns
Number (of subject), 166–168
Numbers
    apostrophes with, 223
    hyphens in spelling, 220

O

Objective case, 54–55, 84
Object pronouns, 59–60, 80
Objects. *See also* Direct objects; Indirect
        objects.
    compound, 77–79
    personal pronouns with, 75
    pronouns as, 85
    whom as one, 66
Objects of prepositions, 44, 51, 59,
        149, 162
    diagramming of, 235
    indirect objects confused with, 91
    personal pronouns with, 75
    pronouns as, 84
    subject-verb agreement and, 172
    whom as one, 66
Objects of the universe, capitalization of,
        193
Observations, writing, 131, 135
Oceans, capitalization of, 193
Of, 148
Off, 148
On, 148
One, 72, 173
Or, 14, 154–155
    with compound subject, 169
    subject-verb agreement and, 182
Order
    of subjects and verbs, 18–20, 33
Organization. *See also* Order.
Organization names, capitalization of,
        196–197
Our, 61, 84, 127
Ours, 61, 84
Ourselves, 64, 84
Out, 148

Outlines
    capitalization in, 190, 192
    periods in, 207
Over, 148
Ownership, 84. *See also* Possessive case.

P

Paragraphs, 258–259
Parentheses, 220–221
Participles, 96–97, 98–100, 118
Parts of sentences
    diagramming of, 232–237
Past, 148
Past participle, 96–97, 98–100, 118
    perfect tenses and, 105
Past perfect, 104–106, 108, 119
Past progressive, 101–103, 108
Past tense, 13, 96–97, 101–103, 108,
        118, 119
    simple, 101–102, 119
Perfect tenses, 104–106, 107–109, 119
Periods, 16, 206–208
    in abbreviations, 207
    capitalization of historic, 196
    for initials, 207
    quotation marks with, 231
    with quotations, 214
Personal pronouns, 54–56
    agreement of antecedents with,
        69–71, 72–74, 244
    in compounds, 77–79
    masculine, feminine, and neuter,
        70–71, 244
    object pronouns as, 59–60
    possessive pronouns as, 61–62
    problems with, 75–79
Person (first, second, third), 54–55, 69–70
Person, of pronoun, 85
Persons
    adjectives and, 133
    adverbs and, 133
    articles and, 123
    capitalization of names of, 186–188,
        202
    demonstrative pronouns and, 67
    initials for names of, 207
    nouns for, 34, 36, 38, 43
    predicate adjectives and, 125
    pronouns for, 54–56
    titles of, 186–187
Photographs
    captions for, 45
    writing about, 135
Phrases. *See also* Prepositional phrases;
        Verb phrases.

INDEX

predicate, 57, 84
prepositions and, 148
problems with, 75–79, 85
reflexive, 64–65, 80, 84
subject, 57–58, 60, 77–79, 80
types of, 84
Proofreading. *See also* Editing; Revising;
Rewriting.
for capitalization, 192, 200
for contractions and possessive
pronouns, 62, 63
for double negatives, 139
of letters, 192
for plural nouns, 39, 40
for prepositional phrases, 153
for pronoun-antecedent agreement,
70, 74
for pronoun errors, 79
for subject-verb agreement, 168
for troublesome verb pairs, 113
Proper adjectives, capitalization of, 123
Proper names, 8
in names of places, 194
titles with, 186–187
Proper nouns, 36, 50, 202
adjectives and, 123
capitalization of, 36
importance of, in writing, 36, 37
Punctuation, 204–231, 269, 270, 271.
See also Commas; Quotation
marks.
checklist for, 231
colons, 218–219
dashes, 220–221
for dialogue, 216, 217
end marks, 206–208, 214–217
hyphens, 220–221
parentheses, 220–221
periods, 206–208
of poetry, 226
of quotations, 214–217
semicolons, 218–219
of titles, 190, 224–225, 230–231

Q

Question marks, 16, 206, 214
with quotation marks, 231
Questionnaires, writing, 67
Questions. *See also* Interrogative
sentences.
interrogative pronouns in, 16
punctuation for, 206
subjects in unusual positions in,
176–177
subject-verb agreement in, 183
Quite, 131

Quotation marks, 214–217, 230–231
with commas, 231
for dialogue, 216, 217
with exclamation points, 231
with periods, 231
with question marks, 231
Quotations, 214–217
capitalization in, 189, 215
direct, 214
divided, 215
indirect, 215
punctuation for, 214–217

R

Races, capitalization of, 188
Raise, 111, 119
Raised, 111
Rather, 131
Real, really 136, 137, 145
Reference, unclear, 75, 76, 244
Reflexive pronouns, 64–65, 80, 84
Regions, capitalization of, 193, 194
Regular verbs, principal parts of, 96–97,
118
Relationships, 84. *See also* Possessive
case.
conjunctions and, 155
family, 187
prepositions to show, 148, 162, 163
Religious terms, capitalization of, 187
Remain, 88
Renaming, 21, 43, 57
Revising, 19, 20, 37. *See also* Editing;
Proofreading; Rewriting.
adding hyphens in, 221
adjectives in, 129
of capitalization, 195
complements in, 45
compound subjects in, 169, 170
conjunctions in, 156
of incorrect verb pairs, 116
possessive nouns in, 42
for pronoun errors, 76
pronouns in, 82
subject-verb agreement in, 167, 169,
170, 179, 180
for verb tenses, 103
Rewriting. *See also* Editing; Proofreading;
Revising
for pronoun-antecedent agreement, 74
pronouns in, 56
for subject-verb agreement, 177
Riddles, writing, 126
Rise, 111, 119
Risen, 111
Rivers, capitalization of, 193

RESOURCES

Stories, writing, 4–5
Streets, capitalization of, 193
Subject case, 54–55
Subject complements, 21–22, 94
  diagramming of, 234
Subject pronouns, 57–58, 60, 77–79,
  80, 84, 85
Subjects, 33. *See also* Compound
  subjects; Plural subjects; Singular
  subjects.
  complete, 6–7, 32
  describing, 21
  indefinite pronouns as, 173–175
  joining, 154–155
  linking verbs and, 88
  nouns as, 43, 51
  order of verbs and, 18–20, 33
  personal pronouns with, 75
  phrases between verbs and,
    171–172, 183
  predicate adjectives and, 94–95, 125
  predicate nouns and, 94–95
  pronouns as, 57, 84, 85
  reflexive pronouns and, 64
  renaming, 21, 43, 57
  simple, 8–9, 20, 32, 232
  subject pronouns as, 58
  in unusual order, 18–20, 176–177
  who used as one, 66–67
Subject-verb agreement, 164–183,
  242–243
  checklist for, 183
  prepositional phrases and, 171,
    176–177, 183
Summarizing, 11.
  information, 199
Superlative form, 133–135, 144, 145
Supporting details, 254
Surveys, creating, 67
Suspense, revising sentences for, 20

T

Taste, 21, 88, 125
Taught, 112
Teach, 91, 112, 119
Television (TV) shows, titles of, 190, 224
Tell, 91
Tenses of verbs, 13, 96–97, 107–110,
  118–119, 248
  perfect, 104–106
  progressive forms of, 101–103,
    107–109
  simple, 101–103, 119
That, 67–68, 84, 127
The, 123
Their, 55, 61, 84, 127, 222

Theirs, 55, 61, 84
Them, 55, 59, 84
  problems with, 77
Themselves, 64, 84
There, sentences beginning with, 19,
  176–179, 183
These, 67–68, 84, 127
They, 54–55, 57, 84
  problems with, 77
They're, 61, 222
Things
  adjectives and, 133
  adverbs and, 133
  articles and, 123
  capitalization of, 202
  demonstrative pronouns and, 67
  nouns for, 34, 36, 38, 43
  pronouns for, 54
Third person pronoun, 54–55, 69–70
This, 67–68, 84, 127
Those, 67–68, 84, 127
Through, 148
Time
  abbreviations for, 196, 218
  capitalization of, 196
  colons in, 218
  tenses showing, 107, 108, 119
Time order, 108, 109
Titles, 224–225
  of book chapters, 224
  of books, 190, 224
  capitalization of, 186–187, 190, 202
  of essays, 224
  italics or underlining for, 224
  of people and cultures, 186–188
  of plays, 224
  of poems, 224
  punctuation of, 190, 224–225,
    230–231
  quotation marks for, 224
  of short story, 190, 224
  of songs, 224
  of written works, 190, 224
To, 59, 91, 131, 148
Toward, 148
Towns, capitalization of, 193
Train names, capitalization of, 194
Transitive verbs, 92
Transportation, writing about, 86, 92

U

Under, 148
Underlining, 224, 225
Until, 148
Up, 148
Us, 55, 59, 84

nowledgments

For Literature and Text

Bilingual Press/Editorial Bilingüe: Excerpt from "The Sand Castle," from *Weeping Woman: La Llorona and Other Stories* by Alma Luz Villanueva. Copyright © 1994 by Alma Luz Villanueva. Reprinted by permission of Bilingual Press/Editorial Bilingüe, Arizona State University, Tempe, Ariz.

Brandt & Hochman Literary Agents: Excerpt from "Scout's Honor" by Avi, from *When I Was Your Age: Original Stories About Growing Up.* Copyright © 1996 by Avi Wortis. Reprinted by permission of Brandt & Hochman Literary Agents, Inc.

Don Congdon Associates: Excerpt from "All Summer in a Day" by Ray Bradbury, published in *Magazine of Fantasy and Science Fiction,* March 1954. Copyright © 1954, renewed 1982 by Ray Bradbury. Reprinted by permission of Don Congdon Associates, Inc.

Houghton Mifflin Company: Excerpt from "All That Is Gold," from The Fellowship of the Ring by J. R. R. Tolkien. Copyright © 1954, 1965 by J. R. R. Tolkien. Copyright renewed © 1982 by Christopher R. Tolkien, Michael H. R. Tolkien, John F. R. Tolkien, and Priscilla M. A. R. Tolkien. Copyright © renewed 1993 by Christopher R. Tolkien, John F. R. Tolkien, and Priscilla M. A. R. Tolkien. Reprinted by permission of Houghton Mifflin Company. All rights reserved.

Excerpt from "Arachne," from *Greek Myths* by Olivia E. Coolidge. Copyright © 1949 by Olivia E. Coolidge. Copyright renewed © 1977 by Olivia E. Coolidge. Adapted by permission of Houghton Mifflin Company. All rights reserved.

Barry N. Malzberg: Excerpt from "Ghost of the Lagoon" by Armstrong Sperry. Copyright © 1961 by Armstrong Sperry. Copyright renewed 1989 by the Estate. Used by permission of the author's agent, Barry N. Malzberg.

Lensey Namioka: Excerpt from "The All-American Slurp" by Lensey Namioka, from *Visions* edited by Donald R. Gallo. Copyright © 1987 by Lensey Namioka. Reprinted by permission of Lensey Namioka. All rights reserved by the author.

Simon & Schuster Books for Young Readers: Excerpt from "Oh Broom, Get to Work," from *The Invisible Thread* by Yoshiko Uchida. Copyright © 1991 by Yoshiko Uchida. Reprinted with the permission of Simon & Schuster Books for Young Readers, an imprint of Simon & Schuster Children's Publishing Division.

Table of Contents

v top illustration by Todd Graveline; **bottom** Photo by Sharon Hoogstraten; **vi, vii** Illustrations by Todd Graveline; **viii** © Getty Images; **ix top** illustration by Todd Graveline; **bottom** copyright © Kenneth W. Fink/Bruce Coleman, Inc.; **xi** Karl Weatherly/Corbis; **xii** Illustration by Todd Graveline.

Illustrations by Todd Graveline

8, 17, 27, 32, 33, 38, 50, 51, 56, 64, 67, 84, 85, 112, 119, 131, 145, 148, 152, 163, 182 top, bottom, 188, 202, 203, 231, 232, 238, 240.

Art Credits

COVER © Ryan Aldrich/McDougal Littell

CHAPTER 1   2–3 © Darren Robb/Getty Images; **4 background** Copyright © Tony Freeman/PhotoEdit; **foreground** Photo by Sharon Hoogstraten; **8, 9** Copyright © Lawrence Migdale; **11** © Pallas de Velletri/SuperStock; **15** The Granger Collection, New York; **25, 27** Copyright © Giraudon/Art Resource, NY.

CHAPTER 2   34 Gail Mooney/Corbis; **36** Photography by D. R. Baston, courtesy of the Center for American Archaeology, Kampsville, Illinois; **40 left, right** Richard T. Nowitz/Corbis; **42** © Richard Pasley/Stock Boston; **45** Nik Wheeler/Corbis; **47 left** © Arthur Gurmankin/Phototake; **right** Eric and David Hosking/Corbis; **48** © The New Yorker Collection 1999 Gahan Wilson from cartoonbank.com. All Rights Reserved.

CHAPTER 3 **52** Photo by Sharon Hoogstraten; **55** © SuperStock; **58** AP/W World Photos; **60** Copyright © Photo Researchers, Inc; **62** AP/Wide World Ph **68** © Ron Cohn/koko.org/The Gorilla Foundation; **71** From Number the Stars Lois Lowry. Copyright © 1989 by Lois Lowry. Used by permission of Random House Children's Books, a division of Random House, Inc; **73** Copyright © R Geographical Society; **79** Brown Brothers; **82** British Museum.

CHAPTER 4 **86** © Jeremy Walker/Getty Images; **93** Schenectady Museum, of Electrical History Foundation/Corbis; **95** © The Granger Collection, New Ye **101** © Lester Lefkowitz /Corbis; **103** U.S. Patent Office; **104** Copyright © Ja Randklev / Stock Connection; **107** Dean Conger/Corbis; **108** Corbis; **116** N

CHAPTER 5 **120 background** Copyright © Vern Clevenger/Adventure Photo Film; **122** © Corbis; **127 top** © Getty Images; **bottom** © 1991 Matthew Borkoski/Stock Boston; **128** © Jay Syverson/Corbis; **129** © Getty Images; **1 left, right** © James D. Watt /www.norbertwu.com; center © Stuart Westmorla Getty Images; **138** Catherine Karnow/Corbis.

CHAPTER 6 **146** Copyright © ILM/Photofest; **149** © Douglas Peebles/Cor **153** © Kenneth W. Fink/Bruce Coleman, Inc; **154** © Wolfgang Baver/Bruce Coleman, Inc; **156** © Roy Morsch/Bruce Coleman Inc; **157** In The Bleachers 1997 Steve Moore. Reprinted with permission of UNIVERSAL PRESS SYNDIC All rights reserved; **158, 159** Illustrations by Daniel Guidera.

CHAPTER 7 **164** © David Madison/Getty Images; **167** © Michael Newman PhotoEdit; **171** AP/Wide World Photos; **173** © Jonathan Blair/Corbis; **174** © Souders/Getty Images; Photo by Sharon Hoogstraten; **180** © SuperStock.

CHAPTER 8 **184** © Kindra Clineff/Getty Images; **187** Andrew Cowin; Travel Ink/Corbis; **189** Photo By Permission of the Folger Shakespeare Library; **191** © Bettmann/Corbis; **bottom** © Kennan Ward/Corbis; **193** © Getty Images; **1** Map illustration by David Fuller, DLF Group; **197** © Getty Images.

CHAPTER 9 **204 background** © Corbis; **foreground** Photo by Sharon Hoogstraten; **206** © Manuela Hoefer/Getty Images; **214** Illustration by Ken Marshall © 1998 from Madison Publishing Inc., a Scholastic/Madison Press Book; **217** Calvin and Hobbes copyright © 1989 Watterson. Dist. by Universa Press Syndicate. Reprinted with permission. All rights reserved; **221** © Bettmann/Corbis.

The editors have made every effort to trace the ownership of all copyrighte material found in this book and to make full acknowledgment for its use. Omissions brought to our attention will be corrected in a subsequent editic